LYNCHBURG COLLEGE LIBRARY

D0287913

*Literature
and Responsibility*

Literature
and Responsibility

THE FRENCH NOVELIST
IN THE
TWENTIETH
CENTURY

Rima Drell Reck

LOUISIANA STATE UNIVERSITY PRESS

BATON ROUGE

1969

LYNCHBURG COLLEGE LIBRARY

PQ
671
.R4

Copyright © 1969 by
Louisiana State University Press

Library of Congress Catalog Card Number: 69–18482
SBN 8071–0301–2
Manufactured in the United States of America by
Kingsport Press, Inc., Kingsport, Tennessee
Designed by Jules B. McKee

For Andrew

Preface

A writer must mediate between his inner needs and the actual historical world in which he lives. The choices he makes bear fundamentally on the literature he creates. The novel reflects and deals with these choices in sensible form. In this book I propose to examine the relationship between literature and social and political responsibility in nine twentieth century French novelists: Jean-Paul Sartre, Albert Camus, Simone de Beauvoir, Georges Bernanos, Julien Green, François Mauriac, Louis-Ferdinand Céline, Louis Aragon, and André Malraux. These nine novelists are the major makers of fiction in France in the period from the end of the First World War to the early 1960's. Other novelists might have been included; however, no study of the novel in France can ignore the contributions of these nine. Their thoughts and their works will stand among the landmarks of the amazingly fertile and challenging French literary spirit.

The interests which led to this book were first stimulated and encouraged when I was an undergraduate at Brandeis University, and I am particularly grateful to Ludwig Lewisohn and David Berkowitz. To Henri Peyre of Yale University, whose encouragement and influence are too great to be measured, I acknowledge my enduring debt. I am grateful as well to Kenneth Douglas for his invaluable questions, and to Victor Brombert, W. M. Frohock, and Germaine Brée for works which helped to light the way. The names of others whose thought furthered my insight into the problems here treated are mentioned in the notes to individual chapters.

Many persons and institutions helped me bring this book to completion. I wish to thank the American Philosophical Society, the American Council of Learned Societies, and the Louisiana State University Research Council for grants which enabled me to undertake the research at the Bibliothèque Nationale and the British Museum Library in 1962, 1964, and 1968. To Louisiana State University in New Orleans I am indebted for leisure time given me at various phases of the writing. To Albert Camus and Julien Green, who discussed with me their conceptions of the relationship between literature and responsibility, I am very grateful. I wish also to thank Charles East of the Louisiana State University Press for his interest in this book and for many very helpful suggestions, and Mrs. Freda Faber for preparing the typescript.

Portions of the chapters on Albert Camus, Simone de Beauvoir, Georges Bernanos, and André Malraux have appeared in different form in journals and quarterlies. For permission to incorporate in revised form material previously published in the pages of their journals I wish to thank the editors of *Modern Language Quarterly, Yale French Studies, French Review, University of Kansas City Review,* and *Criticism.*

My analysis of all texts has been based upon a reading of the originals. All translations from the French are mine.

To Andrew J. Reck, my special thanks for his troubling and illuminating questions, his forbearance, and his encouragement during the years of writing.

Rima Drell Reck

New Orleans
December, 1968

Contents

Introduction

Literature in France has always been a vital part of national life. Writers have considered themselves legislators of opinion and oracles of truth in areas other than purely literary ones. Literature has frequently assumed a polemic character. It has been defended, changed, has become an issue. Even the exemplars of art for art's sake such as Flaubert made a judgment about their responsibility as artists when they decided to detach literature as thoroughly as possible from the common concerns of their own time. They in effect judged the artist's role in his world and decided that the highest form of artistic responsibility lay in refusing to allow art to be tainted by the meanness of an era which did not value art highly enough. Their ultimate commitment was to the future rather than to the present of art.

In the French novel of the twentieth century, social and political forces have assumed an importance greater than at any time in the past. These forces have frequently determined the fortunes of writers, to the extent that their works answered or did not answer the worldly temper of their audience. Novels have influenced as well as reflected national life. The period from after the First World War to the early 1960's has been a time of engaged literature, as the subject matter of fiction has tended to deal with political and social actuality in more obvious fashion, as novelists have grown more conscious of their role as shapers of national morality and guides of conscience.

The present study deals with the theories and fictional works of nine novelists who illustrate the major issue in contemporary French literature—that of artistic responsibility. The two *grands maîtres* of the French novel in the early part of this century, André

Gide and Marcel Proust, are excluded, since their major works were neither conceived under the reign of the attitude described here nor expressive of a reaction to it. The most recent fashion in fiction, the *nouveau roman*, marks the end of the period discussed. The Second World War, which led to the Occupation of France, the Resistance, the Liberation, and the highly charged years after 1944, marks the signal common point of experience of these nine novelists, four of whom were born before the turn of the century (Mauriac, 1885; Bernanos, 1888; Céline, 1894; Aragon, 1897), and five after (Green, 1900; Malraux, 1901; Sartre, 1905; Beauvoir, 1908; Camus, 1913).

Responsibility in literature is a far broader issue than the definition supplied by the existentialist writers in the 1940's. The artist's relation to the world in which he lives, historical, political, and social, has been a principal concern of all major novelists in France since the First World War. Under the banner of engagement Sartre, Camus, and Beauvoir presented as uniquely theirs and wholly new the central problem which significant writers who preceded them had already recognized and dealt with—namely, how to elaborate an individual work in a given historical moment. The earlier responses were more varied and frequently less political, but no less responsible. The existentialists, by their narrow definition of responsibility, created a climate of opinion in which fiction frequently became a tool of political objectives rather than an expression of a unique artistic choice. By their standards, only they and novelists who followed them could be truly responsible artists.

Artistic responsibility should be conceived in its broader sense as the authenticity of a writer's expression of his individual needs and his response to the world in which he lives. In this light, members of the post-1944 generation can be seen as the inheritors of a tradition which they brought to a climax.

This study seeks to clarify a group of individual outlooks on the question of artistic responsibility, rather than to trace the evolution of an attitude. The novelists under consideration are not presented in chronological order. As Henri Peyre has pointed out, it is often misleading to classify writers by the major characteristics of the literary period in which their works fall. The actual products do not always fit the overall classifications. A writer's concerns, attitudes, and reactions are often as easily related to the past as to his present period. Similarly, if he is sensitive and original, he may well be totally at ease conceptually in the future. My aim here is not to demonstrate that all the novelists under consideration were primarily concerned with the question of engaged literature. This would be difficult to prove in the instance of Mauriac during his major fictional period, of Green during all his work, of Malraux even when his novels appeared most rooted in recent history. Rather, I wish to examine the validity of the extraliterary criteria for fiction which became dominant after 1944 for about fifteen years. During this period, tastes and reputations were shaped by standards of judgment formed by the political and moral upheaval the Second World War created in France. And these tastes were frequently applied retroactively. The political stands writers had taken or refused to take during the Occupation determined their literary fortunes. The cataclysmic events of the *épuration* (settling of accounts) which followed the Liberation were but extreme instances of a tenor of mind which prevailed long enough to create some literary reputations in lightning fashion, to destroy other existing ones overnight, to relegate to almost total oblivion opuses which neither upheld the banner of engagement nor overtly repudiated it.

On the issue of artistic responsibility the novelists treated here are the most significant in the period roughly spanning the years from 1920–60. Sartre, Camus, and Beauvoir, the chief exemplars of the post-1944 literary era, are discussed first, because they shaped and expressed the judgments of their generation so vividly as to temporarily rewrite French literary history of several decades prior to their own. Popularized, their criteria reflected the temper of the years after the Second World War and determined the retrospective revaluation of writers who preceded them. I hope to correct the balance, to measure with objectivity the extent to which the criteria for responsible literature popular after 1944 can be applied to the novelists who preceded Sartre, Camus, and Beauvoir. I wish to examine how fiction as an art form is always to some degree concerned with the issue of responsibility. If in the process some of the post-1944 group seem to be less engaged than they have heretofore appeared, and if writers of the pre-1944 group are found to have anticipated the later issues in their private concern with fiction and with the life of France after the First World War, then my purpose will have been served.

For the break between the pre-1944 and post-1944 groups is more apparent than real. The Second World War only further intensified factors which had been present in French literature since the experience of 1914–18. Engaged literature has been a vital issue for nearly fifty years in France. The emergence of the *nouveau roman* in the early 1960's marks the first significant turn away from a preoccupation with fiction as an overt judgment on man's life in relation to his historical moment.

The problem treated here is threefold, and its aspects are interrelated. First, how does the novelist conceive the nature and function of the novel? Second, how important does he feel a sense of social and political responsibility to be for the novel? And third, how successful are his novels as fiction? An examination of the theories and works of Jean-Paul Sartre, Albert Camus, Simone de Beauvoir, Georges Bernanos, Julien Green, François Mauriac, Louis-Ferdinand Céline, Louis Aragon, and André Malraux sheds light on the way in which a novelist's assessment of the artist's political and social responsibility affects his fiction.

These nine novelists represent a broad spectrum of political persuasions, from Céline's apparent Fascist leanings at one end to Aragon's Communism at the other. Between these extremes lie the Catholic novelists, Bernanos, Green, and Mauriac, each of whom adopted a different stance with respect to political and social issues. The remaining four, Sartre, Camus, Beauvoir, and Malraux, illustrate varying conceptions of the notion of engaged art, despite the common and inaccurate tendency to group them together as existentialist writers. The fictional products and literary theories of these nine are as varied as their attitudes towards politics.

Jean-Paul Sartre is the leading spokesman for engaged art in the twentieth century. His intense preoccupation with social and political issues has led him to write novels primarily determined by extraliterary concerns and ultimately to abandon completely the writing of fiction. Albert Camus struggled during the whole of his short life to reconcile his commitment to art with his growing awareness of politics and the effects of history on the life of men in his own time. Simone de Beauvoir has simultaneously developed as an ethical thinker and as a novelist, bringing to the vogue of engaged art her own special emphasis on emotional values. Georges Bernanos, a man of strong polemic spirit, divided his life and his energies between pamphlets and novels. His novels reflected this duality and frequently suffered from it. The least engaged of the nine, Julien Green, has deliberately attempted to exclude political and social considerations from his fiction. His hatred of politics has affected his fortunes as a novelist; it has isolated him in an era which favored engaged art. François Mauriac has had two consecutive careers, first as a novelist and then as a political journalist and moral commentator. Louis-Ferdinand Céline published his major novels during the thirties, was quickly recognized as an extraordinary writer, and then fell under a heavy cloud because of his unfashionable politics in the years immediately preceding and during the Second World War. Although he claimed an aversion to politics as strong as that of Green, political and social issues led to a decline of Céline's reputation only now beginning to be reversed. Louis Aragon, since his youthful abandonment of the Surrealist movement and subsequent adhesion to the French Communist Party, has continued to elaborate a theory of literature as a social and moral force in the life of men. His fiction has reflected this emphasis on artistic responsibility, for better and for worse in aesthetic terms. Finally, André Malraux, whose life and fiction are among the most active and engaged of this century in France, has demonstrated the power of an aesthetic commitment to lead to a unique form of engaged art and engaged political action.

The choice of novelists is of course motivated by a personal judgment of aesthetic value. It is generally accepted that Sartre, Camus, Mauriac and Malraux are among the major novelists of this century in France. The novels of Beauvoir, Bernanos, Green, Céline and Aragon are valued highly by some, much less highly by others. By any objective assessment, however, the latter five also deserve a permanent place in the distinguished history of the French novel in this century. Perhaps detailed consideration of their works will contribute to a more judicious appreciation of their contributions. To some extent particular conceptions of the relationship between literature and responsibility shared by many critics account for the uncertain reputations of novelists such as Bernanos and Céline. Further, other conceptions of this relationship explain some of the weaknesses in the novels of Sartre and Beauvoir. Finally, it becomes possible to direct further attention to the writings of Julien Green, a talented novelist who because of his apolitical conception of literature has been accorded less attention than he deserves.

The nine novelists form a generation with common problems and common concerns. This fact is illustrated by a number of confrontations on a variety of issues. Céline and Sartre, Céline and Mauriac, Aragon and Malraux, Malraux and Bernanos, Sartre and Camus, Camus and Beauvoir, Beauvoir and Céline, Bernanos and Céline, Camus and Green, Green and Sartre, Mauriac and Camus —the clashes, debates, divergences and points of accord on literary, political, and social issues are many and varied. From these confrontations indirectly arises the portrait of an era in which literature and society, radically altered by a rapid succession of crucial historical events, have been indissolubly related. The literary theories treated here represent varying attempts to cope with these events within the domain of individual creation. The novels themselves have been variously mirrors, weapons, escapes, refutations. Their quality has varied from novelist to novelist and from novel to novel for each individual author.

The approach used here may provide a broader critical perspective on the novels themselves. Basic judgments of fictional value are independent of a novelist's political and social theories. The novels he writes must be evaluated primarily for their literary merits. However, this evaluation may be furthered by situating the novels within the era which saw their creation and which affected the thinking of their creator. The reciprocal interaction of fiction on life and life on fiction supplies the living context in which, during a large part of the twentieth century, French writers have sought to respond each in his own way to historical actuality. Their works and their lives have been shaped by the events of the years from the 1920's to the 1960's. Insight into the relationship between literature and responsibility in this period may serve to illuminate not only the novels but also the character of life and thought in France.

Literature
and Responsibility

Jean-Paul Sartre

AMBIGUITIES
OF MORAL CHOICE

Jean-Paul Sartre is the most influential intellectual of his generation. As philosopher, novelist, playwright, political critic, and psy-
choanalyst of art he has reflected the major historical events of his
era in France. Born in 1905, Sartre was shaped by the literary and
philosophical idealism taught in his youth. Affected slightly by the
events of 1914 to 1918, he came to his "age of reason" in the late
1930's. The fall of France, the Occupation, and the turmoil which
succeeded the Liberation turned the brilliant, detached young philosopher and novelist into a moral guide for the postwar era. As
Sartre elaborated the existentialist philosophy which he had begun
to develop earlier, he found himself, along with Albert Camus, the
diagnostician of France's moral uneasiness. In his continuing role
as a non-Communist Marxist, Sartre has peculiarly exemplified the
quixotic character of the French intellecutal Left during the past
twenty years. Above all, he has written and lived the internal
contradictions of engaged art more fully than any writer of his
time.

Francis Jeanson has described the unity of Sartre's thought as
that of "a real existence, an effective experience of the world . . . a
unique consciousness." [1] Jeanson attempts to demonstrate how
Sartre transcended the "stalemate" of existence described in *L'être*

[1] Francis Jeanson, *Sartre par lui-même* (Paris: Editions du Seuil, 1963),
4–5.

et le néant (1943) by moving on to a concern with "the concrete undertaking" placed in its historical dimension.[2] Sartre's *La critique de la raison dialectique* (1960) seems to bear out Jeanson's contention. However, in the latter work another type of stalemate appears, a type consistent with the underlying rhythm of Sartre's thought in all its forms. In his attempt to fuse existentialism with Marxism, Sartre once again reveals a unity not of progression but of contradiction, a preference for antinomies over directives. Sartre has managed in his literary as well as political and philosophical writings to absorb apparently irreconcilable views and to make them his own. If, as he has said, "passion exists only in the form of contradictory demands," he is himself the most passionate of men.[3] Directing his passion toward concrete experience, at first his own, then the experience of other men as perceived by him, Sartre has insisted that "every truth and every action imply a human milieu and a human subjectivity." [4] An ethics is impossible and necessary; man is free and historically determined; the future for all men lies in the ascendency of the proletariat, yet all men (including Sartre himself) except the proletariat would perish in that future; art is the product of human freedom; art is a social byproduct. These are some of the fundamental antinomies his writings bring to light.

Sartre's portrayal of the twentieth century bourgeois intellectual as a man of bad conscience is fundamental to understanding his view of art and its relation to engagement. In the *Critique de la raison dialectique* Sartre describes how the young men of his generation became aware of history first through learning about Marxism, then through direct experience of history in the war. In the beginning Marxism was

a heavy presence on the horizon of working masses, an enormous somber body which was *living* Marxism, which was *practicing* it, and which exercised at a distance an irresistible attraction on the intellectual *petits bourgeois*. . . . It irresistibly attracted us without our knowing it and deformed the whole of our acquired culture. . . . We had been

[2] *Ibid.*, 31.
[3] "Beyond Bourgeois Theatre," translated by Rima Drell Reck, in *Tulane Drama Review*, V (Spring, 1961), 8; originally a lecture reprinted in *World Premières Mondiales* (Paris: Institut International du Théâtre, June, 1960).   [4] *L'existentialisme est un humanisme* (Paris: Nagel, 1946), 12.

raised in bourgeois humanism and this optimistic humanism was falling apart because we sensed, all around us, the immense mass of "sub-men conscious of their sub-humanity." . . . The authors we loved explained to us . . . that existence is a *scandal*. But what interested us was real men with their labors and their pains; we demanded a philosophy which would take account of all this without noticing that it already existed and that it was this philosophy, precisely, which gave rise to this demand in us.[5]

The crucial moment of recognition came with the convulsive events of the Second World War. "Political events led us to utilize as a sort of key, more useful than accurate, the schema of the 'class struggle'; but it took the whole bloody history of this half century to make us grasp its reality and to situate us in a ravaged society. It was the war which exploded the old categories of our thought."[6] Sartre has insisted that existentialism supplies the human emphasis on the individual man whom Marxism tends to subsume under a type, and this insistence has made Sartre a sympathetic critic, at times a gadfly, of Communist thought in France and in Eastern Europe. George Lichtheim has pointed out that Sartre, Merleau-Ponty, and the *Temps Modernes* group as a whole can be classified as a recognizable form of Marxist revisionism, one based on a special reading of the early Marx fused with the unique tonality of existentialist thought.[7] Lichtheim further argues, with convincing force, that men like Sartre, despite the way they appear to critics in the United States and Great Britain, have never been and can never be Communists. Sartre's passion for such contradictions and ambiguities is clearly expressed in the *Critique*, where he states, "The ambiguity of political and social action results, most frequently, from the profound contradictions between the needs, the motives of an action, the immediate project on the one hand—and on the other the collective apparatuses of the social field, that is, the instruments of practice (*praxis*)."[8]

From Simone de Beauvoir's description of Sartre's position in

---

[5] *Critique de la raison dialectique* (Paris: Gallimard, 1960), 23.
[6] *Ibid.*, 24.
[7] See George Lichtheim, *Marxism in Modern France* (New York and London: Columbia University Press, 1966), 89–102.
[8] *Critique de la raison dialectique*, 77.

the last volume of her autobiography, he appears as the embodiment of bourgeois intellectual bad conscience. She writes:

Suspect to the bourgeois, cut off from the masses, Sartre condemned
himself to having no public, only readers; he assumed this solitude
willingly, because it flattered his taste for adventure. There is nothing
more desperate than this attempt, nothing more joyous. By rejecting
him the Communists politically condemned him to powerlessness; but
since to name is to unveil and to unveil to change, by deepening the
idea of engagement he discovered a form of *praxis*. Reduced to his
petit-bourgeois singularity, refusing it, he experienced himself as an
"unhappy consciousness." [9]

Viewing Sartre's predicament from a more detached standpoint,
Lichtheim judges it in much the same way when he says, "His star
rose over a landscape which left little room for hope that the world
might be shaped (or shape itself) in accordance with the heart's
desire. This was all he needed. Sartre had always been at his best in
fighting hopeless battles. Indeed it is arguable that the whole of his
gigantic intellectual *oeuvre* is proof of the capacity of the human
mind to engage itself *contra mundum*." [10] The call for a revolutionary public Sartre voiced in his programmatic essay, "Qu'est-ce que
la littérature?", was of course never answered.[11] But he has continued to protest and to denounce with his pen, even if forced to
admit as he does in *Les mots* (1964) that he can perhaps accomplish nothing at all.

Sartre has himself called the dissenting intellectual "a traitor,"
"a slimy rat" (*un rat visqueux*) who is clear-sightedly outside of
any effective political organization. His dramatic refusal in 1964 of
the Nobel Prize for Literature publicized widely Sartre's determination to remain intellectually independent. In a statement to the
Swedish press on October 22, 1964, he explained his refusal. To
accept the prize would be to accept transformation into an "insti-
tution" sanctioned by the West. He further said he would be
equally unable to accept the Lenin Prize if it were offered him. Not
as idealistic as some of Malraux's heroes, who engage in political

[9] Simone de Beauvoir, *La force des choses* (Paris: Gallimard, 1963),
146.   [10] Lichtheim, *Marxism in Modern France*, 98.
[11] Collected in *Situations II* (Paris: Gallimard, 1948). See 276 ff.

action but condemn the results they help to achieve (li⊦ dez in *L'espoir*), Sartre is nevertheless caught in what Jea.. called "the contradiction of our era" for the intellectual. Aware that action is necessary to bring about the changes he *feels* must take place, Sartre is too lucid to ignore the fact that active *means* are by definition impure and that the *ends* will be colored by the means employed. There is no resolution to his dilemma; he cannot rid himself of his bad conscience; he cannot stop himself from being aware of injustices in the world. Nor can he effectively change the world. All he *can* do is voice his malaise and his criticisms. Some of Sartre's most characteristic and most successful writings are precisely those essays which articulate his impossible situation. In "D'une Chine à l'autre" Sartre reflects on the ease with which Maurice Barrès celebrated blood, misery, his own pleasures, the glory of death. Writes Sartre, "Happy Barrès: he died when his time came, carrying with him into his grave the secret of a good conscience." [12]

The role of the writer is an ambiguous one for Sartre. "I can only assume a mandate no one has given me: this is the contradiction I have to live," he confesses.[13] Beauvoir presents Sartre's commitment to literature as an almost involuntary choice: "Sartre lived to write; his mandate was to testify to all things and to reexamine them on his own in the light of necessity . . . ." [14] Sartre has always felt "there is something to be done" on any occasion, while continuing to question the ultimate efficacy of what is done. Despite his predilection for moral prescriptions in the realm of *praxis*, Sartre has studded his writings with doubts about the actions themselves. For Sartre the role of the writer embodies these apparent contradictions in rather consistent fashion. The writer must testify, but the fact that his testimony is necessary implies an insoluble situation; if the situation were clearly soluble, the testimony would be unnecessary. The act of writing is in fact an expression of freedom within a situation which is determined by

---

[12] *Situations* V (Paris: Gallimard, 1964), 16.
[13] From an unpublished text cited by Jeanson in *Sartre par lui-même*, 187.
[14] Simone de Beauvoir, *La force de l'âge* (Paris: Gallimard, 1960), 18.

social and historical factors. On this subject Sartre's thought has evolved in the direction of growing pessimism. After the "honeymoon" following the end of the war when diverse factions on the Left were briefly united and when Sartre felt a community of responsible action was possible, a gradual disillusionment set in. His break with Camus in 1952 and with Merleau-Ponty a few years later were in a sense symbolic of the weakening of Sartre's group. These breaks also demonstrated Sartre's obvious relish in declaring openly his uniqueness and isolation.[15]

From 1946 to 1947, Sartre's fundamental pessimism was still buoyed by the exhilaration of the Resistance period. Beauvoir attempts to describe the *social* function of this pessimism when she writes:

He refused "a priori hope." At that time he had an idea of action which was intermediate between a certain moralism inspired by the Resistance and the realism of *praxis*; the undertaking must not be based on an assessment of possible success: the undertaking is itself the only hope permitted. The writer must not promise glorious tomorrows; rather, by describing the world as it is, he must arouse the desire to change it. The more convincing his depiction of it, the better he achieves his aim: the darkest work is not pessimistic once it appeals to individual freedom in favor of freedom." [16]

Beauvoir is here summarizing Sartre's ideas from unpublished notes preliminary to "Qu'est-ce que la littérature?", which appeared shortly afterwards in 1947. In this work Sartre defines art as the assumption of the world by an individual freedom.

"Qu'est-ce que la littérature?" is an essay primarily prescriptive in its aims and often simplistic in its formulations. It has been thoroughly discussed in many books on Sartre.[17] Here we need only highlight several of Sartre's major points in his conception of the role of art. Defining prose as essentially utilitarian, Sartre says it is "first of all an attitude of mind . . . ." [18] In order to arrive at this

[15] See "Réponse à Albert Camus," and "Merleau-Ponty," in *Situations* IV (Paris: Gallimard, 1964).   [16] Beauvoir, *La force des choses*, 129.
[17] See for example the thorough discussion of the essay in Philip Thody, *Jean-Paul Sartre, A Literary and Political Study* (London: Hamish Hamilton, 1960).   [18] *Situations* II, 70.

judgment, he makes some highly questionable statements about the way in which *poets* use language: in fact, he says they do *not utilize it* at all. Their effort to grasp reality involves a totally uncritical and nonanalytical use of words. All this is by way of getting at his central point, namely that *prose* can and should be conceived as "a mode of secondary action one might call action by unveiling. . . . The engaged writer knows that words are action: he knows that to unveil is to change . . . ." [19] Prose must involve all men, so that no one will be able to declare himself innocent of the moral factors which will henceforth be the subject matter of prose. Considerations of style are secondary, beauty is in fact a byproduct which "hides," which "acts by persuasion." The work of art is "an act of confidence in the freedom of men," and the writer, a free man addressing himself to free men, "has only one subject: freedom." [20] Rejecting both the "literature as martyrdom" and "literature as vocation" conceptions which he and his contemporaries absorbed during their early education, Sartre hails the "divorce between . . . the literary myth and the historical reality" which was forced upon them.[21] The experience of the war led them to realize they were indeed *situated* and that evil could in no way be redeemed.

The essential experience which determined this radical change in the conception of literature was the brutal advent of a sense of *historicity*, the taste of which Sartre eloquently describes as "a bitter and ambiguous mixture of the absolute and the transitory." [22] Recognizing that the surest way to be duped by one's era is to turn one's back on it, Sartre calls for writers to *choose* themselves within the era. In *La critique de la raison dialectique* Sartre stresses that the important thing is not what is done with us, but "what we do with what is done with us." [23] "Qu'est-ce que la littérature?" calls for a literature of "extreme situations," written by metaphysical writers, because "metaphysics is not a sterile discussion on abstract notions unrelated to experience; it is a living effort to grasp from the inside the human condition in its totality." [24] One of the engaged writer's most essential tasks is to evaluate the *means*

---

[19] *Ibid.*, 73. [20] *Ibid.*, 111, 112. [21] *Ibid.*, 241. [22] *Ibid.*, 243.
[23] *Critique de la raison dialectique*, 63. [24] *Situations II*, 251.

politics employs. (It is curious that Malraux and Aragon, rather than Sartre himself, most effectively addressed themselves to this task within the novel.) For *novels of situation* new fictional techniques are needed, ones which will express the freedom of the novelist and the reader. Above all this freedom will be shown through characters who are "half lucid, half obscure consciousnesses . . . none of whom would have a privileged point of view either on the event or on himself . . . ."[25]

Sartre's basic points in "Qu'est-ce que la littérature?" are two: literature must take account of the changes in man's situation brought about by history; literary techniques must reflect the realities of this situation, and no longer rely on outmoded idealisms. Sartre's call for engaged writing is the natural corollary of the recognition of historicity. In a brief critical essay written several years earlier, Sartre had already formulated the central assumption of "Qu'est-ce que la littérature?", the assumption that art more readily than philosophy can undertake to express the subjective quality of experience. He had written: "I cannot judge this world, since my judgments are part of it. If I conceive it as a work of art or like a complicated mechanism, it is by means of human notions; and if I declare it absurd . . . it is by means of human concepts. . . . How can man judge the world as a totality, the world with man inside of it? . . . The artist persists, where the philosopher has given up."[26]

In this programmatic essay of 1947, Sartre's concern with specific political actions obscures to some degree his earlier insight into the nature of art. However, further political experience and continued writing have led him to synthesize his differing perspectives on the role of art. Answering the charge that he has subjugated literature to politics, Sartre told an interviewer in 1960, "I would find it more logical to accuse me of overestimating literature. Its beauty lies in wanting to be everything and not in sterilely seeking beauty." He insisted further that every written sentence must "reverberate at all levels of man and society. . . . The literature of an era is the era digested by its literature."[27] His definition of engaged art has lost

[25] *Ibid.*, 253.   [26] *Situations I* (Paris: Gallimard, 1947), 136.
[27] Madeleine Chapsal, *Les écrivains en personne* (Paris: Julliard, 1960), 211.

the combative tone ot 1947, but it has otherwise remained constant: "Man lives surrounded by his images. Literature gives him the critical image of himself. . . . A critical mirror. To show, to demonstrate, to represent. That's engagement." [28]

In 1940, according to Simone de Beauvoir, "Sartre was thinking a great deal about the period after the war; he had definitely decided no longer to keep out of political life. His new morality, based on the notion of authenticity and which he was trying to put into practice, demanded that man 'assume' his 'situation'; and the only way to do this was to go beyond it by engaging in action: any other attitude was an evasion, a vain pretence, a masquerade based on bad faith." [29] Sartre realized that a man's *generation* does not define him, but is only a *situation*.

Sartre spent a brief period of captivity in a German prison camp and, armed with this experience, returned to Paris in 1941 determined to put into practice his new assessment of human existence. He attempted to organize a resistance movement and found, as he was again to find even more dramatically at the end of the war, that the problems of uniting disparate political groups into unified action were so great as to be almost insurmountable. For the moment, however, the choices seemed eminently clear, the hopes very high. As he wrote in 1944 in "La république du silence": "We were never freer than under the German occupation . . . every just thought was a conquest . . . every word became as precious as a declaration of principle . . . each of our gestures had the weight of an engagement." [30] During the Occupation, in 1943, Sartre published *L'être et le néant* and wrote and produced his first two plays, *Les mouches* and *Huis clos*. Already he was discovering that his pen provided him the only fully satisfactory form of engagement. Much has been written about the relatively uncourageous form of resistance undertaken by intellectuals like Sartre, Camus, and Beauvoir, who continued to write and to publish under the German occupation rather than taking to the *maquis* or carrying on other more active forms of opposition as did Aragon or Malraux.[31]

---

[28] *Ibid.*, 225.   [29] Beauvoir, *La force de l'âge*, 442.
[30] *Situations III* (Paris: Gallimard, 1949), 11.
[31] See for example R. L. Bruckberger, "A View of Sartre," *New York Times Book Review* (November 15, 1964), 2.

It is not the aim here to evaluate this judgment, but it should be noted that to the "mandarins" of Paris, who spent the years between 1940 and 1944 writing while enduring the physical and emotional hardships of life under enemy rule, the pen did indeed seem to be a kind of sword.

When the war ended in 1945 Sartre found himself at the age of forty definitively stripped of his youthful illusions and in the process of trying to find a definition of action which could take account of his sense of historicity and its concomitant concern with the future of the working classes. As Beauvoir admits, "Sartre respected literature to the point of confusing its destiny with that of humanity . . . ." [32] Hence at that moment he defined engagement as "nothing more than the total presence of the writer in the writing." [33] In his essay on Merleau-Ponty, Sartre later explained how his own struggle to achieve literary freedom led to the discovery of all other freedoms. [34] By attempting to change the social condition of man and the conception man has of himself the writer could rediscover "a professional good conscience." Literature could once again become what it should never have ceased to be, a *social function*. "All writers of bourgeois origin," Sartre wrote, "have known the temptation of irresponsibility . . . ." [35] He was himself determined to transcend this temptation; he would not let his life be "stolen by immortality." His role henceforth would be "to decide and to write," and this determination has persisted into the present.

Like the majority of French intellectuals of his generation, Sartre has been sympathetic to the fundamental objectives of the Communists since the early forties. However, for several reasons, he has never joined the French Communist Party. First and most obvious is the demand for intellectual honesty, which has forced Sartre to criticize the Party's *means* on countless occasions. "When politics must betray its morality, to choose morality is to betray politics." [36] Sartre has continued to play the role of "traitor," that is, of self-conscious critic who values truth and ethics above the

---

[32] Beauvoir, *La force des choses*, 54.   [33] *Ibid.*, 53.
[34] *Situations IV*, 193.   [35] *Situations II*, 9.   [36] *Situations IV*, 230.

comforts of solidarity, who feels that a perspective "from the outside" is the most clear-sighted. The second reason for Sartre's abstention from joining the Communists seems to be a form of pride. His role as critic of the Communists is evidently one he enjoys. It reinforces his earlier predilection for isolation while coming to terms with his later decision to be actively engaged. His justification for this preference is ingenious. "In an era when being engaged meant making a revolution, it was necessary to write the *Manifesto*. In an era like ours, where there are different parties each claiming to be revolutionary, engagement consists not in joining one of them, but in trying to clarify the concepts . . . ." [37]

Sartre revealed that his early commitment to art was essentially personal and nonpolitical: "Literature was at first for me the search for a justification in the future, a transposition of eternal life: to accept a vague and contingent existence in the present, in order to be recognized after death by Society." [38] He continued to seek the Absolute until the era of *La nausée* (1938), which served as a kind of ascesis. It marked his entry into fiction and already contained within it the reasons for which he would later abandon fiction. Simone de Beauvoir tells us that in the mid-thirties Sartre was obsessed by the problem of contingency, that for him it was not an abstract notion but a real dimension of the world; he wanted "to utilize all the resources of art to make sensible this secret 'flaw' which he recognized in man and in things." [39] Sartre's desire to "express in literary form metaphysical truths and feelings" led him to write novels.[40] However, his subsequent resolution not to evade his responsibility led in its turn to his abandoning novels for less ambiguous forms of engagement. He states explicitly in *L'existentialisme est un humanisme* (1946) that the artist will not be judged solely by his works of art. In recent years, Sartre has admitted that he has perhaps changed nothing at all by his writing,[41] and has said ironically that he has chosen the useless, ques-

---

[37] *L'existentialisme est un humanisme*, 105.
[38] Jeanson, *Sartre par lui-même*, 173.
[39] Simone de Beauvoir, *Mémoires d'une jeune fille rangée* (Paris: Gallimard, 1958), 342.   [40] Beauvoir, *La force de l'âge*, 293.
[41] See Chapsal, *Les écrivains en personne*, 220.

tioning, perilous enterprise of literature "against death and because I had no faith—it's a kind of weakness." [42] Literature is in fact the practice of contradiction, trying to fix motion by immobility, to use language for ends which are extralinguistic. Applying his method of social-psychological analysis of artists to himself, Sartre sees his own role and that of his contemporaries as a transitional failure with perhaps only edifying value. "The real task of the engaged writer . . . [is to] show, to demonstrate, to demystify, to dissolve myths and fetishes in a little bath of critical acid. . . . Others will invent new myths through him; or—as happened for Pushkin—the purest or most flamboyant style will be the equivalent of a political action because the writer will make his nation discover its language as the ultimate moment of its unification. We were not given such a chance." [43]

Sartre has no critical canon in the usual sense. His comments on literature are generally directed toward *situating* the writer and his work in an historical context which is then used to demonstrate something about the present. Here Sartre's critical technique resembles the fictional method Aragon uses in *La semaine sainte*, an apparent historical novel whose real subject is contemporary France. (See the chapter on Aragon.) For Sartre the literary work becomes a kind of social phenomenon which bears examination with extraliterary tools. He writes, "The profundity of a work comes from the national history, the language, traditions, specific and often tragic questions that time and place ask the artist through the living community of which he is a part." [44] And unlike the purists who feel that the work, once completed, stands separate from the writer, Sartre goes so far as to maintain that the significance of a work changes according to *who* wrote it.[45] Sartre always concentrates on the *writer*, and from his scattered essays and comments on writers, certain concerns emerge as central to his conception of literary art.

When asked by an interviewer why, if he believes that prose is only an instrument, he has devoted so much attention to writers

---

[42] *Ibid.*, 226.   [43] *Ibid.*, 230.
[44] *Situations* VII (Paris: Gallimard, 1965), 324.
[45] See "Gide vivant," *Situations* IV, 87.

(Flaubert, Genet, Mallarmé) for whom literature was an end in itself, Sartre replied, "Flaubert serves to show that literature seen as a pure art, which draws its only rules from its own essence, conceals a fierce stand on all levels—including the social and political—and an engagement on the author's part." [46] Of Mallarmé he speculates that the poet must have been very different from the image of him we generally have. "His engagement appears as total to me as possible: social as well as poetic. . . . He refused his era, but he conserved it as a transition. . . . Mallarmé related his Orphic and tragic conceptions of poetry to the communion of a people rather than to an individual hermeticism. *That* kind of hermeticism was only a rejection of bourgeois stupidity. . . . He imagined that for a united people the obscure would become clear." [47] It is interesting to note in Sartre's more recent writings the recurrent references to an Orphic conception of literature. His concern with Pushkin and Mallarmé (on whom he is planning to write a book) seems to indicate Sartre's nostalgia for a literature quite different in tone and in substance from the one he has himself produced. While never able to condone the spirit which inspired the works of Baudelaire and Flaubert, on whom he has written extensively, Sartre nevertheless stands in obvious admiration of their writings. One senses that the ideal situation, in his eyes, would be one in which the writer *could* concern himself with literature per se and still be responsible because his audience would have achieved a state of community where moral dicta would be superseded. Unfortunately, such a time seems to be nowhere in sight. Unlike Malraux, for whom the artist *is* the creator of culture standing above the common man, Sartre longs for a culture in which the artist and his audience will be equal: the only difference between them will be that the artist will supply the words for those verities his audience already knows.

In his well-known essay on François Mauriac (1939), Sartre voiced objections to Mauriac's fictional techniques which expressed his own evolving demands for fiction. To capture the reader in the time flow of the novel, the novelist must "trap" him. He must

---

[46] Chapsal, *Les écrivains en personne*, 209–10.   [47] *Ibid.*, 210–11.

make his characters *free;* he must not define or explain, but *present* directly their actions and passions. For Sartre the idea of destiny is inimical to the novel. "The introduction of absolute truth, or the point of view of God is an . . . error of technique in a novel." [48] A novel, made of "free consciousness and of time," must scrupulously avoid the absolute, which is timeless. "A novel is written by a man for men. From the perspective of God, which penetrates appearances . . . there is no novel, there is no art, since art lives on appearances. God is not an artist; neither is M. Mauriac." [49] In his zeal to demystify art, to concretize and link it with the world of things and events, to stand against the idealization of creativity and creation, Sartre undertook to demolish *La fin de la nuit,* one of Mauriac's weakest novels—an attack for which Mauriac never forgave him (see the chapter on Mauriac). Sartre's essay reveals little insight into Mauriac's considerable talents. It *does* highlight those technical dicta which Sartre was to apply in his own fiction: strict use of point of view, no authorial intrusion, dialogues and actions "in motion," a strong sense of time.

Faulkner's use of time fascinated Sartre, who wrote, "A novelistic technique always refers back to the novelist's metaphysics. . . . The metaphysics of Faulkner is a metaphysics of time." [50] In Faulkner's heavy style Sartre saw an effort to capture the "nauseating and pompous monotony" of quotidian existence in a stagnant social situation. Sartre imposed his own concern with contingency on the Faulknerian novel when he wrote, "to be present is to appear without reason and to be immersed." [51] Noting that most great modern authors have tried to mutilate time (Joyce, Dos Passos, Gide, Woolf), Sartre went on to say that Proust and Faulkner simply cut its head off and took away its future; they eliminated from the novel the dimension of actions, the dimension of freedom.

Sartre also greatly admired Albert Camus' *L'étranger* when it appeared in 1942. To Sartre the novel seemed to embody in effective fictional form precisely those qualities lacking from conventional narratives. *L'étranger* did not try to *explain;* it *showed* the

[48] *Situations I,* 47.   [49] *Ibid.,* 57.   [50] *Ibid.,* 71.   [51] *Ibid.,* 72.

absurdity of the human condition and demonstrated the "gratuity" of the novel. "The absurd creator has lost even the illusion that his work is necessary," Sartre wrote, basing his comments on a reading of Camus' *Le mythe de Sisyphe* (1942) as a key to the fictional work.[52] Camus' hero Meursault did indeed seem to be an illustration of the absurd man described in his essay. However, by juxtaposing the novel and the essay so assiduously, Sartre exercised a critical method which perhaps revealed as much about himself as it did about Camus. Interested in *ideas* as they are illustrated by fiction, Sartre depicted Camus' novel as a kind of *roman à thèse* which aimed to demonstrate the contingency of the novel and the prolixity of bad faith among men. He saw Meursault as an opaque consciousness created above all to question the assumptions of the world around him. (We shall discuss this interpretation in the chapter on Camus.) Several of Sartre's comments on Camus' style, sentence structure (anti-lyrical, connected only by simple conjunctions), and use of an artificially objective point of view are quite incisive and demonstrate Sartre's ability to discuss fictional techniques per se when he is so inclined. His main point in the essay, however, is once again occasioned more by his own preoccupations than by those of the writer he is discussing: feelings do not exist as such, they arise *in action;* Meursault is an honest man because he refuses to talk about emotions abstractly.

In another critical essay Sartre marvels at the graceful *essentialism* which underlies Giraudoux's work. How can a man living in Sartre's own time preserve an Aristotelian view of the world? Sartre writes:

"To enter fully the universe of *Choix des élues,* we must first forget the world in which we live. I therefore pretended I knew nothing about this soft paste traversed by undulations whose cause and end come from outside, this world without a future, where everything is fortuitous, where the present comes like a thief, where the event by its very nature resists thought and language, where individuals are accidents, pebbles in the past for which the mind creates general classifications after the fact." [53]

---

[52] *Ibid.,* 105.   [53] *Ibid.,* 83.

In the essay on Giraudoux, written in 1940, we find a concise statement of the emotional tonalities which underly the elaborate description of existence contained in *L'être et le néant* (1943). The author of *La nausée* seems amazed at the view of the world Giraudoux has managed to preserve.

Sartre's essay on Dos Passos (1938) is in fact a manifesto on behalf of the new technique he was to apply himself several years later in *Le sursis*, the second volume of *Les chemins de la liberté*. He admires Dos Passos' manner of telling a story, a manner which allows events to stand, irreducible, like things, by simply adding them one to the other. "Dos Passos' time," Sartre writes, "is his own creation: neither novel nor narrative . . . . It is the time of History." [54] For Sartre passions and gestures are also *things*; he feels that Dos Passos tries to preserve their character as facts by refusing to explain them or to *state* their relationship. In a narrative style which Sartre feels meets the need for an existential fiction he recognizes still another technique in harmony with his own preoccupations. Dos Passos' characters retain their uniqueness and individuality, but within the total framework of the novel they are part of a "statistical determinism." In Sartrean terms, these characters are presented *in situation*. In an essay on Husserl (1939) in which Sartre described the relevancy of phenomenology to his own era, he wrote that Husserl delivered us from Proust, from "la vie intérieure." "We shall not discover ourselves in some hidden retreat; but on the road, in the city, in the midst of a crowd, a thing among things, a man among men." [55]

The practitioners of the *nouveau roman* who have come to prominence in France in the 1960's and who appear as obvious inheritors of the phenomenological tradition do not, with the exception of Butor, seem to satisfy Sartre's moral exigencies. Although he early recognized the originality of Nathalie Sarraute's novels and wrote a preface to her *Portrait d'un inconnu* (1957), Sartre more recently criticized her fiction for its amorality and exclusion of history. She believes she is reaching fundamental rela-

---

[54] *Ibid.*, 16.   [55] *Ibid.*, 34–35.

tionships between people, Sartre says, by her "protoplasmic exchanges," when all she does is "show the abstract and infinitesimal effects of a very limited social milieu, comfortable, bourgeois, a bit worldly, where work and leisure are never differentiated. . . . The individual is never situated in the milieu which shapes him, nor the milieu in the individual. . . . In Nathalie Sarraute's books, the totality is glaring by its absence." [56] Sartre recognizes the importance of Robbe-Grillet's attempt to make *tabula rasa* of any pre-established meanings. Ideally, this stripping away of conditions should free us from the bourgeois vision, but, Sartre comments, "The total object which has its place in a novel is a *human* object, one which is nothing at all without its human meanings. The de-conditioned objects of Robbe-Grillet float. . . . If you take away man, objects are neither far nor near, they no longer exist." [57] Of all the "new novels" Michel Butor's *La modification* seems best to satisfy Sartre's evolving conception of the relation between man and objects. In this novel, Sartre says, Butor has given the object its *real meaning:* "an instrument which transforms the one who uses it." [58]

Sartre has written some excellent essays on the plastic arts. Perhaps because painting and sculpture employ nonlinguistic media, Sartre is less often tempted to impose on these arts his brilliant ability to impart to words a context which is *his* rather than that of the writer he is discussing. He is fascinated by Calder's mobiles, which he describes as "strange creatures, half-way between life and matter." On Swiss sculptor-painter Alberto Giacometti, a close friend, Sartre is truly eloquent. He tries to explain Giacometti's originality and modernity, to understand the sense of isolation, of alienation which emanates from his thin plaster figures. Distance, Sartre speculates, has become part of the object:

The fact is that Giacometti was the first to sculpture man as he is seen —from a distance. He confers *absolute distance* on his plaster figures just as the painter confers absolute distance on the inhabitants of his canvas. He creates a figure 'ten steps away' or 'twenty steps away,' and

[56] Chapsal, *Les écrivains en personne*, 214.
[57] *Ibid.*, 215.   [58] *Ibid.*, 217.

do what you will, it remains there. The result is a leap into the realm of the unreal since the relation to you of the block of plaster no longer depends on your relations to it—the liberation of Art.[59]

Sartre's essays on painters are less satisfying aesthetically. On Tintoretto and Michelangelo he writes psychological and social biography similar in approach to his studies of Baudelaire, Genet, and Flaubert. Sartre is interested in the artist as a man, in the human situation in which art is produced, rather than in painting itself. Social, economic, political, and psychological forces form the canvas upon which Sartre's characters (for that is what these artists become in his imaginative reconstructions of their lives) produce art. Because the artist lives in a society, he is bent by it, imbued with its values. Thus Sartre says of Tintoretto that he hid his genius under his opportunism and considered social success the sole obvious sign of a mystical victory. Sartre pities Tintoretto for this attitude, because despite the fact that his art goes beyond his own era the painter can only see it with the eyes of his time. In Sartre's essay, Tintoretto becomes typical of the social forces of his time: he incarnates bourgeois puritanism in a declining aristocratic republic. With audacity Sartre limns the character of a city and of an era—Venice in the sixteenth century. Tintoretto, a man involved in "a passionate love affair between a man and a city," is an artist as well. He is symbolic of an eternal dilemma: how to reconcile man's submission to time with the independence of the artist.[60]

Sartre's most characteristic literary form is the essay. He has written essays on literature, politics, philosophy, social thought, artistic biography, and on himself. He revealed his preference for the essay in 1943, when he wrote, "Pascal's death saved his *Pensées* from being composed into a strong colorless Apology; by giving them to us in their disorder, in striking down their author before he had time to gag himself, death made of these fragments the model of the genre. . . ."[61] Sartre's own essays constitute a varied ambiguous mass of writings which reflect the man, brilliant, passionate, often self-contradictory, above all intensely modern in his

[59] *Situations III*, 299.   [60] *Situations IV*, 291–346.
[61] *Situations I*, 144.

preoccupations and in his mood. Sartre's essays analyzing writers are among his most interesting. They express the dilemma which has always concerned him, the dilemma his essay on Tintoretto also highlights—how to reconcile the artist's historical situation with his creative independence. In the conclusion to *L'être et le néant* Sartre describes existential psychoanalysis as "a *moral description,* because it reveals to us the ethical meaning of different human projects." [62] Of all human projects the creative most vividly comes to grips with Sartre's conception of freedom as *freedom within a given situation.* Simone de Beauvoir says of Sartre in her autobiography, "His preface to the works of Genet became a fat book in which he tried more deeply than in his *Baudelaire* to encompass a man. He had moved closer to psychoanalysis and to Marxism and it seemed to him at present that situations tightly limited the possibilities of the individual; his freedom consisted in not enduring situations passively, but, by the very movement of his existence, in interiorizing them and going beyond them to meanings." [63] As Sartre points out in "Question de méthode," the introduction to the *Critique de la raison dialectique,* only by a fusion of existentialism and Marxism can we hope to understand *why* one individual in an historical situation will react as he does, create what he creates, be what he is. For example:

Contemporary Marxism shows . . . that Flaubert's realism is in direct reciprocal and symbolic relation to the social and political evolution of the *petite-bourgeoisie* of the Second Empire. But Marxism *never* shows the genesis of this reciprocity of perspective. We do not know why Flaubert preferred literature to all else nor why he lived like a hermit, nor why he wrote *these* books rather than those of Duranty or of the Goncourts. Marxism situates but it reveals nothing further . . . .[64]

Sartre calls his method structural and historical anthropology. Philosophy used to be "a cultural milieu for contemporaries." Now, Sartre maintains, philosophy must be *practical* because "method is a social and political weapon." [65] "Anthropology will remain a confused mass of empirical knowledge . . . as long as we

[62] *L'être et le néant* (Paris: Gallimard, 1943), 720.
[63] Beauvoir, *La force des choses,* 217.
[64] *Critique de la raison dialectique,* 45.   [65] *Ibid.,* 16.

shall not have established the legitimacy of dialectical Reason, that is to say as long as we shall not have acquired the right to study a man, a group of men or a human object in the synthetic totality of his meanings and of his references to totalization in process. . . ." [66]

In the *Critique* Sartre briefly examines Flaubert in the light of the method he calls for, anticipating his book-length study of Flaubert, parts of which have already appeared in *Les temps modernes*. The method consists in synthesizing the analysis of an individual childhood in its family relationships with a knowledge of class structures; that is, to understand the man at his "point of insertion into his class . . . the unique family as a mediation between the universal class and the individual. . . ." [67] Hence we can read *Madame Bovary* as the product of an author who, though a Romantic schoolboy in 1830, was in 1847 a member of a generation disgusted with Romanticism. Finally, the *work* becomes a sign, a question for History to answer: "What must the era have been which demanded *this* book?" [68] Sartre's method is then both psychological and sociological. Beginning with the individual, it ends with an insight into History; conversely, an insight into History is the starting point for an understanding of the individual. Sartre admits that the writer himself is not concerned with these questions, that he wants only to write the sentence, the paragraph, the book. But his ultimate aim, whether or not he is conscious of it, is "totalization," an enterprise which deals with the total situation and attempts to go beyond it.

The circularity of Sartre's method is vividly illustrated by his recent essays on Flaubert (*Les temps modernes*, 1966). Basing the major portion of his analysis on Flaubert's early writings, Sartre evokes the young writer first as he experiences the bourgeoisie as the class of his origin around 1837, then as affected by his reading of Vigny's *Chatterton*, which concretized for him the antagonism between the bourgeois and the poet. Sartre points out that Flaubert was unable to see the bourgeoisie *as object* because he was inside of it. But because he was determined to see it from the

[66] *Ibid.*, 10–11.   [67] *Ibid.*, 47.   [68] *Ibid.*, 95.

outside he could not see it *as subject* either. Hence we have "the irreality in virulence" which Sartre judges to be Flaubert's hallmark. "The result," Sartre writes, "is that he can know neither others nor himself, because in spite of his efforts to view the world 'as an aristocrat,' this bourgeois dichotomy imposes on him a bourgeois point of view on the bourgeoisie." [69] At once accepting and condemning the class of his origin, Flaubert lived in bad faith in his desire to "become classless through merit, but to do so with the approval of his own class." [70] Sartre's most ingenious comments on Flaubert deal with matters of style and subject. Flaubert, writes Sartre, made *la bêtise* (stupidity) a thing; he made "nothing" the subject of language. These creative transformations were the result of his situation—he was what was made of him. Flaubert's famous objectivity is for Sartre an a posteriori judgment: "Flaubert never *thinks*: the defender of 'objectivity' has no objectivity." [71] His mockery of bourgeois speech was after the fact; he thought that way himself, then tried to separate himself from the social and artistic implications of that mode of thought by the style which expressed it.

Ultimately Flaubert sought to escape his bourgeois condition by conceiving a superior role, that of the Artist. Sartre writes, "Gustave's aim—to be separated from himself by leaning like a stony witness above his life—is the aim of all those who . . . believe they escape culpability by admitting themselves to be guilty. . . . Recourse to the infinite is an attitude: humiliated, one climbs up." [72] Sartre condemns Flaubert for refusing a solidarity which would have situated him in history. (This is much the same criticism he leveled at Camus in 1952.) In trying to join a community "out of history" Flaubert created a specious objectivity; the artist is in the object, but hidden. Flaubert's style is his way of groping for the absolute. One of Sartre's most interesting remarks in his generally tedious analysis of Flaubert's early writing is his comment that

[69] "La conscience de classe chez Flaubert," *Les temps modernes*, No. 240 (May, 1966), 1,943.   [70] *Ibid.*, 1,951.
[71] "La conscience de classe chez Flaubert (fin)," *Les temps modernes*, No. 241 (June, 1966), 2,125.
[72] "Flaubert, du poète à l'Artiste (II)," *Les temps modernes*, No. 244 (September, 1966), 467–68.

Madame Bovary is the book with "the invisible subject matter" of which Flaubert dreamed. This subject matter, Sartre writes in a footnote, is "The world is Hell." [73] We shall have to await his book to find out how Sartre comes to grips with a novel which has always fascinated him and which he evidently admires, but which certainly does not fulfill his own criteria for fiction.

Sartre's comments on Naturalism have generally been unfavorable, for several reasons. First, he is inclined to condemn its deterministic framework. Second, he has always been irritated by the adverse reactions to his own fiction which have labeled it Naturalism because of similarity of mood and atmosphere. (The ugliness which pervades the novels of Zola is not unlike the ugliness present in Sartre's depiction of lives lived in bad faith.) However, because Naturalism did in fact take account of history, Sartre judges it favorably by comparison with the objectivity of Flaubert. He writes:

The Naturalistic novelist . . . although he posits himself as creative subject, does not claim to leave the world; rather, he aims to reconstitute a social ensemble (events and structures) *in a particular perspective.* And in spite of everything this perspective reveals the writer's roots: Zola speaks of courtesans, of bourgeois men, of peasants, of workers, never of *Man.* This is because he is *of his time,* because he sees things from his milieu. For example, he totalizes the temporal destiny of a family. Thus the problem of Naturalism—and of realism as well—is that of the truthfulness of fiction.[74]

By contrast, Flaubert exhibited bad faith in his attempt to become part of a community outside of history. In this he resembled Baudelaire. By claiming separateness from his milieu, Flaubert "concealed from himself his gratuitousness, the unjustifiable freedom of his choice," Sartre wrote in *Baudelaire.* "He replaced the fallen nobility by a spiritual confraternity, he safeguarded his mission as an intellectual (*clerc*)." [75]

Sartre's book on Baudelaire (1947) was his first extended ven-

---

[73] "Flaubert, du poète à l'Artiste (fin)," *Les temps modernes,* No. 245 (October, 1966), 659, 49 *n.*
[74] *Ibid.,* 601.   [75] *Baudelaire* (Paris: Gallimard, 1947), 164.

ture into existential psychoanalysis. In many ways it remains his most successful to date. Better written, more compact and concentrated than his study of Jean Genet (1952), less jargonistic than the excerpts so far published from the study of Flaubert, *Baudelaire* contains the essential Sartrean canon. A lonely introspective man severely affected by his mother's remarriage to a man he hated, Baudelaire turned his situation into a choice; he assumed his situation. "He claimed his solitude so that at least it would come to him from himself, in order not to have to endure it passively." [76] Sartre's Baudelaire is a typically Sartrean hero, obsessively self-conscious, always leaning inward upon himself, unable to be "natural." Sartre describes the famous Baudelairean *ennui* as a metaphysical feeling, as Baudelaire's "interior landscape." In poetic creation he seeks pure freedom, by inventing his own ends, by making the gratuity of consciousness into an end in itself. Sartre finds in Baudelaire the same bad faith evident in Flaubert, with this difference: in Baudelaire bad faith is evinced in his fundamental inability to take himself seriously. Hence his love of artifice, of dressing up like a dandy, his attraction to frigid women. As Sartre paints it, Baudelaire's desire is a solitary one, the result of his hatred of *things* because they exist so completely. (Baudelaire is Roquentin with pretensions.)

"From childhood, in a deterministic era," Sartre writes of Baudelaire, "he had the intuition that the spiritual life is not given but made; and his reflective lucidity allowed him to formulate the ideal of self-possession: man is truly himself, in good as in evil, at the extreme point of tension." [77] Sartre made the reading of *Chatterton* the key psychological experience which led Flaubert to decide to become an artist. Sartre's Baudelaire finds in Poe the image *of an existence which is a destiny.* He decides to become the *elected one.* In Baudelaire's pursuit of "the impossible ideal of creating himself" totally, Sartre finds the paradigm of the creative contradiction. He writes, "Each poet pursues in his own way this synthesis of existence and being which we know to be impossible. This quest leads him to choose certain objects in the world which appear to

[76] *Ibid.,* 20.   [77] *Ibid.,* 155.

him the expressive symbols of this reality where existence and being may be fused and to try to appropriate them to himself by contemplation." [78] Sartre interprets Baudelaire's choice of imagery as an effort to "objectify his consciousness." There is no doubt some truth in this remark. However, and here we see the weakness of Sartre's comments on poetry, this would apply to almost any poet. It provides no special insight into Baudelaire's unique poetic genius.

Sartre's "progressive-regressive method," as he names it in the *Critique*, stumbles over its own circularity. The poet is a product of his time—thus we must try to understand his poetry in terms of his historical situation. But the history must also be interpreted in the light of the poetry. What Sartre fails to do for Baudelaire, for Flaubert, for Genet, is to explain precisely what he himself admits is most important, namely, *why* in any given historical situation some men become creative artists and others do not. Beginning with his long-standing love for certain poems and novels, Sartre imposes on their creators an elaborate analysis which fuses Marxism with existential psychoanalysis. He constructs some ingenious psychoanalytical interpretations of the creators *as men*. Their works remain as they were, intact in their fundamental mystery as objects outside the pale of Sartre's method. What he actually creates is a mythology of creative artists, a mythology in which the creator is the existential hero of his time.

Nowhere is Sartre's method, with its brilliance and its flaws, more evident than in *Saint Genet, comédien et martyr* (1952). In 573 pages Sartre attempts to reconstruct Genet the man through the mythical representations Genet himself has given us. Sartre's aim is to find the original event to which Genet endlessly refers.[79] Actually, this event is described quite early in the book; it is the moment of "ontological malediction" when the young orphan is accused of stealing by his foster parents. From that moment he becomes what others define him as, a thief, the eternal Other, the Wicked One. Through an overlong account of Genet's life as thief,

---

[78] *Ibid.*, 199–200.
[79] *Saint Genet, comédien et martyr* (Paris: Gallimard, 1952), 12.

pederast, and traveler in the marginal world of prisons and perversions, Sartre eventually leads us to an insight into Genet's choice of writing. Finding that Beauty alone offers him a weapon against the society which has cast him out, Genet chooses the beauty of evil: by choosing evil he can destroy *value* and thus have a defense against the world which condemns him.[80]

In *Saint Genet* Sartre comes closer to defining genius than in his studies of Baudelaire and Flaubert, when he writes, "Genius is not a gift but the 'out' one invents in desperate cases." The case history of Genet thus illustrates "the choice the writer made of himself, of his life and the meaning of the universe right down to the formal characteristics of his style and composition, right down to the structure of his images . . . ."[81] Sartre's interpretation of Genet is more convincing than his interpretations of Baudelaire and Flaubert because his evidence is drawn almost entirely from Genet's writings. In these writings the images and the mythology are already unified into the schema Sartre employs. In other words, Sartre tells us what Genet says, and what he says about what he says. The connecting prose is Sartre's; the mythology is Genet's own. The overall result is a tedious narrative by Sartre illuminated by quotations from Genet. Sartre's Genet is Genet himself; Baudelaire and Flaubert are interesting fictional characters in the Sartrean anthropology of art.

"I have always written literature of circumstance," Sartre admitted to an interviewer in 1960.[82] He went on to say that he had wanted to write novels and plays long before he knew what philosophy was. Now, with the experience of more than twenty years of writing, including philosophical as well as creative work, Sartre admits more readily than he once did that thought alone cannot explain or take account of a unique work of art. "No one will write philosophy on *Madame Bovary*, because it is a unique book. More unique than its author, like all books."[83] Any evaluation of Sartre's novels must of course take into consideration his ideas on fiction. However, the theory cannot and does not wholly account for the

---

[80] *Ibid.,* 521.   [81] *Ibid.,* 536.
[82] Chapsal, *Les écrivains en personne,* 207.   [83] *Ibid.,* 209.

success or failure of the imaginative product. The great temptation with Sartre is to apply his own method to his characters. However, if we keep in mind that Sartre applies his method for the most part to the artists themselves and not to the characters, we can avoid the error he generally avoids, that of equating the characters with their creator.

When Sartre says that he has always written literature of circumstance, he is reaffirming his commitment to a conception of literature which refuses to separate the actual world from the world of art. He prefers a dramatic literature which deals with man in situation and which does not ignore the historical consciousness to which his generation fell heir. "It's no longer a question of contemplating the immobility of substances which are what they are, nor of finding the rules for a series of phenomena," he says of contemporary philosophy. "It's a question of man—at once an *agent* and an *actor*—who produces and performs his drama by living the contradictions of his situation . . . ." [84] Since 1949, when he published chapters of the fourth and unfinished volume of *Les chemins de la liberté*, Sartre has abandoned fiction for the theater. A theater of situations is better suited to his dramatic conception of philosophy than is the novel. "A play . . . is the most appropriate framework today for showing man in action. . . . Philosophy . . . claims to concern itself with that man. That is why the theater is philosophical and philosophy is dramatic." [85] As Sartre's thinking has evolved he has exhausted the limits of novelistic fiction as he conceived them. His plays have continued to grow in complexity and depth. It is likely that in the future he will be valued more highly as a dramatist than as a novelist. Nevertheless, the fiction he published between 1938 (*La nausée*) and 1949 (*La mort dans l'âme*) represents a unique period in literary history.

Sartre's fictional style is indeed what Jeanson has called "a refusal of style." Simone de Beauvoir tells us that as a young man Sartre was concerned with not being overwhelmed by emotion for the thing he wished to describe. This "distance between the word and the thing, between the created work and the given world" was

---

[84] *Ibid.*, 208.   [85] *Ibid.*

for Sartre "the very condition of literature and its reason for being. The writer should make use of this disparity, for his success . . . [lies] in assuming this stalemate." [86] In an early critical essay, Sartre further refined his conception of the language of fiction. He wrote that an idea cannot be captured totally by a sentence, a chapter, a volume; an *idea* may well be "inexpressible and represent only a method for viewing certain problems." [87] He was well aware that his philosophical concerns were related to his fiction; they did not, however, define it. Germaine Brée has pointed out that Sartre's realism is perhaps "intellectual" in origin; it is nonetheless disturbingly alive.[88] Merleau-Ponty explains the characteristic ugliness which generally constitutes the mood and atmosphere of Sartre's fiction as "the collision of man, to the extent that he is nothing or that he is free, with nature experienced as plenitude and destiny." [89] Essentially Merleau-Ponty is describing the same *décalage* which is present in the fictional world of Camus, with this difference: in Camus the disparity between man's desire for meaning and certainty and the indifferent separateness of the universe gives rise to a lyrical nostalgia. This nostalgia then becomes for Camus the basis for the stoic resignation of the "absurd man." The defeat is transmuted by a logic of the emotions into a peculiarly human kind of victory. On the other hand, in Sartre's fictional world, where "the feeling is built by the actions one carries out" [90] and where his characters are depicted as incapable of acting freely, the collision of man with nature gives rise to a feeling of disgust, of self-contempt, in extreme cases to a feeling of nausea.

Sartre was aware of and sensitive to the comparisons made between his fiction and Naturalism. His defense was based primarily on the crucial factor of freedom: "When the existentialist author depicts a coward, he is saying that this coward is responsible for his cowardice. . . . What readers obscurely sense and what horrifies them is that the coward we present is guilty of being a

---

[86] Beauvoir, *La force de l'âge*, 44–45.   [87] *Situations I*, 298.
[88] Germaine Brée and Margaret Guiton, *The French Novel from Gide to Camus* (New York: Harcourt, Brace and World, 1962), 205.
[89] Maurice Merleau-Ponty, *Sens et non-sens* (Paris: Nagel, 1948), 80.
[90] *L'existentialisme est un humanisme*, 45.

coward." [91] In this matter of fixing responsibility existentialist fiction perhaps appeared uglier than Naturalism; it intended to be morally beautiful because it was honest.

In the present day, when a literature of ugliness and of pornography is so widespread as to be commonplace, Sartre's novels no longer shock. We are little inclined to judge them as they were judged in the 1940's. Further, the man of bad faith has become a fictional cliché. (Indeed, the hero who surprises today is the one who acts in good faith—*he* is the one who seems unusual and faintly archaic.) Thus, with the perspective of some twenty years, we judge Sartre's novels without shock and without the historical anxieties which made his earlier readers identify with his situations and react so violently. The novels themselves gain stature in some respects and lose in others. The particular dilemmas of choice his novels present seem less urgent, more moralistic, far less exciting. His use of colloquial crudity barely touches us. However, his fictional gift for creating mood and atmosphere, his talent for psychological analysis clothed in antitraditional form emerge as the hallmarks of a unique imagination.

By his own admission Sartre was strongly influenced by the techniques of John Dos Passos. In *42nd Parallel* Sartre found in concrete form a mediation between freedom and social determination. As Simone de Beauvoir writes, Dos Passos "had invented with respect to his heroes a distance which permitted him to present them at once in their minute individuality and as a pure social product. . . . Dos Passos furnished us with a new critical instrument which we used liberally." [92] Hemingway's technique of presenting objects only as they appeared from the perspective of a unique subjectivity guided Sartre in his own novels. [93] And Sartre's reading in 1932 of Céline's *Voyage au bout de la nuit* was a crucial moment in his literary development. Beauvoir writes that Céline "attacked war, colonialism, mediocrity, commonplaces, society, in a style and tone which enchanted us. Céline had forged a new instrument: a style of writing as alive as the spoken word. What a release after the marmorean sentences of Gide, Alain, Valéry!

[91] *Ibid.*, 59–60.   [92] Beauvoir, *La force de l'âge*, 143.
[93] *Ibid.*, 144–45.

Sartre profited from this. He once for all abandoned the stilted language he had used in *La légende de la vérité*." [94] Céline was to complain bitterly and with cause during his persecution and exile following the war that Sartre, his most virulent attacker, owed him a great deal in literary terms. (See the chapter on Céline.) In retrospect, Beauvoir finds a "pre-Fascist" attitude in *Mort à crédit* because of the contempt Céline expressed for the "little people." [95] It is interesting to note that the epigraph to *La nausée* is from Céline's *L'église*.

In the *Critique de la raison dialectique* Sartre demonstrates how his view of *things* has changed since his productive fictional period. He says that all things are "signs," that man gives meaning to things through his projects. Man understands these meanings only to the extent that he is himself meaningful. [96] He shapes his tools and is shaped by them. The position is one which has evolved from Sartre's growing concentration on moral and historical issues. This shift of emphasis is fundamentally inimical to the creation of fiction as he earlier conceived it. For fiction can succeed as an illusion of reality only when it is primarily descriptive. Once prescriptive, it is no longer fiction; it is instead the moral essay. In Sartre's recent writings such as the *Critique* and *Les mots* we find the sources of the fictional dead end he apparently reached in 1949.

In his youth Sartre was above all concerned with the "irreducible reality of things." When Raymond Aron returned from a year of study in Germany and jokingly said to Sartre that to talk of the cocktails before them on the café table was philosophy, Sartre realized that phenomenology made it possible for him to do precisely what he had longed to do—to speak of things. [97] If he wanted to encompass the world of things, it was not enough to look at them and be moved by them; he had to capture their meaning and fix it in words. [98] Fusing his preoccupation with phenomenological reality with a growing contempt for *la vie intérieure* as the primary subject of literature, Sartre's thought moved toward his early essay

---

[94] *Ibid.*, 142. *La légende de la vérité* is a very early work which Sartre never published.
[95] *Ibid.*, 142, 2 n.   [96] *Critique de la raison dialectique*, 98.
[97] Beauvoir, *La force de l'âge*, 141.   [98] *Ibid.*, 151.

on the transcendance of the Ego and the collection of short stories, *Le mur* (1939). The stories in *Le mur*, written between 1936 and 1938, contain the basic elements of Sartrean fiction: fundamentally unsympathetic characters acting in bad faith; carefully controlled use of point of view to convey subjective perspectives on things and events; brilliant visual and sensory description; complex psychological analysis achieved primarily by perceptual descriptions and ironically false self-analysis on the part of the characters. Within their compass, the stories "La chambre" and "Intimité" are among Sartre's finest achievements in fiction.

La nausée (1938), Sartre's first novel, in many ways remains his most successful work of fiction. Roquentin, a lonely introspective intellectual, retires to the Norman town of Bouville in 1932 in order to complete a historical biography of the Marquis de Rollebon, an eighteenth-century nobleman. Roquentin has previously traveled extensively and seems in his present sedentary situation to have decided tacitly that his past life of adventure has not brought him whatever he was seeking. The novel is written in the form of a journal, apparently discovered and published after Roquentin either died or went mad, as is suggested by the "Avertissement des éditeurs" which precedes the journal proper and which provides the aforementioned objective information. Sartre himself described the novel as a tract on contingency (*un factum sur la contingence*).[99]

After the initial installation in Bouville, Roquentin begins to find his days haunted by an undefined uneasiness. He works desultorily in the public library, spends his leisure time in the ugly streets or depressing cafés of Bouville, and becomes more and more bored and dispirited. He begins to discover that available objective information on the Marquis de Rollebon does not add up to a clear picture of a life, that eighteenth-century contemporaries provide disparate pieces of information which could be put together in almost any way at all. As Roquentin's research proceeds, the Marquis de Rollebon begins to disappear into an incoherent mass of unassimilable facts. Roquentin becomes less and less interested in

[99] *Ibid.*, 111.

his project and begins to concentrate his attention on the problem which his discouragement has brought into the open—what constitutes a human existence? He turns inward upon himself and finds that he can say as little about his own biography as about that of his historical subject. Memories, snapshots, dead desires form no coherent pattern. He cannot reconstruct his own existence *as it really was* since he is viewing it from the vantage point of the present, that is, with the sense that it is indeed a story. As it actually transpired, it *was,* simply. It was happening. Once he *thinks about it* he is imposing on his existence in the past the perspective of the present, that is, a *form* external to the actual day-to-day events.

Roquentin marvels at the men in the cafés who are able to talk about "what happened to them" with confidence. He realizes that his own existence has no form, is not a story he can tell. Having thus abandoned biography (Rollebon) and autobiography (himself), he is reduced to contemplating the naked fact of his existence, which is formless, meaningless, and terrifying. (His own face in the hotel room mirror is only a blob with protuberances that seem to be covered with fish scales—his eyes.) He has already noticed that things, objects around him, a pebble, some old newspapers, the purple suspenders worn by a café owner, terrify and disgust him. In Simone de Beauvoir's autobiography we find a concise summary of the rest of the novel as Sartre himself related it to his understandably confused publisher. "Beginning with Sunday there is no further welding in the narrative. . . . There is nothing but the fear, the museum, the discovery of existence, the conversation with the Autodidacte [the self-taught man], contingency, the end." [100]

The novel's central scene takes place in the public park, where the gnarled roots of some ancient trees reveal concretely to Roquentin the utter superfluity, the supreme contingency of his own existence.[101] (This scene apparently takes place on the Monday following the Sunday to which Sartre referred.) Naked existence is an obscenity, an imperfection; Roquentin himself is *de trop.*

[100] *Ibid.,* 307.   [101] *La nausée* (Paris: Gallimard, 1938), 159–60.

"Every existent," he realizes, "is born for no reason, goes on through weakness and dies by chance." [102] At this point Roquentin decides to go to Paris to see Anny, a woman he thinks he loves. That attempt to find a meaning to his life also fails. He returns to Bouville, decides he must do something. He cannot justify writing, for example, because "to do something is to create existence, and there is already enough of that." [103] In the last few pages of the novel Roquentin listens to a blues recording of "One of these days." (Sartre mistakenly cites the lyrics as "Some of these days/ You'll miss me honey.") In the necessity and harmony of the music he thinks he glimpses some solution to his present impasse —to create something, like the music, which will need no justification. Perhaps he should write something; certainly not a history, since that speaks of what used to exist, and "never can one existent justify the existence of another existent. . . . Another kind of book . . . beautiful and hard as steel and which will make people ashamed of their existence. . . . A book. A novel." [104] Roquentin hopes that this work will perhaps give a form and a justification to his existence. And at this point Roquentin falls back into the web of irony which holds the novel together—once the book is published, he hopes he will be able to accept himself. The novel ends, ambiguous in its conclusion. Did Roquentin go mad, like the man he used to see in the public park staring fish-eyed at his own foot? Did he indeed go on to write something? All we know is that the journal was found among his papers.

The richness and complexity of *La nausée* is poorly conveyed by a statement of its structure or its capital events. Sartre's gift for visual detail is revealed in brief descriptions (the Boulevard Noir in the evening, the café scenes) as well as in the scenes where Roquentin confronts his own existence in its substantial obscenity. The character portrayals of Lucie, the maid in the hotel whose ability to suffer Roquentin admires, and of the Autodidacte, who is reading his way alphabetically through the Bouville public library and who is also a pederast, are incisive and memorable. An extended critique of literary traditions (the novel of adventure, the

[102] *Ibid.,* 169.   [103] *Ibid.,* 216.   [104] *Ibid.,* 222.

Proustian deification of memory, the Gidian journal) is subtly woven into the strictly maintained first-person narrative. *La nausée* is indeed a metaphysical novel; it is also a lively, humorous account of an individual crisis in the life of man who without knowing it questions the bad faith in which most men (including himself) live. It is a literary *tour de force* mocking literary *tours de force*. Germaine Brée has aptly called Sartre's critical method in the novel "the indirect use of negative formulations." [105] In a critical essay on the "new mysticism" of Maurice Blanchot written in 1943, Sartre described Blanchot's technique in terms which apply equally well to his own method in *La nausée*: "Tools, acts, ends, all is familiar to us, and we are in such a relationship of intimacy with them that we scarcely notice them; but, just at the moment when we feel ourselves closed into a warm atmosphere of organic sympathy, they are presented to us in a cold and strange light." [106] Roquentin's *nausea* is an ascesis preliminary to any assessment in good faith of the relationship between man's freedom and his existence.

La nausée has been widely examined and frequently criticized as fiction. The severest critiques have come from those who read the novel as a purely philosophical work which illustrates the ideas Sartre expressed nonfictionally in *L'être et le néant*. Iris Murdoch has written that *La nausée* is not a novel; she calls it "Sartre's philosophical myth." [107] This reading tends to ignore one crucial fact. *La nausée* was written in the 1930's. Sartre later insisted that prose must be a tool of communication, and literature a depiction of situation. We have no reason to apply exclusively his later criteria for fiction to his first novel and therefore to judge that it is not, in fact, a novel. It is a novel of a very special kind and quite successful within its own framework. A critical and ironic portrayal of an isolated existence and its struggle to cope with the realization of contingency, *La nausée* uniquely fuses a subjective point of view with objective considerations of others and the world—that is, it fuses *being* with *meaning*. Sartre's fictional marriage of two fundamentally disparate domains into a unified narrative is highly origi-

---

[105] Brée, *The French Novel*, 209. [106] *Situations I*, 137.
[107] Iris Murdoch, *Sartre, Romantic Rationalist* (Cambridge: Bowes and Bowes, 1953), 17.

nal and his writing very talented. Ever since Sartre published *Les chemins de la liberté* between 1945 and 1949 critics have wondered *when* Sartre would write a truly outstanding novel. The fact is that he did so in 1938—*La nausée*. As his thinking evolved, however, Sartre began to conceive that the metaphysical discovery embodied in his first novel was perhaps a malady with political causes and political remedies. *Les chemins de la liberté* was the next phase in his search for a literature to deal with his growing sense of historicity.

Les *chemins de la liberté* comprises three novels, *L'âge de raison* (1945), *Le sursis* (1945), and *La mort dans l'âme* (1949). Of the promised fourth and final volume Sartre published only a section entitled "Drôle d'amitié" in *Les temps modernes* (November and December, 1949). The trilogy deals primarily with the personal situations of several central characters during the period from the pre-Munich days of 1938, through the crucial last week of September, 1938, to the fall of France in 1940. Mathieu Delarue, a thirty-four-year-old teacher of philosophy, is the prototype of the *salaud*, the man of bad faith who justifies his inability to commit himself to anything or anyone by his abstract ideal of freedom. Daniel Sereno is a well-to-do homosexual who is unable to accept the fact of his perversion and spends most of his time in self-hatred, playing a variety of insincere roles aimed at self-punishment. The third major character, Brunet, is an active member of the Communist Party, a rough and determined man to whom the self-analyses of his friend Mathieu seem idle frivolity. In addition to these three, there are many other characters of lesser importance (though not always of lesser fictional density): Boris and Ivich Serguine, children of Russian expatriates; Marcelle, Mathieu's pregnant mistress; Lola, the middle-aged mistress of young Boris.

L'âge de *raison* is set in the summer of 1938, and revolves about Mathieu's dilemma when he learns of Marcelle's pregnancy. The plot itself is simple and unremarkable, except perhaps for the resolution, when Daniel offers to marry Marcelle, relieving Mathieu of the decision between marriage and an abortion. However, the novel is unique in its deliberate application of Sartre's pronounced fictional theory. All events are seen subjectively, by the different characters. There is no deterministic view of human nature. His characters are free, even though they do not realize it, and their situations are shown rather than explained by the novelist. Their thoughts are expressed through interior monologues, their values and fears through the way they perceive things and people around them. Sartre's use of mood and atmosphere is excellent. He conveys the personal doubts, hesitations, unspoken feelings of his characters effectively without ever departing from the restricted points of view he has set himself. As each character lives his indetermination, he muses on how others see him. In this way Sartre elaborates a network of relationships in bad faith which exudes a feeling of inauthenticity. Lack of commitment is shown by skillful indirection. Certain scenes (Marcelle's suffocating pink room where she vegetates in fleshy uncertainty, the penny arcade where Daniel makes a homosexual contact while detesting the cheap vulgarity of the situation) match in intensity the brilliance of Sartre's best short stories. The conversational idiom of *L'âge de raison* is crude and convincingly aural.

The novel's major weakness becomes apparent when Sartre is forced to confront the *moral* implications of the situations he so brilliantly describes. The dialogues in which his characters discuss and attempt to judge themselves falter badly. Too much is stated. The reader finds it hard to believe that creatures with such obvious lack of insight into the meaning of their existences can so eloquently state the true nature of these existences. The overall effect of the longer dialogues is one of preaching. The style of Sartre's essays on moral ambiguities destroys the illusion of fiction. The task Sartre set himself in *L'âge de raison* is impossible: to explain inauthenticity by incarnating it. Despite his determination to make freedom his *subject* and his *technique,* he cannot do both. Whereas in *La nausée* the subject evolves naturally from the situation, in *L'âge de raison* the characters *are already* examples of the problems with which Sartre tends to deal. Contingency seems to grow out of the very texture of the prose in *La nausée*. Inauthenticity is already present when *L'âge de raison* opens; it is then analyzed, discussed, thought about endlessly. The graceful irony of Sartre's first novel is of no use to him in his second. In its place he must resort to an analysis of motives which differs from traditional psychological analysis, which he claims to discard, only in the manner in which it is presented. As Victor Brombert has acutely remarked, what are these "situations" if not a series of inalienable subjectivities? [108] The characters themselves provide the analysis the traditional novelist supplied. The end result is the same. *L'âge de raison* is a psychological novel dealing with peculiarly contemporary characters. Its claim to indeterminancy is belied by its substance.

Le sursis finds the characters now dispersed in various parts of France. Sartre employs the technique he so much admired in Dos Passos, shifting from one place to another, from one character to another without transition. The unifying factor is of course the Munich crisis which creates a new element to which each character must now relate himself, the possibility that war will break out over the occupation of Czechoslovakia and that France will become involved. Many of the familiar characters, Mathieu, Daniel, and a host of newly introduced ones, find that they are to be mobilized into the army. The ubiquitous shifting from place to place (including the chambers in Munich where Chamberlain waits) is highly effective. The personal and the historical situation become indissolubly interrelated. The scope of the novel moves beyond the petty hesitations and doubts of *L'âge de raison* to a confrontation of the individual with history. Henri Peyre has pointed out that the influence of Jules Romains' Unanimism is probably as large a factor in Sartre's method as Dos Passos' narrative technique.[109] The novel's most effective moments are those in which Sartre evokes in quick sketches, composed of incisive dialogue and brief evocations of atmosphere, the feelings and actions of minor characters (the virginal Philippe who is afraid to be drafted and has his first sexual adventure in a night of drunkenness, the invalids from the sanitorium at Berck who are loaded like packages into a train). But the fictional success of these sketches is

[108] Victor Brombert, *The Intellectual Hero* (Chicago and London: University of Chicago Press, 1964), 199.
[109] Henri Peyre, *French Novelists of Today* (New York: Oxford University Press, 1967), 266.

in some ways a contradiction of Sartre's theory of existentialist fiction. These characters are not free; they are straws in the rising wind of history. Sartre maintains the strictness of his subjective points of view. However, his total narrative effect is fundamentally deterministic. His time is, like that of Dos Passos and of Romains, "the time of History." "Statistical determinism" is not freedom, even if it works "by addition." At the end of *Le sursis* war seems to be averted. But the individuals who were frightened by the prospect of armed conflict and who began during the terrible week to reflect on the issues are now ashamed. The reprieve is not a resolution, it is a compromise.

La mort dans l'âme describes the French defeat in 1940. Divided into two parts, it views this defeat first from the point of view of Mathieu, then from that of Brunet. The only one of the three volumes which deals directly with engagement, it shows two different responses to the dilemma of the individual immersed in history. Mathieu, now in the army, finally assumes his freedom in a futile and rather suicidal holding action designed to slow down the German advance. He has at last realized that freedom would not "happen" to him, no matter how long he waits. It consists instead in doing something. He is much like Hugo in Sartre's play *Les mains sales,* who ironically has himself shot in order finally to exist. Hemingway's "Short Happy Life of Francis Macomber" is probably the prototype of both these situations, with this difference. In Sartre we consistently find a virulent anti-Romanticism. Sartre's heroes do not "become what they are," they simply decide in a paroxym of self-hatred to accept *that they are* and then act in order to give their being a form. Brunet, the Communist, allows himself to be captured, believing that he can be useful politically within a German prison camp. His experience in prison begins to undermine some of his doctrinaire certainties. *La mort dans l'âme* ends with a scene of carnage and desolation of striking power, as Brunet wonders what the next day will bring besides vultures to pick the bones of the dead prisoners. The impression conveyed by both parts of *La mort dans l'âme* is that of a man confronting an impasse, a kind of stone wall beyond which there is nothing. Mathieu seems likely to die; Brunet watches the death of his fellow prisoners. Nothing is gained, and many things which seemed to become clearer in *Le sursis*—the issues, the moral stands—become blurred.

In the published excerpts from the unfinished fourth volume Brunet is further caught in the conflict between his personal convictions, his friendships, and the discipline demanded of him by the Party. In the light of his character as presented in *L'âge de raison*, Brunet has grown, assumed depth and ambiguity. However, the moral imperatives which buttressed him have weakened. Commitment has become an elusive thing, an impossible necessity which can never be clearly defined. From Mathieu's vacillating inauthenticity at the beginning of the trilogy we have come to Brunet's vacillating honesty. Brunet has become the central character and he has reached an impasse. Simone de Beauvoir admits frankly that she prefers *La mort dans l'âme* to the earlier volumes of *Les chemins de la liberté* because "in the transparency of each individual vision the world preserves its opaqueness." She goes on to explain why Sartre lost interest in finishing *Les chemins*. With all the characters disposed of (as he apparently planned for the unfinished fourth volume), there was no one to confront the problems presented by the war's end.

There was nothing he could say about the Resistance because he viewed the novel as a form of questioning and under the Occupation we knew unequivocally how to act. . . . To skip ten years and plunge his characters into the anxieties of the present era would have had no meaning: the last volume would have contradicted all the hopes of the next to last. Everything was so clearly and imperiously prefigured there was no way for Sartre to change the plan or for him to enjoy conforming to it.[110]

In his concern with creating a literature relevant to life, Sartre wrote himself into a dead end in *Les chemins de la liberté*. Perhaps, as Robert Champigny speculated in 1955, Sartre can no longer write fiction because his conception of prose as a critical instrument precludes its depicting anything but dead ends.[111] The

[110] Beauvoir, *La force des choses*, 212–14.
[111] Robert Champigny, *Stages on Sartre's Way* (Bloomington: Indiana University Press, 1955), 191.

intervening years tend to bear out Champigny's judgment. Nevertheless, Sartre has continued to write. As he says in *Les mots*, "It's my habit and besides it's my craft. For a long time I mistook my pen for a sword: now I know our powerlessness. No matter, I make, I shall make books; they are necessary; it all serves some purpose. Culture saves nothing and no one, it does not justify. But it's a product of man; only this critical mirror shows him his own image." [112] Sartre is no less bound to literature than those writers who attributed to it a divine office. Sartre's reasons for his attachment are expressed in the language of our time. His moral concerns have perhaps made it immoral for him any longer to write fiction. Fiction is not ideally suited to expressing moral injunctions. Neither can it successfully be molded to purely political ends. Sartre's love of irony has survived the demise of his fiction. In *La nausée* he employed irony to demonstrate the bad faith of all prior attitudes toward human existence, including his own. As he explains in *Les mots*, "At thirty I managed to put down in *La nausée* . . . the unjustified brackish existence of my contemporaries and to place my own beyond question. *I was* Roquentin, in him I showed without self-indulgence the pattern of my life; at the same time I was *myself*, the elected one, the analyst of hell, with my high-powered microscope of glass and steel focused on my own protoplasmic syrups." [113] But in the confession itself, in the analysis of his own impostures which constitutes *Les mots*, Sartre's irony prevails. We are no closer to the reality of the man than we were to that of his character Roquentin. Both judge themselves harshly; both are conscious of postures and unable to avoid assuming them. *Les mots* is a unique autobiography, characteristic of the writer who produced it and of his significance for this era. In this work Sartre's concern with responsibility and authenticity has led him directly to what he sought to avoid—a special form of posturing, the pose of perfect understanding of his own motives in the past. By applying the method of his own existential psychoanalysis to his childhood, Sartre has perhaps invented a new type of fiction.

It is too soon to estimate the importance future generations will

[112] *Les mots* (Paris: Gallimard, 1964), 211. [113] *Ibid.*, 209–10.

accord to Sartre's philosophical writings. His fiction has been evaluated in widely different ways. His rank as a playwright is very high. And he continues to write essays at an alarming rate. Any assessment of Sartre as a writer must await the completion of his work. However, of all the writers in this study, he most completely embodies in his life and in his work a conception of literature as a *total experience* inextricably bound up with the life of modern man. This conception may well result in an *oeuvre* which is defective because of its effort to mirror the complexity of human existence. In the eyes of later generations, Sartre may be only a minor figure in the intellectual history of the twentieth century. His synthesis may lose in stature what it aims to gain in breadth. The overall meaning of his work may lie precisely in its desire to unite life and art into an indissoluble whole. In this sense he reflects a period of change whose struggles will ultimately result in a new perspective; from this perspective the struggles themselves may appear purely transitional and fundamentally derivative.

From literature as an absolute value in itself in Flaubert, to literature as an instrument for social change in Aragon or Sartre, the distance appears very great. Perhaps in the writings of Sartre lies the indication that this distance is smaller than we think. For if Sartre is correct, Flaubert and Aragon embody the same essential situation: each produced a human product meant for a human audience, and each tried in his own way to be a man in the only way he could. There is no evasion for the writer, there are only varying postures in bad or better faith. As Sartre expressed it, "Every piece of writing has a meaning, even if this meaning is very far from the one the author wanted to give it. . . . The writer is neither Vestal nor Ariel: he is in it up to his neck, whatever he does, marked, compromised, right into his most distant retreat." [114]

[114] *Situations II*, 11–12.

Albert Camus

THE ARTIST
AND HIS TIME

The death of Albert Camus in an automobile accident in 1960 marked the abrupt end of a career which had captured the imagination and attention of a wide audience. Born in Algeria in 1913 into a very poor family, Camus determined at an early age to become a writer and man of importance.[1] He came to prominence in France in 1942 with the publication of a novel, *L'étranger*, and an essay, *Le mythe de Sisyphe*. Hailed by the general reading public and by influential intellectuals such as Sartre, Camus quickly became an integral part of the literary elite of Paris under the Occupation. Although these two books were actually begun and elaborated primarily in Algeria in the years preceding the war, they struck a responsive chord in the confused and desperate emotions of the metropolitan French under German rule. The intense, ambitious, highly charming young writer found himself famous beyond his own hopes.

After joining a Resistance group in 1943 and participating in the writing and dissemination of its clandestine publication, Camus became director of the newspaper *Combat* when it began to appear openly on the eve of the liberation of Paris in the summer of 1944. His stature as a writer was reinforced by the publication in 1947 of a second novel, *La peste*.

[1] See Camus' *Carnets, mai 1935—février 1942* (Paris: Gallimard, 1962). Hereinafter cited as *Carnets I*.

Camus found himself involved in moralistic journalism on a scale much larger than his earlier forays into this field.[2] He met Sartre, who had greeted *L'étranger* as a unique and significant work of fiction, and became part of an unsuccessful movement by the intellectual Left to form a workable coalition with the Communists. (See the chapter on Sartre.) In the years from 1944 to 1952 Camus was generally regarded as a member of the existentialist group, although he frequently said he considered himself neither an existentialist nor a philosopher. In fact, he pointed out, *Le mythe de Sisyphe* was intended as a refutation of that philosophy. After his gaudy public break with Sartre in 1952 over the unfavorable review in *Les temps modernes* of *L'homme révolté* (1951),[3] Camus moved into a clearer position of independence from any definable political movement or group.[4] He also became famous abroad. The apogee of his almost universal popularity in Western countries was of course the receipt of the Nobel Prize for Literature in 1957. Freshest in the public mind at that moment were *L'homme révolté* and his third novel, *La chute* (1956).

No attempt will be made here to repeat the many excellent analyses of Camus' work as a whole.[5] He has probably received more critical attention than he himself would have believed justified. His work consists of five volumes of essays (three lyrical, two philosophical), three novels, a collection of short stories, four original plays and several adaptations, and numerous journalistic pieces. Much of this will probably fall into deserved oblivion. The concern

[2] For an account of Camus' early years as a journalist, see Germaine Brée, *Camus* (New York: Harcourt, Brace and World, 1964).

[3] A detailed account of this quarrel is given in Emmet Parker, *Albert Camus: The Artist in the Arena* (Madison: University of Wisconsin Press, 1965).

[4] Camus' very brief adhesion to the Communist Party in Algeria is described by Brée in *Camus*.

[5] In addition to Germaine Brée's book, some of the most notable are: Philip Thody, *Albert Camus, 1913–1960* (London: Hamish Hamilton, 1961); Roger Quilliot, *La mer et les prisons, essai sur Albert Camus* (Paris: Gallimard, 1956); John Cruickshank, *Albert Camus and the Literature of Revolt* (London: Oxford University Press, 1959); and Thomas Hanna, *The Thought and Art of Albert Camus* (Chicago: Regnery, 1958).

here is his attitude toward artistic responsibility and how it is related to his fictional writings.

Albert Camus provides the interesting example of a writer who was naturally disinclined to political engagement but who found the "force of circumstance" carrying him into the political arena at a dizzying pace. By his own admission he was fundamentally fuzzy-minded on politics; yet he was obliged to speak loudly and publicly on any and all issues and to justify each statement he made. Camus had become in the mid-forties the focus of an era which allowed for no retreat on the writer's part, none at least if he wished to remain in the public eye. In a sense, Camus was the product of the history of his era and also in part its victim. His fame was based in large measure on the notoriety he achieved, much less on the quality of his fiction. The recently published volumes of his notebooks reveal the extent to which he was aware of this fact.

In the 1950's Camus was uneasy over the political dogmatisms to which Sartre had turned. It was precisely Camus' uneasiness over the fusion of existentialism with Marxism which broadened his appeal beyond the borders of France. In France as well his evident weariness with the stress on engagement, authenticity, and the burdens of freedom found an audience. His beautifully written, if conceptually thin, essays invoking individual happiness, Man, and eternal values seemed an attractive respite from the intense self-questioning and constant moral choices demanded by Sartre and his group. When Camus, in an irate letter to *Les temps modernes*, attacked both the reviewer of *L'homme révolté* (Francis Jeanson) and Sartre himself, Sartre responded in a lengthy reply which expressed two attitudes toward Camus. On the one hand Sartre cuttingly indicted Camus' pretensions, confusions, and overly sensitive pride. On the other, he eloquently voiced what Camus had represented to the French in the early and mid-forties: "You encompassed in yourself the conflicts of the era, and you went beyond them in your ardor to live them. You were . . . the last and best of the heritors of Chateaubriand." [6] And Sartre con-

[6] Jean-Paul Sartre, *Situations IV* (Paris: Gallimard, 1964), 111.

tinued, "You were for several years what might be called the symbol and the proof of the solidarity of classes. And that is what the Resistance also appeared to be. . . . Thus a confluence of circumstances, one of those rare accords which make a life the image of a truth. . . ."[7]

Despite Sartre's insistence in his reply to Camus' letter on their common position as bourgeois intellectuals ("For you *are* a bourgeois, Camus, like me, what else could you be?"),[8] Camus did not in fact have the same bad conscience over his origins as did Sartre. Camus felt his childhood had indeed been privileged, but in a manner quite different from that of the writers with whom he became associated in Paris. His childhood had been financially impoverished.[9] But his love of natural beauty which forms the backdrop for the early lyrical essays and for *L'étranger* and *La peste* apparently more than compensated for a lack of material comforts. As he wrote in his *Carnets*, "To rich people the sky, an additional gift, seems a natural gift. To poor people, its character as an infinite grace is restored."[10]

Camus' central theme of justice and its ambiguities in man's life was born directly out of that "luxury of beauty" which so deeply affected him in his youth. "Beauty is unbearable," he wrote. "It makes us despair, the eternity of a minute which we would want to stretch out for all time."[11] Unlike Sartre, who tried deliberately to identify himself with the working classes because of a sense of social injustice, Camus did not readily identify himself with any class. Instead, he simply felt himself at one with all victims, that is, with all men. His desperate desire for happiness, so vividly revealed in the *Carnets*, was intensified by his recurrent bouts of tuberculosis, the first in his late teens. He ironically called happiness "the pathetic sense of our misery,"[12] and valued its attainment, or at least the right of each man to pursue it, above all political or ideological ends. Georges Bernanos called this world "a universe glistening with beauty." Camus differed from Bernanos only in insisting that there was no world beyond this one. He affirmed, "I am happy in this world because my kingdom is of this world."[13]

[7] *Ibid.*, 118.   [8] *Ibid.*, 100, 1 n.   [9] See Brée, *Camus*, 15 ff.
[10] *Carnets I*, 15–16.   [11] *Ibid.*, 18.   [12] *Ibid.*, 19.   [13] *Ibid.*, 22.

While Sartre could find Camus' insistence on the *absurdity* of man's situation in the world sympathetic, he could never fully understand or appreciate that Camus' "philosophy" sprang from fundamentally emotional rather than rational sources. It was natural for Sartre eventually to label Camus' concern with personal values a form of selfishness.[14]

Camus' Algerian origins were fundamental to his way of seeing and understanding the world. In a sense, he was himself a "stranger" in the literary world of Paris, much like his character Meursault who described Paris as a dirty place full of pigeons, a place where people had pale faces. The early years of Camus' life, which Germaine Brée calls "the Algerian summer," formed a Mediterranean sensibility which colored all his writings. Even in those works from which the sun is conspicuously absent, such as *La chute* or the play *Le malentendu*, brilliant light and numbing warmth play a role by their very absence. Henri Peyre described the lyrical essays [15] as "the reflections of a moralist . . . a Pagan who refuses to sacrifice the present to the future, the concrete possession of a rich experience to mere hope." [16] An interesting, if highly tendentious, study of Camus' work is presented by Anne Durand in *Le cas Albert Camus*. She attempts to demonstrate from firsthand knowledge of French Algerian life the extent to which Camus' individuality, and even his hypersensitivity, were traits common to his native milieu.[17]

Camus' break with Sartre was inevitable. They saw the world in different lights. Although he had studied philosophy, Camus was essentially anti-historical in his thinking. He admired the ancient Greeks for their lack of a sense of history,[18] and often confessed that he considered Hegel and the influence of Hegelian thought

[14] For a clear picture of Sartre's attitude toward Camus after their quarrel, see Simone de Beauvoir, *La force des choses* (Paris: Gallimard, 1963), 126–27.

[15] *L'envers et l'endroit* (Alger: Charlot, 1937); *Noces* (Alger: Charlot, 1938); *L'été* (Paris: Gallimard, 1954).

[16] Henri Peyre, *French Novelists of Today* (New York: Oxford University Press, 1967), 312–13.

[17] See Anne Durand, *Le cas Albert Camus* (Paris: Editions Fischbacher, 1961).   [18] *Carnets I*, 100.

the principal evil of his time. He remarked bitterly in *L'homme révolté* in 1951 that because of Hegelianism, "truth, reason and justice are suddenly incarnated in the 'becoming' of the world." [19] Sartre was accurate in his assessment of Camus' anti-historicism, although he repeatedly misquoted a sentence from Camus' *Lettres à un ami allemand* (1948) in his attack in *Les temps modernes*.[20] While Sartre felt that he and his fellow Frenchmen were "never freer than under the Occupation" (see Chapter I), Camus detested the moral state the Occupation imposed. In preference to *une morale commune* Camus desired, as he always had, the position of an isolated individual, at once proud and guilty, that is, fundamentally human. He wrote in the late forties, "The Resistance . . . never appeared to me a happy or an easy form of history." [21] The lessons of those bitter years seemed to Camus to have no lasting application: "The war and the Resistance taught us nothing except about themselves . . . ." [22] Simone de Beauvoir tells us in her autobiography that the ideological and political opposition between Sartre and Camus had existed as early as 1945. It merely became clearer in the years that followed. She writes, "Camus was idealistic, moralistic, anti-Communist; forced to give in for a moment to History, he wanted as quickly as possible to withdraw from it; sensitive to the misery of men, he imputed this misery to Nature. . . ." [23] Her assessment is essentially accurate. Camus had written in the early forties, "More and more, before the world of men, the only reaction is individualism. Man is his own end." [24]

The Second World War was as much a turning point for Camus as it was for Sartre, Beauvoir, and Mauriac. In Camus' case the change imposed might best be described as an abrupt intrusion of historical and extraliterary concerns into the development of a man

---

[19] *L'homme révolté* (Paris: Gallimard, 1951), 169.
[20] Camus' original sentence was: ". . . j'en ai tiré d'autres conclusions que celles dont vous me parliez alors et que, depuis tant d'années, vous essayez de faire entrer dans l'Histoire." Sartre quotes it as: "Depuis tant d'années, vous essayez de *me* faire entrer dans l'Histoire." (italics mine). Camus, *Lettres à un ami allemand* (Paris: Gallimard, 1948), 75; Sartre, *Situations IV*, 115.
[21] *Actuelles II* (Paris: Gallimard, 1953), 105.   [22] *Ibid.*, 155.
[23] Beauvoir, *La force des choses*, 279.   [24] *Carnets I*, 203.

whose moral convictions had up to that time been shaped by personal and eternal considerations. In the late thirties, as he became aware that war was on the horizon, Camus wrote, "To be made for creating, loving, winning, is to be made for living in peace. But the war teaches one to lose everything, and to become what one was not." [25] The fatality he once attributed solely to nature, to its beauty and its indifference to man's mortality, now took on a more specific face, that of war.[26] Once war has come, Camus confessed, "it is futile and cowardly to try to separate oneself from it with the excuse that one is not responsible for it." [27] He tried to convert the unwelcome event into still another personal trial of his own strength. (The first had been his tuberculosis.) "It's from this struggle to remain a normal man in exceptional conditions that I have always drawn my greatest strength and my greatest usefulness." [28] Camus refused the existentialist equation of man with history. For Camus, history was in fact, as Sartre had observed, something imposed on man from the outside. Sartre's efforts to reconcile individual freedom with historical situation appeared ludicrous and positively dangerous to Camus. We find an ironic note in the *Carnets*, written in 1947: "Sartre or the nostalgia for the universal idyll." [29]

Camus conceived his work in terms of three cycles. The first, including *L'étranger*, *Caligula* (a play), and *Le mythe de Sisyphe* constituted the cycle of Sisyphus, the cycle of the Absurd. The second cycle, labeled Prometheus, the cycle of Revolt, included *La peste*, the plays *Les Justes* and *L'état de siège*, and *L'homme révolté*. The *Carnets* reveal that he had planned a third cycle, that of Nemesis, or measure, which was to deal with love and compassion.[30] The third cycle was barely begun when Camus died at the age of forty-seven. The fragments of *Le premier homme*, the novel on which he was working in 1960, are still unpublished. *La chute,*

---

[25] *Ibid.*, 168.   [26] *Ibid.*, 170.   [27] *Ibid.*, 172.   [28] *Ibid.*, 173.
[29] *Carnets, janvier 1942–mars* 1951 (Paris: Gallimard, 1964), 218. Hereinafter cited as *Carnets II.*
[30] See *Carnets II*, 328. See also Germaine Brée, *Albert Camus* (New York and London, Columbia University Press, 1964), 11–12.

to which we shall return later, occupies a special place in the work, marking a kind of transition from the second to the third cycle, and commenting on the total work up to that time. It seems to embody in fictional form, ambiguously and ironically, the theme of justice which remained Camus' most constant moral preoccupation. Camus commented, in a preface to Konrad Bieber's book on the literature of the Resistance, "I make no claims to being exemplary and I am very far from virtue. Something in me shivers when you write that I am a man of justice. I am a man without justice and whom that infirmity torments, that's all." [31]

It is remarkable how much of Camus' work has been interpreted and elucidated as political philosophy.[32] He is taken seriously as a political thinker, as a "liberal moralist," according to Roy Pierce. Pierce defines a liberal moralist as a man who has an ethical theory without a sociology, who is concerned with individual behavior but not with institutions.[33] Camus himself described the "absurd reasoning" of Le mythe de Sisyphe not as an attempt to state ethical rules, but as "illustrations and the breath of human lives." [34] Except for his many editorials and journalistic pieces, which have no firm ideological unity, the only thing resembling a political philosophy in Camus' work is L'homme révolté. This essay is no more systematic than Le mythe de Sisyphe, and lacks the stylistic excellence and suggestive brevity of the earlier work. In Camus' Carnets we find how hard he labored over L'homme révolté. It appears to have been a work he found very difficult to write; but he felt the unpleasant task a duty. "In the time of ideologies, we must take account of murder." [35] For the notion of the absurd, which had unified Le mythe de Sisyphe, Camus substituted that of revolt.

[31] See Konrad F. Bieber, L'Allemagne vue par les écrivains de la résistance française (Genève: Droz, 1954), 5.
[32] See, for example: Roy Pierce, Contemporary French Political Thought (London and New York: Oxford University Press, 1966); Fred Willhoite, Camus's Political Philosophy (Baton Rouge: Louisiana State University Press, 1968).
[33] Pierce, Contemporary French Political Thought, 144.
[34] Le mythe de Sisyphe (Paris: Gallimard, 1942), 95.
[35] L'homme révolté, 14.

Revolt is a positive notion because it reveals "that in man which must always be defended." [36]

L'homme révolté is essentially a plea for the preservation of human values in the face of abstract ideologies, a defense of "the creators" against "the conquerors." Camus examines historical and literary figures who exemplify the notion of revolt. He is far more convincing in his literary illustrations; his historical knowledge, as has been pointed out by Sartre among others, is often weak and secondhand. Camus' assessment of the Marquis de Sade is strikingly similar to that of Simone de Beauvoir in her "Faut-il brûler Sade?" Camus says of Sade that he demanded total freedom, that by his erotic and literary adventures he sought to substitute man for God. (Sade in Camus' description begins to resemble Dostoyevsky's Kirilov, one of the principal illustrations of the absurd man in *Le mythe de Sisyphe*.) Ultimately, Camus condemns Sade because his "claim to total freedom" led to a "dehumanization coldly carried out by the intelligence." [37] After Sade, the Romantics committed evil in a nostalgia for an unattainable good. Baudelaire's dandyism is an aesthetic of individuality and of total negation for Camus. For Sartre this same love of appearance is instead a search for being. (See the chapter on Sartre.)

With Romanticism, which makes art its own morality, also begins the age of the *directeurs de conscience*, according to Camus. The primary evil to be born with Romanticism, therefore, is the temptation of conformity. For if the *directeurs de conscience* elaborate an ethics according to their own lights, that is, which is the fruit of their own revolt, they also by extension demand that others follow them. What began in freedom ends in loss of freedom. If we apply Camus' own conception of the role of the *directeur de conscience* to himself, Sartre, and Beauvoir, we are tempted to understand them as fundamentally Romantics with a special twentieth-century historical consciousness. Perhaps this is what Camus indirectly intended.

With the advent of Hegel, Camus reasons emotionally, Western

[36] *Ibid.*, 32.   [37] *Ibid.*, 67.

thought enters the realm of violence "as one enters religion." [38]
Hegel justifies the will to power of twentieth-century ideologies by
giving them the sanction of the historical process. In contradistinction to Hegelian historical thought Camus defines "true revolt"
in this century as a demand for freedom, "an inner submission to a
value which takes a stand against history and its successes." [39] He
criticizes Marxism because, "an end which requires unjust means is
not a just end." [40] This is the point which apparently aroused the
ire of Jeanson and Sartre, who felt that Camus was making specific
reference to the slave labor camps in the Soviet Union and consequently justifying Western capitalist thought indiscriminately.
Historical reason, Camus argues in *L'homme révolté*, is the history
of nihilism and of overpowering ideologies, that is, of theories
which sacrifice man to abstractions. [41] Thus, he concludes, Marxism
makes history innocent by condemning man. It is easy to see why
Camus' essay had such great success in non-Communist countries.
Unsystematic, suggestive, it lent itself perfectly to condemnations
of the Stalinist regime. It also presented the viewpoint of a French
intellectual of the Left who was not by definition pro-Marxist. In
retrospect the book's structural and rational flaws are glaring. From
its dense confusion one is left only with the impression of a strong
sense of justice on Camus' part. His distinctions between conquerors and creators are not always convincing; his attention to detail is
at times overwhelming, at other times vague.

L'homme révolté* is no more a work of political philosophy than
it is one of literary criticism. The paragraph in which Camus sums
up his indictment of historical reason by poetically arguing that
Prometheus has now become Caesar is characteristic of his
thought; images and myths predominate; they are used to demonstrate the logic of the heart. [42] Revolt is finally what Camus wants
it to be and not what he has shown it became through history:
"man's refusal to be treated as a thing and to be reduced to simple
history." [43] In his *Carnets* Camus stated perhaps more clearly than
anywhere in *L'homme révolté* what his intention was when he
undertook that long and laborious book. He wanted to find out if

[38] *Ibid.*, 171.   [39] *Ibid.*, 231.   [40] *Ibid.*, 259.
[41] *Ibid.*, 272–73, 288.   [42] *Ibid.*, 301.   [43] *Ibid.*, 307.

there was any middle ground. "To be in history by referring to values which transcend history, is this possible, legitimate?"[44] In an interview conducted in 1952 for the *Gazette des Lettres* Camus was asked if he planned a sequel to *L'homme révolté* or if he planned to revise the book in any way. He replied that a sequel was not out of the question. As for revisions, he felt they were totally unnecessary, given the true nature of the book. "I am not a philosopher and I have never claimed to be one. . . . The book is a sort of confession, the only kind, at least, of which I am capable. . . . With respect to myself I do not believe in isolated books. In certain writers, it seems to me that their works form a whole where each is illuminated by the others and where all are interrelated."[45]

W. M. Frohock maintains that for writers like Camus, no single form is adequate for what they want to express and that they are in a sense forced to write in several genres at once. Frohock concludes from this fact that Camus was perhaps not what one calls a born novelist and that his commitment to prose fiction was not only far from exclusive; it was indeed weak.[46] The observation is an interesting one. However, from Camus' own admissions, it appears that his inner commitment to fiction was very strong. Rather, his conscience did not allow him to devote himself exclusively to writing novels and lyrical descriptive essays, although his greatest talents lay in those directions. The same thing happened to him as happened to Sartre. Bad conscience over historical events disturbed an isolated devotion to literature for its own sake. But Camus did not abandon fiction. Instead he tried to divide his energies, to broaden his commitment by dispersing it. He found the effort tiring and discouraging. He noted in March, 1951: "Finished the first draft of *L'homme révolté*. With this book the first two cycles end. And now, can creation be free?"[47]

Camus' most moving statement of the artist's moral obligations is his essay, "L'artiste en prison," the preface to a French translation of Oscar Wilde's "Ballade of Reading Gaol." Camus inter-

---

[44] *Carnets II*, 202.   [45] *Actuelles II*, 63–64.
[46] W. M. Frohock, *Style and Temper, Studies in French Fiction, 1925–1960* (Cambridge: Harvard University Press, 1967), xiv–xv.
[47] *Carnets II*, 345.

prets Wilde's *De Profundis* as "the confession of a man that he was not so much mistaken about life as about art." [48] Wilde had made the error of assuming that art could exist independent from all else; thus, he had cut art off from its true roots, which lie in the condition of all men. Camus continued:

> Why create, if not to give a meaning to suffering, even if just to say that it is inadmissible. Beauty rises at that instant from the ruins of injustice and evil. The supreme aim of art then is to confound the judges, to suppress all accusations and justify everything, life and men, in a light which is only beautiful because it is true. No great work of genius was ever based on hate or contempt. Somewhere in his heart, at some moment in his life, the true creator ends up by reconciling. [49]

In his analysis of the metaphysical foundations of Surrealism in *L'homme révolté*, Camus pointed out that the revolt of the Surrealists eventually led to new forms of conformism and suppression of freedom, although their original aim had been the total liberation of art. The destruction of language led to a pragmatic attitude which, in the case of men like Louis Aragon, ended up in a new form of servitude, Communism. [50] But if he betrays man in any way at all, the artist is guilty. The only just stance for art, and consequently for the artist himself, is at once to refuse reality and to exalt some of its aspects. Creation is the demand for unity and refusal of the world. "The artist recreates the world on his own account," Camus wrote in *L'homme révolté*. [51] The only thing the artist can do is to accept the fact that he is human, that is, imperfect, guilty, and then use his art in the service of men. The end result will not be perfect justice; that is unattainable. The result will be art, which for Camus was inextricably bound up with the imperfections of the human condition. He confessed, "If the world seemed to me to have a meaning, I would not write." [52] No judgment can account for the world as it is; but art can "repeat" it. That is, art can recognize and accept, in the form of images, the imperfections which constitute human life. The artist who recog-

---

[48] "L'artiste en prison," *La Ballade de la geôle de Reading* (Paris: Falaize, 1952), 18.
[49] *Ibid.*, 20.   [50] *L'homme révolté*, 122.   [51] *Ibid.*, 316.
[52] *Carnets II*, 54.

nizes that in this "middle ground" lies the essence of creativity, the artist who like Wilde comes to admit his solidarity with other men, is the only one likely to create great art. In Camus' *Carnets*, he noted, "Inability to be alone, inability not to be. One accepts the two. Both gain." [53]

Camus' thought was essentially conservative, as Philip Thody has pointed out.[54] Camus longed for a sense of measure. In *Noces* he wrote, "It is not easy to become what one is, to rediscover one's essential balance." [55] Camus' work is fundamentally the expression of "tragedy in modern dress." His novels, plays, and essays portray men struggling with the emotional and psychological facts of alienation by means of man-made justice. For example, the terrorists of his play, *Les Justes* (1949), attempt to redeem the myth of absolute justice with their lives, sacrificing love, beauty, and the other relative truths which alone are available to man.[56] Those who seek absolute justice fail to recognize the futility of such a quest in an absurd universe. In "Réflexions sur la guillotine," an essay on capital punishment, Camus wrote:

There are no just men, only hearts more or less poor in justice. Living permits us, at least, to learn this and to add to the sum of our actions some good which will compensate a bit for the evil we have put into the world. This right to life which coincides with the chance for reparation is the natural right of every man, even the worst. The lowest of criminals and the most incorruptible of judges here find themselves side by side, equally miserable and equally united.[57]

Men who live by absolute transcendent values intensify rather than relieve human alienation. For Camus total peace, absolute justice, inexorable logic are all misunderstandings of the essential nature of man, which is eternally and pathetically distant from supreme ends. "An unpunished crime, the Greeks believed, infected the city," Camus noted. He went on to add, "But condemned inno-

[53] *Carnets I*, 45.   [54] Thody, *Albert Camus, 1913–1960*, 66.
[55] *Noces*, 15.
[56] For a more complete analysis of Camus' plays, see: Rima Drell Reck, "The Theater of Albert Camus," *Modern Drama*, IV (May, 1961), 42–53.
[57] "Réflexions sur la guillotine," in *Réflexions sur la peine capitale*, with Arthur Koestler (Paris, Calmann-Lévy, 1957), 169.

cence, or crime punished too much, in the long run soils it no
less." [58] The tragedy of our modern era stems from a misunderstanding, a fatal misunderstanding not of the divine ways of the
gods, but of the finite, physical way of man. Camus' ideal of measure is one in which man is related both to his natural environment,
the earth, and to other men. Relationship to other men means a
tolerant acceptance of mortality; it demands compassion; it implies
responsibility. When the essential balance is disturbed the scales
jangle and dance in the frenzy which characterizes the history of
our era. For all these reasons, Camus could not justify a single-
minded devotion to art, an art for its own sake, much as he would
have liked to do so.

In his speech accepting the Nobel Prize in 1957, Camus stated
his conception of responsible art quite clearly. "In my eyes, art is
not a solitary pleasure. It is a means of moving the greatest number
of men by offering them a privileged image of common sufferings
and common joys. Thus art forces the artist not to isolate himself;
it subordinates him to the most humble and most universal
truth." [59] Moved on the one hand by a sense of responsibility for
the history of his time and on the other by a longing for the
solitude and impassibility requisite for artistic creation, Camus
sought to formulate a theory of literature which could reconcile
these two desires. He confessed the dangers of his ambiguous
position in his essay, "L'artiste et son temps," when he wrote, "In
this day to create is to create dangerously. Every publication is an
action and this action exposes one to the passions of a century
which pardons nothing. . . . The question . . . is simply to know
how, among the troops of so many ideologies (oh how many
churches, and what solitude!) the strange freedom of creation

---

[58] *Ibid.*, 163.
[59] *Discours de Suède* (Paris: Gallimard, 1958), 13. This volume also
includes an essay, "L'artiste et son temps," 26–57, which is directly
connected with the Nobel Prize speech. In conversation with me in
Paris in winter and spring, 1954–55, Camus revealed that he had been
working on this essay for many years prior to its appearance in two
earlier versions: in *Actuelles II*, 173–82; and in *Quaderni ACI*, XVI
(Turin: n.p., 1954–55), 5–23. All subsequent references to this essay
are to the 1958 version, unless otherwise indicated.

remains possible." [60] Camus speculated that in 1957 Racine would perhaps have been forced to make excuses for writing *Bérénice*, instead of fighting to defend the Edict of Nantes.

Trying to understand the difference between his own time and that of artists in other eras, Camus decided that the artist's social involvement is dictated by the historical form of the world in which he lives. The nineteenth century creative artist (Rimbaud, Nietzsche, Strindberg) may well have been morally justified in choosing to break completely with his society, a mercantile society with respect to which the only responsible form of action was complete refusal. But the social and political circumstances of the twentieth century, this time when law and idealism are invoked to justify repression and murder, make an "art for art's sake" pose irresponsible and dangerous. Camus noted that since the First World War writers have suffered an intensification of self-consciousness to the point of guilt. It is precisely this guilt which forced Camus to ask himself again and again whether art was not "a dishonest luxury" (*un luxe mensonger*).

Not a fancier of most modern poetry and modern plastic arts, Camus found it easy to condemn contemporary poets for their pointless "gargling" and wasteful self-consciousness. (The one contemporary French poet he thoroughly admired was René Char, a close friend.) Many references to "poetry" as a mode of forgetting the world and one's moral relation to it are scattered throughout Camus' lyrical essays. He used the term poetry rather inconsistently; above all, he wanted it to convey the opposite of lucidity and the corollary of lucidity in the Camusian rhetoric—responsibility. The romantic artist had been stirred by the perspective of the perpetual movement of history, the grandiose epic, the prophecy of a miraculous event to come at the end of time. The "modern" artist must define quite a different realm of experience, Camus insisted: "The common existence of history and of man, everyday life to be built in the most enlightened possible way, the obstinate struggle against one's own degradation and that of others." [61] The useless subtleties and abstractions of contemporary art compare

[60] "L'artiste et son temps," 29.   [61] *Ibid.* (1953 version), 175.

unfavorably with the work of a Tolstoy or a Molière, where universal communication was the aim and the result. "Contrary to the common notion, if there is anyone who has no right to solitude, it is precisely the artist," Camus argued. (He did not clarify *who* commonly held this notion. It was certainly not common in the existentialist circles in which he moved at the time he began to work out the ideas of "L'artiste et son temps.") He concluded, "Art cannot be a monologue." [62]

The work of art, when it deals with everyday reality, provides life with a form which it does not normally have. As Camus noted in *L'homme révolté,* "Life . . . has no style. It is only a movement which pursues its form without ever finding it." [63] Thus in the very act of *re*-creating reality, that is, of representing it in images and words, art fixes the real and gives it a more satisfactory unity. By this reasoning Camus managed in part to resolve his dilemma: by its very nature artistic creation is an act of responsibility, since the "new world" which the work of art fashions out of reality is at once a protest against and an acceptance of the world as it is. Reality is controlled by choice and by treatment, that is, by style. By fixing it, the artist in some measure possesses the alien world in which he lives; he also demonstrates his essential dissatisfaction with it. "The highest work will always be, as in the Greek tragedies, in Melville, Tolstoy or Molière, the one which establishes a balance between reality and man's refusal of reality. . . . Then there arises . . . a new world, different from the everyday one and yet the same, particular yet universal, brought to life for a few hours by the power and dissatisfaction of genius." [64]

Very much aware that he was using the term freedom quite differently from the way Sartre used it, Camus defined artistic freedom as a search for classical strictness and purity, as an individual discipline of style and mind: "The free artist is the one who . . . creates his order himself. . . . The art which is most free . . . will be the most classic . . . ." [65] Camus insisted that art can flourish only under self-imposed constraints. It cannot exercise its unique liberty if under an injunction to prove a particular political

[62] *Ibid.,* 42.   [63] *L'homme révolté,* 323–24.
[64] "L'artiste et son temps," 56.   [65] *Ibid.,* 61–62.

point of view.[66] "To judge contemporary man in the name of a man who does not exist is the role of prophecy. The *artist* can only appreciate the myths proposed to him in relation to their repercussions on living man." [67] By classifying specific political engagements as "myths," Camus attempted to deal with his personal dilemma. Since he felt himself to be first of all an artist, and second, a classical moralist obliged to deal in all too specific problems of a very troubled era, he used the highly charged words of the forties—freedom, engagement, responsibility—to mean what he wanted them to mean. Art is the advocate of man and his mortal life; the artist must refuse to sacrifice man to absolutes. The artist is not a religious or a political prophet. Above all, he is not a judge and does not deal in absolutes.

If [the artist] judged absolutely, he would divide reality clearly between good and evil, he would create melodrama. But the aim of art, on the contrary, is not to legislate or to reign, it is above all to understand. . . . That is why the artist, at the end of his road, absolves instead of condemning. He is not a judge but an advocate. He is the perpetual advocate of the living creature because this creature is alive. . . . The great work ultimately confounds all the judges. Through it the artist at once pays homage to the highest form of man and bows down before the lowest of criminals.[68]

Camus defined the engagement of the artist as a higher form of non-engagement. (In Sartrean terms this is an argument in bad faith, of course.) He demanded that the artist serve not the makers of history, but those upon whom history is inflicted. Camus' sincere concern with individual freedom made him the favorite of the existentialists in the early forties; in the fifties, when they had fixed upon definite distinctions between right and wrong in the political domain, he became their most striking opponent. In a little-known essay, *Prométhée aux enfers,* Camus expressed in 1945 the idea which was later to inform *L'homme révolté* in 1951: "The man of

---

[66] In the earliest drafts of "L'artiste et son temps," Camus had in mind the Nazis and their violations of human and artistic freedom. In the succeeding versions Camus' growing antagonism toward Communism became the focus for these remarks. The terms he uses are vague enough to support many readings.

[67] "L'artiste et son temps," 57.   [68] *Ibid.*, 57–58.

today has chosen history. . . . But instead of making it serve him, he consents a bit more day by day to being its slave. . . . Thus he returns to the misery of the men Prometheus wanted to save." [69] Fundamentally, Camus believed that an honest concern with art was a valid vantage point from which to judge a great many other matters. His definition of the artist as the external advocate of man implies that every artist is also qualified to be a moral critic. He stated this quite clearly in an article which appeared in *Combat* in 1948. "The first choice an artist makes is precisely that of being an artist. And if he has chosen to be an artist, it is in the light of what he himself is and because of a certain idea he has of art. And if these reasons seemed to him to justify his choice, there is every likelihood that they will continue to be good enough to help him define his position with respect to history." [70]

Camus' extensive journalism, much of it presently collected in the three volumes of *Actuelles* (1950, 1953, 1958), reveals the effort he expended to take a stand on the shifting historical and political issues of the years between 1944 and 1958.[71] These journalistic writings share certain common qualities indicative of Camus' discomfort in the role of political commentator. On the one hand, his gift for strikingly expressed formulations of a general nature makes many of these articles highly enjoyable reading. In them, Camus' style reflects his usual flair for classical language and abstract formulations. On the other hand, Camus' curious admixture of volatile personal sensitivity and general vagueness with respect to specific political and social issues leaves the reader with no clear idea of what he was driving at. No doubt many of these articles made sense to the specific audience of the time when they were written; their anxieties and Camus' were after all the same. In retrospect, however, Camus' journalism appears high-mindedly unclear. As he explained, he wanted to carry on "the political and moral commentary of events" through "the periodic exercise of

[69] *Prométhée aux enfers* (Sceaux: Le Palimugre, 1947), n.p.
[70] *Actuelles I* (Paris: Gallimard, 1950), 254–55.
[71] A great many other uncollected journalistic articles are included in Parker, *Albert Camus*, and indicate an even larger body of journalism than was realized up to now.

some rules of conscience which, it seems to me, have not been used very much by politics up to now." [72] He wanted to reconcile justice with freedom, to instill values into the political arena. Camus confessed that he did not believe in "political realism" and that his method was different from that of other journalists. He wrote in 1944 that he wanted "to introduce the language of ethics into the exercise of politics." [73] The goal he set himself was indeed an exalted one: "It is not sufficient to criticize one's era; one must also try to give it a form and a future." [74]

Although Camus was aware that journalism "is not the school of perfection," that "in politics error . . . follows conviction like a shadow," [75] he nevertheless tried to formulate a few specific rules of conduct and to warn against the errors he felt inherent in the political stands of the day. He noted the tendency of the "intellectuals" to further contemporary nihilism in its two most common forms, the bourgeois and the revolutionary, and cautioned, "None of the evils which totalitarianism claims to fight is worse than totalitarianism itself." [76] He took a brief utopian stand on the Algerian war which aroused infinite displeasure among the majority of his fellow writers, who felt that his desire for a compromise was in fact a betrayal of the ideal of justice they single-mindedly equated with complete independence for the Algerian nationalists. [77] What Sartre and others failed to understand was Camus' very real sympathy for the French Algerians from whose community he had sprung.

Occasionally, Camus' journalism reveals his realization that he had in fact made an error of judgment. For example, in 1945 in an editorial in *Combat* he called for swift and unhesitating punishment of alleged collaborators; the editorial addressed itself to François Mauriac's plea for charity. [78] (For a fuller account of Mauriac's position, see the chapter on Mauriac.) However, in 1948, Camus admitted that Mauriac had been correct in cautioning against the hasty and bloodthirsty action which was widespread during the

[72] *Actuelles I*, 37, 40.   [73] *Ibid.*, 51.   [74] *Actuelles II*, 11.
[75] *Actuelles I*, 51, 14.   [76] *Actuelles II*, 56, 1 *n.*
[77] For an account of Camus' proposed solution to the Algerian question, see Parker, *Albert Camus*, 164–65.   [78] *Actuelles I*, 73, 78.

period of the *épuration* (settling of accounts) immediately following the Liberation.[79] While Sartre has always enjoyed the position
of the dissenting leftist intellectual, the role of *le rat visqueux*,
Camus found this role an uncomfortable one which frequently led
him to judgments he later regretted. First of all he felt obliged to
admit his errors of judgment when he recognized them. Second, he
disliked the task of defending his views against critics. In his
prefatory remarks to replies occasioned by criticism of *L'homme
révolté*, Camus wrote, "A writer who dares to meddle in public
things is also obliged to refuse the deformation or falsification of
his theses." [80] He found that his efforts to correct these falsifica-
tions generally led him into still further disputes and misunderstandings.

The *Carnets* reveal that as early as the late 1940's Camus had
been aware that his determination to be first and foremost an
artist, to follow his natural inclinations, was being undermined by
his daily involvement in political and social issues. "I have reread
all these notebooks—from the very first one," he wrote. "What
struck me: the landscapes are disappearing bit by bit. The modern
cancer is destroying me too." He wondered how this personal
deformation had come to pass: "No one as much as I was certain
of conquering the world by the right roads. And now. . . . Where
was the flaw, what weakened all of a sudden and undermined the
rest?" [81] He recognized that his era had forced upon him an obligation to be engaged which resulted in precisely the opposite of the
righteousness he had sought. "The misery of this century. Not so
long ago, it was evil actions which had to be justified; today it's the
good ones." [82]

By 1950, when he was approaching the completion of *L'homme
révolté*, Camus knew that his efforts to be responsibly engaged had
destroyed a part of himself which had been the inspiration for his
earliest lyrical and fictional writings. "I have tried with all my
might, knowing my weaknesses, to be a man of ethics. Ethics
kills." [83] He became far less certain in his political judgments and
began to view those writers whose engagement had led them to

[79] *Ibid.*, 212–13.   [80] *Actuelles II*, 37.   [81] *Carnets II*, 206, 232.
[82] *Ibid.*, 210.   [83] *Ibid.*, 254.

political certainties in a bitter and ironic light. "Recruiting. Most of the *littérateurs manqués* are going to Communism. It's the only position which permits them to judge from on high." [84] He regretted what had happened to him and began to interpret his passionately involved years in the forties as the result of weakness rather than, as he had earlier tried to persuade himself, of strength. He wrote, "Modern man is forced to concern himself with politics. I do so against the grain and because, more through my faults than my good qualities, I have never been able to refuse obligations which I encountered." [85] Camus had unwillingly moved far from the conviction which made him write in his notebooks before the war, "Those who have a grandeur in themselves do not engage in politics." [86]

Except for his few articles on the Algerian conflict, Camus became silent in the journalistic field after 1952. He returned to his earlier preoccupation with the theater, and produced adaptations of plays by Calderón, Buzzati, Lope de Vega, Faulkner, and Dostoyevsky. In 1956 he published *La chute* and in 1957 *L'exil et le royaume*, a collection of short stories. Except for the brief period following his acceptance of the Nobel Prize, Camus devoted himself to his earliest and most fundamental concern, literature. The fruits of his political period had indeed been bitter.

Camus never elaborated a consistent theory of literature. As we have seen, he tended to invoke rather than to explain his literary admirations for Tolstoy, Melville, Molière, among others. He admired greatly the classical French writers, whose style had an obvious influence on his own. A short psychological novel such as *La princesse de Clèves* seemed to him a breviary of psychological complexity,[87] a landmark of an art which says "less," that is, which achieves by condensation and strict attention to form an ambiguity of meaning which reflects the ambiguity of life itself. In the novels of Melville and Defoe Camus recognized the symbolic method which was his own most natural mode of expression. In Gide he admired the manuals of sensualism which so strongly resembled his

---

[84] *Ibid.*, 272.   [85] *Ibid.*, 273.   [86] *Carnets I*, 99.
[87] *Carnets II*, 60–61.

own early lyrical essays; he also recognized there the tone of the moralist which was not unlike his own. Some passages in the *Carnets* seem directly inspired by Gide's early style.[88] The admiration for Kafka expressed in the final pages of *Le mythe de Sisyphe* is repeated in a notation from the *Carnets*, where he groups Kafka, the outstanding mythological writer of this century, with others equally concerned with "justice and its absurd functioning": Gide, Dostoyevsky, Balzac, Malraux, Melville.[89]

Camus was also very much interested in the writings of André Malraux. Around 1936 he noted plans for an essay on Malraux which he never wrote.[90] In a comment apparently inspired by Malraux's *La tentation de l'Occident*, Camus wrote, "Nothing great or new is possible—at least in this Occidental culture. There remains only action. But whoever has a great soul will enter action only with despair." Further on, he added, "The revolutionary spirit lies in man's protest against the human condition. In this sense, the only eternal theme of art and of religion." [91] In Malraux Camus recognized a new form of humanism, what C. D. Blend has called a tragic humanism, which was not unlike the one Camus later developed in his own work. However, there is a crucial difference between Camus' expression of tragic humanism and the form Malraux evolved. Although Malraux's novels are as much shaped by a mythical imagination as Camus', they depict directly and concretely the major historical events and political choices through which the myths are expressed. Camus' depiction of the real world is shadowy with respect to times, places, and political engagements. He presents his myths as myths, rather than as realistically narrated historical events. This difference in style is due in large measure to a difference in imagination. For Camus, the relation between art and reality is determined by a theory of art whose key terms are limitation and refinement.

Camus conceived artistic creation as a form of *mime*. As he explained in *Le mythe de Sisyphe*, artists "choose to write in images rather than in thoughts" because they are convinced "of the

[88] See, for example, *Carnets I*, 74.   [89] *Carnets II*, 14.
[90] *Carnets I*, 47.   [91] *Ibid.*, 58, 105–106.

futility of any principle of explication and convinced of the telling message of sensible appearance." [92] An art which says "less," which is above all symbolic in conception and classical in style, was Camus' ideal. "The work is only a piece cut out of experience, a facet of the diamond where the inner brilliance is focused without being confined." [93] Whereas Malraux conceived of art as a statement of the human condition which can speak to men at large and shape the culture it expresses, Camus tended to conceive the work of art as a more personal quest. "Perhaps," he wrote, "the great work of art is less important in itself than in . . . the occasion it furnished . . . [the artist] to surmount his phantoms and to approach his inner reality a bit more closely." The work of art, said Camus, "is born when the intelligence renounces its reasoning on the concrete. . . . The work of art incarnates a drama of the intelligence, but proves it only indirectly . . . [in] an art where the concrete means nothing more than itself." [94] Camus continually pondered the relation between the artist's personal experience and his writings. He found what he believed to be the essence of this relationship in a midway point. In the *Carnets*, he noted, "The writer who speaks, who exploits what he has never experienced is detestable. But be careful, an assassin is not the man best suited to speak of crime. . . . One must imagine a certain distance between the creation and the act. The true artist stands midway between his imagination and his acts." [95]

The artist's basic practical, as well as personal, problem for Camus was to find the proper *distance* between himself and his subject matter. In attempting to outline some rules for establishing this distance, Camus revealed the extent to which he was preoccupied with this problem. In the early forties, when he was finishing *L'étranger* and *Le mythe de Sisyphe*, he wrote in his *Carnets*, "The problem of art is a problem of translation. The bad writers are those who write in the light of an inner context the reader cannot know. One must be double when writing. The first thing . . . is to learn to dominate oneself." [96] His notebooks indicate that his first

[92] *Le mythe de Sisyphe*, 138.   [93] *Ibid.*, 135.   [94] *Ibid.*, 156, 134.
[95] *Carnets II*, 20.   [96] *Carnets I*, 234.

novel was the result of a constant process of limitation and shrinking down of his original plans and ideas. From his early plans for *La vie heureuse*, which was to be a semi-autobiographical novel presented through a third-person hero, Patrice Mersault, a would-be writer, Camus moved through several versions to his final novel. *L'étranger* is in many ways a much smaller book both in size and scope than the original project. On the other hand, in its attention to concrete detail, to tone and structure, it is a striking example of how Camus solved the problem of distance.

Unity of tone was a quality which Camus frequently noted in writers he admired. For example, he saw in Molière's Alceste "monotony . . . the absurd consequence of a character pushed to his limit." Here he found "the true work of art . . . the one which says less." [97] Camus admired novels which called themselves "chronicles": Defoe's *Journal of the Plague Year*, Stendhal's *Le rouge et le noir*, whose subtitle *Chronique de 1830* Camus noted with particular interest. On Stendhal he commented, "In the disproportion between the tone and the story lies the secret of Stendhal (like some of the Americans). . . . Would have failed if Stendhal had assumed the pathetic tone." [98] Camus' concern with unity of tone stemmed from his view of the fundamental nature of nineteenth and twentieth century art as differing from that of earlier periods. The earlier centuries, he believed, produced works which were critical, even negative in their approach to reality. However, in our time, the only valid art is one which is essentially positive, defending values which are threatened: "It defines styles of life." [99] Camus recognized the self-consciousness characteristic of modern literature as something he himself experienced. [100] However, he tended to measure the success of a work by the extent to which it managed to cloak this self-consciousness in impersonal or indirect styles. "Art has moments of modesty. It cannot say things directly." [101] He sought in his own fiction to express the modern temper in classical style in order to achieve a "historical universal."

[97] *Ibid.*, 215, 127.   [98] *Carnets II*, 14.   [99] *Ibid.*, 28.
[100] Frohock calls this the personal, poetic tone. See Frohock, *Style and Temper*.   [101] *Carnets II*, 107.

(He contrasted this modern subject with the "eternal universal" of earlier centuries.) In this era, when passions are collective, the characteristic works are *reportages* or *récits*, because "at the same time one experiences [these collective passions] one is devoured by them."[102]

Camus recognized that the modern artist's greatest opportunity for authenticity lies in personal experience of the collective passions, the most dangerous of which is politics. However, politics is the passion most likely to consume the artist's time, hence to destroy art itself before it is born. Defending himself against reproaches for not making politics the subject matter of his books, Camus noted bitterly, "They want me to depict parties. But I depict only individuals, opposed to the machine of the State, because I know what I am saying." He was against "engaged literature" because, he said, "Man is not *merely* social. At least his death belongs to him."[103] If this is an era in which man is devoured by the collectivity, then only an art which represents "creation corrected" (*la création corrigée*) can defend man. Camus ultimately defined his artistic responsibility as a passionate devotion to art. "Engagement," he wrote in 1950. "I have the highest and most passionate conception of art. Much too high to be willing to put it second to anything. Far too passionate to want to separate it from anything."[104] Camus occasionally came to the defense of writers who were apolitical, as when he expressed his admiration for Julien Green because Green managed to rediscover "tragic grandeur" through an admirable "ambiguity," "a fatal equivocation" which Green's critics did not perceive.[105]

Camus' most extensive essay in literary criticism is his preface to the *Oeuvres complètes* of Roger Martin du Gard, written in 1955. At this time Camus had, as we have seen, moved out of the political arena and was devoting his time primarily to creative work. His preface reflects a calmness and maturity of thought frequently lacking in his earlier unsystematic comments on literature. In Martin du Gard Camus recognized that "third dimension"

[102] *Ibid.*, 130.   [103] *Ibid.*, 233–34, 157.   [104] *Ibid.*, 329.
[105] From a letter to Julien Green cited in *Le Figaro Littéraire* (October 16–22, 1967), 18.

he so much esteemed in Tolstoy, that expression of human beings in their total personal and historical setting rendered by a literary form which had the ease and scope of a *total* view of life. Camus contrasted the Tolstoy-Martin du Gard manner with that of Dostoyevsky, who depicted "passionate inspired shadows who trace the gesticulating commentary of a reflection on destiny." [106] He admitted that his own heritage was of course that of Dostoyevsky, Kafka, and the American novel. Our era no longer allowed for that breadth of vision and ease of conception necessary to the creation of vast historical novels. Perhaps one day, Camus wrote nostalgically, "after having assimilated *The Possessed*," some one of our generation will be able to write another *War and Peace*.[107] By the term historical novel Camus meant one in which the individual is depicted as existing in his own right, coequal with history. The changes which have taken place since Tolstoy's day have produced "tired individualities" and "a history stiffened and diseased by several wars and the anguish of the latest destruction." [108] The artist of this day is faced with two possibilities: he can either allow history to dominate his writings (the engaged, political novel); or he can decide, as did Camus, to concentrate on the individual and reveal his relation to history symbolically, indirectly, with "shadows." In Martin du Gard Camus saw a writer whose method actually marked the transition from Tolstoy's world to our own, whose work lay "along the road."

According to Camus, Martin du Gard was neither an absolute realist nor an artist who stylized reality. Martin du Gard had his "obsessions" like every true artist, Camus affirmed. These were the obsessions with death and with the limitations imposed on the individual's strivings by forces outside of his control. (We see here the extent to which Camus, like all original artists, tended to impose his own view of the world on what he read.) Camus wrote

[106] Preface to Roger Martin du Gard, *Oeuvres complètes* (Paris: Bibliothèque de la Pléiade, 1955), I, p. ix.   [107] *Ibid.*, x.
[108] *Ibid.*, xvii. Like Malraux, Camus obviously used Tolstoy for his own purposes. Camus tends to minimize the extent to which individuals are secondary to the dialectic of history in Tolstoy's novel. Malraux concentrated on single scenes in which he found "that confrontation of man and the universe" he admired and used in his own novels.

of one of Martin du Gard's characters, "He knows that pure individualism is impossible, because life is not limited to the egoistic splendor of youthful force. . . . What else can he do except to accept himself within his limitations and to try to reconcile his duties toward himself with his duties toward others?" Martin du Gard's art was real art, "never utilizable for propaganda or hatred . . . ." [109] Camus called *Les Thibault* "the first engaged novel." The appellation was an expression of approval, because Martin du Gard's novel defended the individual against the nascent historical forces which threatened him. Eloquently Camus wrote:

The community of griefs, struggles and death exists; it alone establishes the hope for a community of joy and reconciliation. He who accepts this confraternity finds there nobility, fidelity, a reason to accept his doubts and, if he is an artist, the profound roots of his art. . . . All men die . . . and in the same violence. How can one henceforth separate himself from any man, how can one ever refuse him the highest form of life which only the artist through pardon and man through justice can restore to him? [110]

For Camus the genre most suited to expressing the modern dilemma was the novel. "Our greatest moralists," he wrote, "are not the creators of maxims, they are novelists. And what is a moralist? . . . a man with a passion for the human heart." The novel is a moral form, Camus argued, because it alone is "faithful to the particular. Its object is not the conclusions of life, but its very unfolding." [111] Camus detested the *roman à thèse*, because it expressed a thought which was "self-satisfied," hence dishonest. [112] In *Le mythe de Sisyphe* Camus wrote at some length on Kafka, whom he greatly admired and whose themes and techniques strongly resemble Camus' own.

Camus found in Kafka the ambiguity he deemed essential to expressing the true nature of man's situation in the world. "All of Kafka's art lies in forcing the reader to reread." Kafka's complexity is achieved by a disproportion between the strangeness of the

[109] *Ibid.*, xxvii, xxx.   [110] *Ibid.*, xxxi.
[111] Preface to Chamfort, *Maximes et anecdotes* (Paris: Livre Club du Librairie, 1961), viii.   [112] *Le mythe de Sisyphe*, 156.

events and the simplicity with which his characters accept these events.[113] *L'étranger* has frequently been compared with some of Kafka's narratives. However, if we examine closely what Camus says of Kafka, we find that their methods are in a sense opposite. Where Kafka's characters accept the strange with utter naturalness, Camus' Meursault accepts what is "natural" with disproportionate intensity, in the second half of the novel. The "others" also react with disproportionate intensity to those things Meursault does with utter naturalness in the first half of the novel. In Kafka Camus recognized the problem of proportion. However, he used Kafka's equation in the opposite direction. Kafka's work is symbolic; it is not tragic. Yet Camus wrote, in the course of his comments on Kafka, "The tragic work could be . . . one which describes the life of a happy man." [114] In other words, Camus glimpsed in Kafka's technique a method which he himself applied, but for different purposes. Instead of showing the mystery which pervades the real world, as Kafka did, Camus elaborated a form which restored to the real world (at least in the physical and mechanical sense) its concrete density. The mystery in Camus' narratives lies in the way the utterly real is somehow destroyed by malevolent forces having nothing to do with reality. Kafka's concrete world is a symbol of transcendent reality. Camus' concrete world is what it is; it is menaced by the unreal, but not informed by it. Camus wrote in *L'homme révolté* that the novelist "claims to give the world its unity by removing from it any privileged perspective." [115]

Camus wrote three novels. Each differs radically from the others, portraying "a style of life" which, in Camus' own mind, represented a stage in the development of his thought on man's relation to the world in which he lives. Camus indicated in his notebooks that *L'étranger* was in fact the "zero point," depicting the individual in the naked "absurd" honesty which was Camus' own preoccupation in the years preceding the war. *La peste* was intended to denote a progress toward "a deeper complexity." The final stage,

---

[113] *Ibid.*, 171, 173.   [114] *Ibid.*, 185–86.   [115] *L'homme révolté*, 331.

final because Camus died before he had time to elaborate still another, is represented in *La chute*, whose central character is "the saint," but a limited saint, "measurable like man himself." [116]

Germaine Brée has perceptively pointed out that one of the striking common characteristics of Camus' novels is their oral quality; that is, each one has a unique tone which is the sound of a particular voice, that of the narrator from whose point of view the story is seen. She further suggests that the mimetic sound Camus achieves is no doubt due to his long-standing interest and participation in theatrical activities. [117] However, because of Camus' deliberate effort to treat his characters and situations with that aesthetic distance he sought, in the first and last of his novels the characteristic *tone* is not necessarily a passkey which unlocks all the problems the narrative raises. "All my work is ironic," he wrote. [118] This is perhaps an overstatement; his journalism, *La peste*, many of the lyrical essays lack the ironic bite of his best work. In his most successful works of fiction (*L'étranger, La chute*), in his best play (*Caligula*), the ironic approach modifies the unity of tone to a remarkable degree. The result is works which, like those of Kafka, demand rereading and seem with each successive examination to yield new and often conflicting meanings.

Frohock ranks Camus with those twentieth-century French writers who have discovered new possibilities in narrating in the first person. He suggests that these novelists were in a sense forced into novelty of approach by their fundamentally poetic temper, that they were perhaps not novelists by nature but poets, and thus forced to stretch the means of the novel in order to use it as a vehicle for the personal thoughts and "epiphanies." [119] Frohock's approach yields remarkable insights into the texts. It does not take account of the possibility that the novel as a form is amorphous enough to include first person approaches and still remain a novel. With Camus, who has variously been called a writer of moral

---

[116] *Carnets II*, 31.
[117] Germaine Brée and Margaret Guiton, *The French Novel from Gide to Camus* (New York: Harcourt, Brace and World, 1962), 232; also Brée, *Albert Camus*, 6.
[118] *Carnets II*, 317.   [119] Frohock, *Style and Temper*.

fables, of parables, we have an outstanding example of one of the roads the novel has taken in the nineteenth and twentieth centuries. We must not forget the narrator of *Notes from the Underground,* or the hero of Lermontov's *A Hero of Our Time,* as Peyre has pointed out. The ironic use of a first person narrator can also be found in the earlier works of Henry James.

In Camus' effort to mediate between realism and lyricism, in his definition of art as "a demand for the impossible put into form," [120] we find one of the most striking illustrations of a literary mode characteristic of a large segment of modern literature. The modern novelist has frequently been more a philosopher than a poet, a metaphysician, as Cruickshank has said. Camus indicated his awareness of this situation in an early entry in his notebooks: "One thinks only in images. If you want to be a philosopher, write novels." [121]

Camus considered himself first of all a creative artist, and his personal notebooks show that fiction was one of his earliest and most enduring preoccupations. What intrigued him was to find a way of expressing in fictional form his most personal obsessions. His original subject was the isolation of the individual in an alien world. "The 'real' experience of solitude is one of the least literary there is," he noted.[122] Camus' cultivation of self, his deliberate pursuit of attitudes he found difficult to maintain, so eloquently expressed in his notebooks, found their uniquely successful expression in his first novel, *L'étranger.* In this brief narrative he created by a willed effort a vehicle to express with perfection and ambiguity the feelings aroused in him by the world, by his era, by his personal experiences.

The tale is simple. Meursault, a clerk in a commercial firm in Algiers, attends the funeral of his aged mother whom he had placed in a home some three years earlier. He meets an attractive young woman, Marie, with whom he begins a casual liaison. He inadvertently becomes involved in the personal vendetta of a neighbor, Raymond (reputed to be a pimp), against Raymond's unfaithful mistress. During a Sunday at the beach cottage of one of

[120] *L'homme révolté,* 335.   [121] *Carnets I,* 23.   [122] *Ibid.,* 118.

Raymond's friends, Meursault becomes involved in a brawl with some Arabs, one of whom is a relative of the mistress. Blinded by the sun and heat, believing he is being attacked with a knife, Meursault, who happens to be carrying Raymond's gun, shoots one of the Arabs. The second part of the novel describes Meursault's arrest, the investigation of his crime and of his personal life prior to the crime, his trial and ultimate condemnation to death by guillotine for murder. From the conduct of the trial and the speeches of the prosecuting attorney, it becomes clear that Meursault is condemned to death not for shooting the Arab (the shooting could clearly be interpreted as murder in self-defense), but because of his attitude toward his mother (he had put her in a home, he did not cry at her funeral) and toward the world in general. Divided into two almost equal parts, the narration is in the first person. Meursault speaks in a deliberate paratactic style part of the time; the rest of the time he expresses himself in a measured lyricism occasioned by his reactions to the physical beauty of the world, by which he is highly moved.

A great deal has been written on the style of *L'étranger*. The earliest piece of intelligent criticism was of course Sartre's "Explication de *L'étranger*," published in 1943. In that essay Sartre stressed the deliberate understated sentences which characterize much of the first part of the novel and some of the second. In this technique Sartre saw reflected the influences of American fiction and of Kafka. Above all, Sartre interpreted *L'étranger* as an illustration of the Absurd Man, the subject of Camus' *Le mythe de Sisyphe*, which also appeared in 1942. By juxtaposing the two texts, Sartre achieved an interpretation of the novel as a fictional illustration of the philosophical theory which has yet to be surpassed.[123] With the recent publication of Camus' *Carnets*, the correctness of Sartre's analysis of *one* aspect of Camus' style has been strikingly demonstrated. Sartre described Meursault's way of seeing others as that of a man viewing another man speaking on the telephone behind a glass partition. He sees the actions but does not interpret them because he cannot hear the accompanying

---

[123] Jean-Paul Sartre, "Explication de *L'étranger*," *Situations I* (Paris: Gallimard, 1947), 99–121.

words. In the *Carnets* Camus writes of a woman who watches her husband speak on the radio from behind a glass; she notes primarily his puppet-like gestures and his absurdity.[124]

Sartre emphasized the philosophical significance of Camus' style. In the notebooks we find indications of how much thought and labor went into the perfection of the deliberately colloquial, understated mode of speech Meursault uses. There is ample evidence that this part of *L'étranger's* style is an artistic transposition of a mode of speech common to Camus' native Algerian milieu. Anne Durand admits this. She also points out that occasionally Camus errs, as when he has Meursault say, "Aujourd'hui, *maman* est morte," in the novel's first sentence (my italics). Durand notes, "In Algeria, 'maman' is used in direct address, never otherwise." [125] Camus called his stylistic effort in *L'étranger* "an exercise in objectivity and detachment . . ." [126] bearing out Durand's contention that Camus' diction was often artificial.

However, there are actually two styles in the novel. The other one, the lyrical, sensitive language which expresses Meursault's reactions to the things he likes, was generally ignored by critics until recent years. Frohock demonstrates convincingly that a large part of the novel's language is metaphoric, in a sense inconsistent with any simple interpretation of Meursault's character.[127] In his early notes on the projected novel, Camus wrote, "I will speak of nothing but my love of living. But I will say it in my own way. . . ." He described a tranquil eternal moment of banal violence seen in the streets of Algiers. Elsewhere he remarked that one of the stylistic problems with which he was grappling was how to express "silence" in words and images.[128]

Camus had set himself a double problem in *L'étranger*, and much of the novel's ambiguity and effectiveness stems from the synthesis he devised. As the tragedy of a "happy man," in love with life, sunshine, ocean bathing, the novel depicts the combination of chance and positive malevolence which ultimately deprives Meursault of his life. Chance is represented by the shooting and in part

---

[124] *Carnets I*, 156–57.   [125] Durand, *Le cas Albert Camus*, 74.
[126] *Actuelles II*, 93.   [127] Frohock, *Style and Temper*, 103–15.
[128] *Carnets I*, 25, 20, 201–202.

by the trial. The positive malevolence is present in the "other face of the coin," in the blinding brutality at high noon of that sunshine and sky Meursault so loves; it is also present in the nature of legal judgment and the unjustifiable fact of capital punishment. René Girard has pointed out that *L'étranger* is fundamentally flawed, that in order for the narrative to move in the direction Camus intended Meursault must be guilty and not guilty at the same time.[129] A careful reading of Camus' plays, of his other novels, reveals that the same contradiction underlies them as well. This contradiction is not a flaw; it is the very heart of Camus' thought and of his feelings, both of which are expressed in his works. Men deal in justice but they are not just. All men are to some degree guilty, all men are innocent.

The ambivalence of Camus' attitude toward justice is perhaps his most original contribution to recent literature. His apprehension of what he called the absurd is precisely that—it makes no sense. But sense, that is, rational explanation, is of the domain of polemics. As Camus once said, if the world made sense he would not have tried to write. *L'étranger* says what it does because it is written primarily in images. Even Meursault's isolated "island-like" sentences are images, spare ones, it is true, of what he sees in the world. He is a man not given, at least until the time of his imprisonment, to trying to understand the world. He is, the world is. These are discrete facts. The *atmosphere* of the novel is its primary unifying thread, expressing above all the beauty of the physical world. This atmosphere reconciles a dual style, now matter-of-fact, now lyrical, into the unified movement of a tragedy.

Meursault is simply a highly sensitive, if inarticulate, fellow who refuses to make any judgments about men or the world until he is forced to do so. In the course of his narrative, a host of minor characters come vividly to life: Salamano and his dog; Marie; his mother; his mother's "fiancé" at the asylum, Thomas Perez; Céleste, the café owner. Meursault's world is full of people, and he generally likes them. He is sympathetic to their situations and their complaints. When he feels they want someone to agree with them,

[129] René Girard, "Camus' *L'étranger* Retried," *PMLA*, LXXIX (Dec., 1964), 519–33.

he agrees just "to be nice," even when he doesn't fully understand their problems. He is obviously very much at one with his milieu, with the crowded, brightly-colored streets of Algiers, and the sounds of its teeming life. He has no desire to be transferred to Paris, which he had once visited and which struck him as a depressing sunless place with lots of pigeons. Meursault is a happy man who does not reason on things or say very much to others about what he feels.

In his 1957 preface to the new edition of *L'envers et l'endroit*, his first volume of lyrical essays (1937), Camus wrote, "One finds many injustices in the world, but there is one of which no one speaks, that of climate . . . . When poverty is joined to this life without a sky and without hope which . . . I have discovered in the horrible suburbs of our cities, then the ultimate injustice, the most repulsive is consummated . . . the double humiliation of misery and ugliness." [130] By these standards Meursault is a happy man; the only negative factor in his life is one of which he is unaware, that he must die. This is brought home to him by his imprisonment and condemnation. Then he begins to reason and to make judgments.

The contrasts in the second half of the novel are primarily between Meursault's inability to detach himself from the world he loves so much and his efforts to "understand," to "reason." [131] Indeed, Meursault is forced to become *un raisonneur*, while in the first part of the novel he never reasoned at all. In a sense, the vehemence of Meursault's outcry against the chaplain at the novel's end is in direct proportion to his growing awareness of rational processes. In the first part he did not reason, and his lyricism was restrained. In the second, when he begins to *understand* what his life means and has meant, his lyrical outcries are overwhelming. After a tirade which purged him of the resentment provoked by the chaplain's insistence that he admit this life to be only a preparation for the next, Meursault once again uses the word "reason," but now in a different sense. He had been right: "J'avais raison"; he had

---

[130] *L'envers et l'endroit* (Paris: Gallimard, 1957), 16–17.
[131] It would be interesting to note the number of times "comprendre" and "raisonner," in their various forms, are used in Part II of *L'étranger*.

been happy. He has realized his attitude of apparent indifference (Part I) was exactly parallel to that of the world, the universe he so loved. "I opened myself for the first time to the tender indifference of the world. By finding it so like myself, indeed so fraternal, I felt that I had been happy and that I still was." [132]

In the carefully constructed ambiguous framework of *L'étranger,* Camus created a justification of life and a condemnation of death. He did so by means of Meursault, whose fundamental innocence and partial guilt illustrate the general condition of all men. The novel remains Camus' most successful. The author's distance from his subject is at once by detachment deliberately great and by lyricism intimately close. The novel achieves that ambiguity of meaning and disproportion of tone Camus most admired in writers with whom he felt kinship.

Camus' second novel, *La peste,* is primarily an account of varying human responses to mass deaths. It is set in Oran, described as an unattractive Algerian plateau city with little historical character, sparse vegetation, constructed to face *away* from its one natural asset, the harbor. The novel details some ten months during which the bubonic plague appears in April, devastates the inhabitants, forces the closing of the city, continues to spread and then, finally, with the arrival of the brief Algerian winter after Christmas, wears itself out and dies away. The tale is narrated in the third person by an inhabitant of the plague-struck city who does not identify himself until the novel's end, but who is obviously the central character, Doctor Bernard Rieux. Rieux attempts to tell the grim story as a chronicle, with deliberate objectivity and few personal comments. He makes use of his extensive medical involvement with the events and occasionally of the journal of his friend Tarrou, who dies just as the plague is coming to an end.

As Camus himself saw it, *La peste* was a step from the isolation of *L'étranger* "in the direction of solidarity and participation." [133] The earlier novel had concentrated on the psychological and metaphysical nakedness of an individual facing the absurdity of man's situation in the world. *La peste* was intended to reveal many

---

[132] *L'étranger* (Paris: Gallimard, 1942), 171–72.   [133] *Actuelles II,* 94.

individual viewpoints on the same absurd situation. Camus wrote in the *Carnets*, "*La peste* shows that the absurd *teaches nothing*" (Camus' italics). The social and the metaphysical meaning of the novel, Camus explained, were precisely the same. In this equation lay the novel's ambiguity, the same ambiguity which informed *L'étranger*.[134] Camus elucidated the connection between the social and metaphysical dimensions of *La peste* when he wrote that in it he wished to express "the suffocation we have all suffered and the atmosphere of menace and exile in which we lived." He referred of course to the experience of the war and the Occupation. He continued, "I also want to extend this interpretation to the notion of existence in general." [135]

Both *L'étranger* and *La peste* deal indirectly with the relation between the actual and transcendental aspects of human existence, and demonstrate that for Camus, the world without God (which is the way he saw it) is no different from the world conceived in a theological relationship. In either case there is no way to justify human suffering and death; in either case man must behave "as if" anything positive done to alleviate man's torments must be carried out by man himself. In *La peste* Father Paneloux delivers two sermons during the siege of the plague. In the first he attempts to persuade his listeners that the disease is a punishment visited on men by God for their sins, that it is in fact justifiable and purposive. In his second sermon, delivered after he has witnessed the slow death agony of a child (described with clinical precision in the narrative), he urges the congregation to fight against the plague, to resist on their own, adding that they must nevertheless continue to believe in God gratuitously, *quia absurdum est*. After a period of intense spiritual crisis Paneloux himself dies of what appears to be a pulmonary form of the disease. His death certificate classifies his as a doubtful case (*un cas douteux*). Thus, Camus suggests that faith is questionable, that man's torments are unjustifiable, that religion offers no answers to the travail of quotidian existence. The figure of Paneloux is a sympathetic one, one of the

---

[134] *Carnets* II, 36, 50.   [135] *Ibid.*, 72.

few characters in the novel who assumes convincing fictional density.

On the whole, *La peste* is an unsuccessful novel. Very well received in 1947 by a public which read it as an account of their own difficult recent experience, it appears after twenty years as a novel whose message is too obvious and whose means are scant. The major characters, Rieux and Tarrou, are obvious symbols, respectively, of the practical man of good faith and the seeker of truth whose experience of the plague leads him to understand that truth is a relative thing. The deliberate unity of tone, designed to convey Rieux's effort to tell his story objectively, becomes monotonous in the course of the novel's 332 pages. There are occasional moments of restrained lyricism: when Rieux and Tarrou indulge in an ocean swim in a rare moment of wordless loving fraternity; when the sounds of life rise again in the streets of Oran as the plague is declared ended. Otherwise the narrative is dry, clinical, deliberately understated in an overly obvious fashion.

The novel's high points are the brief vignettes of minor characters whose reactions to the mass peril are illustrative of personal manias rather than of any cohesive pattern of human behavior: the old man whose habit of spitting on stray cats from his window is interrupted by the disappearance of the cats; the elderly asthmatic patient whose determination to survive in bedridden obstinacy is expressed by his little pots of sweet peas which he is continually transplanting. Characters of intermediate importance—the journalist Rambert, who is prevented from rejoining his mistress in Paris by the closing of the city; some of the doctors and city officials who attempt to deny the reality of the plague by refusing to recognize it —are obvious illustrations of the author's theses.

The novel's principal flaw, however, lies in the confusion of Camus' message. On the one hand, *La peste* is meant to illustrate the evils of war. War is unjustifiable, it destroys human life and reduces men to objects. The only positive values of the situation war imposes are the rare times when individuals realize their solidarity through common grief and deprivation. On the other hand, the symbol Camus adopted for the war, that is, the natural disaster of a plague, is unsuitable to the message he wished to convey. One can attribute the evils of war to human actions. A plague arrives *ex nihilo*. The resistance of men to war is a moral recommendation; their reactions to a plague are fundamentally descriptive, rather than prescriptive. If one reads *La peste* as an image of men in time of war, it is a preachy demonstration that war is a bad thing. Nothing could be more banal. If one reads it as a description of man's moral condition, its message is not ambiguous; *that* would be artistically valid. It is distinctly confused. Are we to understand that all reactions to the injustices of man's situation are equally valid? Are we to accept such injustices as tests of man's courage and ingenuity? If the answer to either of these questions is affirmative, then the novel contradicts itself. The plague is shown to be terrible, unjust, unjustifiable. And yet the narrative in a sense exonerates the plague.

It is perhaps unfair to demonstrate the rational flaws of Camus' novel. There are equally glaring rational flaws in *L'étranger*, but, in the earlier novel, the lyrical epiphanies turn contradictions into poetic truths. In *La peste*, the artistic means are too scantily deployed to support the rational machinery. Written during the height of Camus' engaged period, *La peste* is tainted with the moralism of his journalism and weakened by the sincerity of his convictions. Along with *L'homme révolté*, it is an inferior product of an artistic imagination better suited to ambiguous symbolism than to obvious parable.

La chute is, as John Cruickshank has pointed out, Camus' most traditional novel with respect to form.[136] A first person narrative primarily focused on an individual existence, it seems to belong to the tradition of the *roman personnel*. However, the novel transcends any such simple classification. An obsessive monologue, a dialogue in which one participant has no chance to say anything, it is reminiscent of *Le neveu de Rameau*, *The Rhyme of the Ancient Mariner*, the first part of *Notes from the Underground*, *Adolphe*, and Baudelaire's "Au lecteur." The narrator, Jean-Baptiste Clamence, formerly a successful Parisian lawyer, now spends most of

---

[136] See Cruickshank, *Albert Camus*, 181 ff.

his time in a waterfront bar in Amsterdam, where he buttonholes
likely victims in order to tell them the story (true, invented, ironically distorted?) of his life and of how he has come to his present
occupation, that of judge-penitent (*juge-pénitent*).[137]

The tone of *La chute* is of course the *sound* of Clamence's voice,
ironic, histrionic, theatrically shaded. He is weak with fever and
faint, laughing, deadly serious, self-pitying, mocking, pleading.
Clamence is a serious clown, a guilty saint, "an empty prophet for a
mediocre era." [138] Through five successive evenings Clamence leads
his listener-victim through a twisting account of his past life, his
successes and sins, his moments of doubt and revelation. He
learned he was a coward when he did nothing to save a woman
drowning in the Seine. The final scene takes place in Clamence's
room, which is bare except for a stolen Flemish painting, "The
Uncorrupted Judges." His feverish voice finally explains the function of a judge-penitent, which is to make his listener realize that
he too is guilty of bad faith with respect to himself and to others.

Most remarkable is Camus' ability, through almost two hundred
pages, to sustain interest and to provide almost infinite variety in
movement, mood, and meaning. The atmosphere is vividly rendered by Clamence's descriptions. He is a master with words, both
because of his former legal profession and his occasional theatrical
experience in the army. Amsterdam is evoked, with its fog, low sky,
circling canals, as the ultimate symbol of the modern Hell, *un
enfer bourgeois*. Briefly, the opposite of Amsterdam, the Greek
isles, are recalled as the image of purity, light, natural Pagan
innocence. Clamence is a narrator of changing moods; he has
moments of sheer inspiration, others when his spirit flags and he
becomes reluctant, almost silent. Through comments he makes, we
notice that the mood of his unspeaking companion also changes.
At moments, the listener is interested, curious; at others, impatient. In the last scene he is obviously troubled, penetrated at last

---

[137] Clamence's name is the subject of much critical speculation. He is
indeed a kind of prophet, crying out (*clamans*) in the desert of modern
society. It is interesting to note that his first name, Jean-Baptiste, is the
same Céline used to address Sartre ("Jean-Baptiste Sartre") in his reply
to the latter's attack on Céline in "Portrait d'un anti-sémite."
[138] *La chute* (Paris: Gallimard, 1956), 135.

by the insidious method of guilt-sharing which Clamence has been exercising for five days.

Clamence is an eloquent inexhaustible talker. He is not only ironic, poetic, and witty; he is also a coiner of striking maxims in the great French tradition of the seventeenth and eighteenth centuries. Literally hundreds of quotable *maximes* can be found in the pages of *La chute*.[139] Many are concerned with the narrative's central theme, guilt and justice. Clamence says, "If pimps and thieves were always and everywhere condemned, honest men would all constantly believe themselves innocent. . . ." And he adds, "And in my opinion . . . that is what we must avoid at all costs." [140] He admits that his method of confession and self-abasement is not born simply out of a desire to humiliate himself and to be pardoned. He confesses only before those who are not themselves guiltless. Thus he can be certain that a complicity exists, and that his own guilt will in some measure be palliated by knowing that his confessor is not spotless. Examining his past life, Clamence notes, "I have no more friends, I have only accomplices. In return, their number has grown, they are the whole human race." [141]

At this point in the narrative (during the fourth day), the general direction of the drama begins to become more explicit. The long confession is a kind of trial, not of Clamence, but of us all. He believes there is no *last* judgment; it is taking place every day. In this particular notion, Camus' novel echoes Kafka's remark that our idea of the Last Judgment is perhaps an error; it is in fact a summary court in perpetual session. However, Camus-Clamence's method differs from Kafka's in one important respect. Despite the extensive religious vocabulary, the biblical references, the overall theological pattern of Clamence's method, he stresses that God's judgment is unnecessary; the judgment of men will suffice.[142] Clamence has, or so he says (he admits that he is not always to be believed), great sympathy for Christ, who was the first man to

---

[139] Some of the more striking ones deal with, for example: avidity and ambition (p. 26); self-love and love of others (p. 41); engagement and the need for variety (p. 45); how we are attached to what we *don't* want (p. 74); the absence of hypocrisy in our pleasures (p. 77).
[140] *La chute*, 49.   [141] *Ibid.*, 87.   [142] *Ibid.*, 128.

know that he was not guiltless. That, in fact, is why Christ had to die; he could not live with that knowledge. The horror and the humor of modern man is that he is able to live with his guilt and to condemn that of others. Judgment is the favorite occupation of "great men of the moment." [143]

Clamence's remarks on contemporary society, on the guilt of the intellectuals, on the self-deluding dream of a classless society, are all obviously directed toward the real problems and bitter quarrels Camus himself experienced during the years from 1944 to the mid-1950's. His irony is directed against himself as well as against others. The contrast between nineteenth century lyricism over lakes and forests and that of the twentieth, *le lyricism cellulaire* (lyricism over prisons), is an obvious allusion to his own eloquent concern with punishment. In fact, through Clamence's ironic narrative, Camus seems to condemn the major preoccupations of his own "moral years": "Formerly, I had nothing but the word freedom on my tongue. I spread it on my biscuits at breakfast, I chewed on it all day, I carried out into the world a breath deliciously refreshed by liberty. I struck anyone who contradicted me with this word, I had put it in the service of my desires and my power . . . ." [144]

When *La chute* appeared, the attack on the prophets of freedom seemed to be directed against Sartre. In a sense it was. But Camus' method in *La chute* is precisely that of Clamence: the confession is also an accusation. No one, including the narrator, is blameless. The truncated dialogue is in fact an immense mirror (Clamence's word) for the whole era in which Camus lived, and in which are reflected the ideals and aspirations he and his fellow engaged writers followed. The reflection is, like Clamence himself, double, a distortion in which the truth, if there is anything that simple, becomes clearer. In this dark rainy landscape, the physical opposite of the Algerian brightness of *L'étranger*, Camus places a *persona* of himself and of others like him.

The themes of *La chute* were already present in Camus' earlier writings. He had written of Oscar Wilde, "He has no other shame

---

[143] *Ibid.*, 91.   [144] *Ibid.*, 153.

. . . except to have been the accomplice of this world which judges and condemns in a moment, before going to dine by candlelight." [145] In the notebooks we find among the earliest entries (around 1935) the following notation: "I deny, am cowardly and weak, I act as if I were affirming, as if I were strong and brave." [146] The character of Clamence is already present, without the mask, without the stage setting of Amsterdam, without the firsthand knowledge Camus was to acquire of the duplicities which would arise from the conflict between his character and the duties he was to feel toward his era.

By 1951, when Camus finished writing *L'homme révolté*, he had already begun to temper his sense of the modern tragedy (*L'étranger*) with the realization that his time was too ambiguous for the tragic genre. "If only the era were simply tragic," he noted. "But it is filthy (*immonde*). That is why it must be tried—and pardoned." [147] *La chute* is the fictional expression of that trial and pardon. Simone de Beauvoir in her autobiography reveals the extent to which she was unable to grasp the ultimate revelation of *La chute*, namely that Clamence's accusations are in fact a form of pardon. She wrote, "In the early pages, I recognized . . . [Camus] as I had known him in 1943. . . . Camus realized his long-standing project; to span the distance between his inner truth and his external pose. . . . Suddenly, his sincerity ran out; he disguised his failures beneath the most conventional anecdotes; first penitent, he became a judge. He took all the bite out of his confession by putting it too explicitly in the service of his resentments." [148] Beauvoir was correct in recognizing the actuality of many of Clamence's comments on politics and contemporary justice. What she missed, however, was the irony with which these comments are expressed. Clamence confesses frequently that he is an unreliable penitent *and* a poorly qualified judge.

La chute is a brilliant fictional representation of the problems of justice and guilt which were Camus' consistent themes. His experience with history, with social and political responsibility, provided

[145] "L'artiste en prison," 16.   [146] *Carnets I*, 39.
[147] *Carnets II*, 328.   [148] Beauvoir, *La force des choses*, 372.

him with insights. He made of these insights a work of fiction which in some ways is one of the most characteristic of our time. Like Meursault, Jean-Baptiste Clamence is likely to stand as a symbol of the dilemma of the artist in the mid-twentieth century. Unable to remain uncommitted, unable to act in total good faith in his commitment, he has frequently become, like Camus himself, the uncertain prophet of universal guilt. Camus' originality as a novelist lay in his ability to state his insights ambiguously, that is, with the density and complexity of human existence. In *L'été* he wrote,

The idea that every writer necessarily writes about himself and paints himself in his books is one of the foolish notions left to us by romanticism. It is quite possible for an artist to be interested first of all in others or in his era or in familiar myths. . . . A man's works often retrace the history of his nostalgias or his temptations, but almost never of his own history. . . . I would have liked to be . . . an objective writer. . . . But the contemporary rage for confusing the writer with his subject does not allow the author this relative freedom. . . . But what else have I done but meditate on an idea I found in the streets of my time? [149]

[149] *L'été*, 131–33.

Simone de Beauvoir

SENSIBILITY AND RESPONSIBILITY

In her three-volume autobiography Simone de Beauvoir reveals the bases of her literary and ethical writings and highlights the major lines of thought of the existentialist school of writers. Essayist and novelist, long-time friend of Jean-Paul Sartre, she is the leading female intellectual of this century in France. Trained in philosophy and strongly influenced by Sartre, she has brought to their common concerns her own particular emphasis on ethics. Any assessment of the concept of social and political responsibility in the twentieth century French novel must take account of her work.

Beauvoir became committed to a life of intellect and art in much the same way as Sartre, Camus, and Malraux—when she realized that religious faith is no longer either possible or even desirable for a morally honest individual. "One day," she said, "I realized I no longer believed in God. For a long time I had found a contradiction between believing in God and living in this century: if there were infinity, eternal life, one should renounce the world." [1] Her strong instinct for happiness, for personal fulfillment which she elaborately chronicles in her autobiography, made any such renunciation of the world out of the question. In Malraux's *La condition humaine* a character asks, "What is to be done with a human life if there is neither God nor Christ?" For Beauvoir the

[1] Cited in Madeleine Chapsal, *Les écrivains en personne* (Paris: Julliard, 1960), 19.

question occasioned by the loss of faith assumes a slightly different emphasis. In *Pyrrhus et Cinéas* she asks, "What is the measure of a man? What goals can he set for himself and what hopes are permitted to him?"[2] Her personal goals and hopes were to be modified through the years; her assessment of the value of an individual existence remained relatively fixed: it was to be judged by a morality of action in relation to others. "Only that in which I recognize my being is mine, and I recognize it only where it is engaged. . . . The only reality which belongs entirely to me is my act . . . ."[3] Not until his *Critique de la raison dialectique* in 1960 did Sartre attempt explicitly to elaborate an existentialist ethic. In *Pour une morale de l'ambiguïté*, however, in 1947, Beauvoir provided the first and probably still the clearest exposition of the moral imperatives implied in a man-centered philosophy such as Sartre's. The central fact of the existentialist ethic is its ambiguity, an ambiguity all the more poignant because action and choice are necessary and inevitable.

The basic theme of Beauvoir's novels is the relation of self to others. This relationship is the key to her ethics as well. She has pointed out that man's unique characteristic, indeed the basis of his condition in the world, is the fact that he is "a sovereign and unique subject in the midst of a universe of objects. . . . In turn object for others, he is in the collectivity on which he depends nothing more than an individual." This then is the eternal "tragic ambiguity" of man's condition.[4] We need others in order to experience our own subjectivity; however, for others we are objects. If we treat others as objects we cannot fully be ourselves. "No existence can fulfill itself if it is limited to itself; it demands the existence of others," writes Beauvoir.[5] "Each man needs the freedom of other men . . . ."[6] Faith in God is an evasion of man's dilemma, since it demands devotion to another world. She stresses the impossibility of evasion: "There is no way for man to escape this world; it's in this world that he must . . . realize himself morally."[7]

There are for Beauvoir two direct results of man's inevitable

[2] *Pyrrhus et Cinéas* (Paris: Gallimard, 1944), 12.   [3] *Ibid.*, 16.
[4] *Pour une morale de l'ambiguïté* (Paris: Gallimard, 1947), 12.
[5] *Ibid.*, 95.   [6] *Ibid.*, 100.   [7] *Ibid.*, 98.

ambiguous situation. The first is that life must be oriented by moral choices; there is nothing "given." She recognizes that Camus' "stranger" is right "in refusing all ties people claim to impose on him from without: no tie is given from the beginning." [8] The ethical world of man must be endlessly formed and defined in action: "The moral world is not a given world. . . . it is the world willed by man as his will expresses his authentic reality." [9] The difficulty of this constant process of moral choice is counterbalanced by its advantages. "It is because man has something to lose and because he can lose that he can also win." [10] The second result of man's ambiguous situation is the privileged role it confers upon art, which is made by man. "The error of theories," Beauvoir observes, "such as art for art's sake is to imagine that a poem or a painting is an inhuman thing which is sufficient unto itself: it is an object made by man, for man. . . . It demands to be understood and justified, men must love it, wish it, prolong it. The artist must concern himself with the situation of the men who surround him. His own substance is engaged in others." [11]

In addition to working out the ethical implications of existentialist thought in action and in art, Simone de Beauvoir has brought to the movement an emphasis which is uniquely hers and which may stand ultimately as her most original contribution. She has expressed the *emotional* side of philosophical and moral issues with striking force. Her pursuit of personal happiness has led her to concentrate on the more immediate less abstract facets of life. She frequently expresses a joy in living uncharacteristic of much of existentialist literature. In *Pour une morale de l'ambiguïté* she writes, "I would like to be the landscape I contemplate, I would like for this sky, this calm water to be thought in me, that it be me they express in flesh and blood, and that I remain at a distance. But it is also true that by this distance the sky and the water exist apart from me; my contemplation is only a tearing asunder because it is also a joy." [12] In what Nelson Algren has called her "steadfast . . .

---

[8] *Pyrrhus et Cinéas*, 15.   [9] *Pour une morale de l'ambiguïté*, 25.
[10] *Ibid.*, 49.   [11] *Pyrrhus et Cinéas*, 111–12.
[12] *Pour une morale de l'ambiguïté*, 18–19.

passion for human justice" [13] she has demanded that the capacity
for joy be allowed to unfold in places where it was absent: in
female sexuality, in oppressed minorities, and underdeveloped
countries. In her monumental (and often incredibly dull) *Le deuxième sexe* she elaborated an existential interpretation of women in
the modern world based primarily on her concern with the self-
other dilemma. In her autobiography she succinctly states her
thesis thus: "Femininity is not an essence or a nature: it is a
situation created by civilizations on the basis of certain physiological facts." [14] The "female condition" is something she has sought
to remedy by illustration in her writings and by example in her own
life.

Female writers have been few, female intellectuals even fewer.
Beauvoir has tried to show in her autobiography how difficult it
was in her generation to become the *intellectuelle-écrivain* she is.
Her early decision to be a writer was motivated in large measure by
a desire to fill the gap left by the loss of religious faith. She
dreamed, "I would burn in millions of hearts. By writing a work
based on my own life, I would create myself anew and I would
justify my existence." [15] She admired the artist's ability to create
"something real and new" and decided quite early that language
was her special medium "because it expressed the substance of
things, it illuminated them." [16] She studied philosophy because "I
perceived the general meaning of things rather than their singulari-
ties, and I preferred understanding to seeing . . . ." [17] This preference has weakened much of her fiction with unnecessary didacticism. When the public reacted favorably to her first novel,
L'invitée (1943), she was delighted that it "existed for others. . . .
I had entered public life." [18] According to Beauvoir, her primary
motive in wishing to become a successful author has been an
emotional rather than aesthetic one: "To penetrate so far into
strange lives that people, hearing my voice, would have the impres-

---

[13] Nelson Algren, "The Question of Simone de Beauvoir," *Harper's* (May,
1965).   [14] *La force de l'âge* (Paris: Gallimard, 1960), 375, 1 *n.*
[15] *Mémoires d'une jeune fille rangée* (Paris: Gallimard, 1958), 143.
[16] *Ibid.*, 70.   [17] *Ibid.*, 158.   [18] *La force de l'âge*, 572.

sion of speaking to themselves: that's what I wanted; if it multiplied itself in thousands of hearts, my existence, renewed and transfigured would be . . . in a certain way saved." [19] She wanted to be heard and ultimately to teach, to have "people like my books and me through them; for people to listen to me, and for me to serve them by showing them the world as I saw it." [20] As she grew older, she emphasized less the pursuit of happiness and more the moral commitment involved in the life of a writer; with the disappointments of time and events, she saw her *métier* less as a joyous personal salvation and more as an existential involvement. "My life stopped being a game, I knew my roots, I no longer pretended to escape my situation: I tried to assume it." [21]

Simone de Beauvoir structures a relationship between art and ethics based on her concern with the self-other dilemma and with the extension of justice to all people. In her view, art above all other forms of action comes to grips with the nature of existence in a manner which can yield positive results. In *La morale de l'ambiguïté* she writes, "The artist and the writer attempt to go beyond existence; they try to realize it as an absolute. What constitutes the authenticity of their effort is the fact that they do not aim to reach being . . . it is existence itself which they try to fix and to eternalize . . . ." [22] To fix and eternalize existence is to uncover its possibilities, that is, to make manifest the prolixity of activities and experiences open to man in his finite situation and to encourage him to assume his existence fully. Art, she continues, "must not aim to create idols: it must uncover for men existence as the reason for existing. . . . Art reveals the transitory as absolute; and as transitory existence perpetuates itself through the centuries, art must also through the centuries perpetuate this revelation which will never be finished. . . . Discoveries, inventions, industries, culture, paintings, books people the world concretely and open up to men concrete possibilities." [23] There is of course no ready guideline for the artist which will guarantee beauty in the finished work. He

[19] *Ibid.*, 577–78.
[20] *La force des choses* (Paris: Gallimard, 1963), 677–78.
[21] *La force de l'âge*, 614.   [22] *Pour une morale de l'ambiguïté*, 97.
[23] *Ibid.*, 113.

too must confront the *ambiguity* of the human situation in his creation of art; but he can be assured of one thing: "In the earthly realm all glorification of the earth is true as soon as it is realized." [24] Beauvoir points out how radically her view of art differs from the traditional one. For example, in the Platonic tradition, art can be a mystification, because there is the realm of Ideas. In an existential view of the world, where there is no recourse to any realm outside the world of man, what *is* is true. "Like ethics, an authentic art confronts the world in its living becoming; to claim to fix the human . . . is to work against it . . . ." [25]

In her earliest literary attempts Beauvoir was still under the shadow of the religious faith she had lost. She spoke of writing as a mission, a salvation, a self-justification. She sought to save her existence. "I want to write; I want sentences on paper, the things of my life put into words," she noted in a journal.[26] Moved by the joy of living, she sought to communicate this joy: "I was enjoined to lend my consciousness to the varied splendor of life and I was to write in order to deliver it from time and extinction." [27] Beauvoir admits that she was a long time in finding a *subject* for writing. Indeed, for ten years during which she began and abandoned many stories, she had nothing to say despite her desperate desire to write. She describes the moment when she at last found a subject in the self-other dilemma which became the heart of her first published novel, *L'invitée*. In retrospect she asks, "In what circumstances, why, how do things reveal themselves as 'something to say?' " Her answer reveals the extent to which her natural inclination to happiness had in effect barred her from the world of literature. "Literature appears when something in life becomes disarranged; for writing. . . the first condition is that reality stop *being a matter of course*; only then is one capable of seeing it and showing it." [28] Up to the time of the Occupation she had tended to think of her life as a story she told herself; with the turmoil of exterior events she realized that her life was instead a compromise between the world and herself. "Since the declaration of war, things had definitively

---

[24] *Ibid.*, 220.   [25] *Privilèges* (Paris: Gallimard, 1955), 164.
[26] Quoted in *La force de l'âge*, 30.   [27] *Ibid.*, 18–19.   [28] *Ibid.*, 374.

stopped being a matter of course; unhappiness had erupted in the world: literature had become as necessary to me as the air I breathed. . . . Conscious of the abyss which separated what I felt from what is, I needed to write, to do justice to a truth in complete disaccord with my feelings . . . ." [29]

Beauvoir points out that others may gain from a writer's literary record of this *décalage* (disaccord) between himself and the world because the work sheds light on existence. "The most commonplace truths can . . . through the writer's pen, be illumined by a new light." [30] However, literature is not simply autobiography; of this she is well aware. In the closing pages of her autobiography she points out that literary sincerity is not what we usually imagine. "It's not a matter of transcribing the emotions, the thoughts which instant by instant pass through you, but of indicating the horizons you don't reach, which you scarcely notice and which are nevertheless there. . . . [The writer] may repeat and correct himself for tens of years, he will never succeed in capturing on paper . . . the multiple reality which is in him. . . . The effort he makes to approach it constitutes a kind of dialectic within the work itself. . . ." [31] With her characteristic tendency to express aesthetic commonplaces as if she were the first to uncover them, Beauvoir tells us that the main problem of literary art is how to go from life to writing.

The literary work becomes for Beauvoir a new and separate form of existence, a special locus of reality in which the complexities of daily amorphous reality may reveal their meaning. In *La force des choses* she writes, "An experience is not a series of facts. . . . One of the essential roles of literature . . . [is] to manifest ambiguous, separate, contradictory truths which no one moment makes total. . . . In some cases one only succeeds in assembling them by placing them within the unity of an imaginary object." [32] There is a strong resemblance between her notion of the literary work as the experimental ground on which the data of experience will reveal their meaning and Zola's claims for the naturalistic novel in the nineteenth century. Of course, she obscures this resemblance by

[29] *Ibid.*, 621–22.   [30] *Ibid.*, 337.   [31] *Ibid.*, 622.
[32] *La force des choses*, 282–83.

invoking existentialist vocabulary at crucial moments: "The art of the novel demands transpositions [of reality] in order to transcend anecdote and to shed light on a meaning which is not abstract but indissolubly engaged in existence." [33] In a sense, however, Beauvoir's conception of the novel is as experimental as Zola's; they differ in their valuation of deterministic forces. As a good existentialist Beauvoir constantly reasserts man's freedom; however, she is forced to admit that there are many limitations on this freedom, not the least of them the very *situation* (personal, social, historical) which allows its exercise. At the end of her autobiography she confesses, "When one lives in an unjust world, it is futile to hope, by any method, to rid oneself of injustice; what is necessary is to change the world, and this I cannot do." [34]

However—and here we find the unique voice of Simone de Beauvoir—she remains quintessentially hopeful and in love with the possibilities life offers. Literary creation "is adventure, it is youth and freedom," and that is why she cannot live without it. [35] In the process of "narrating herself" she finds at least a partial solution to the self-other ambiguity; when the writer comes alive in the hearts of others, he becomes part of their subjectivity, he breaks through the wall which closes each man into his subjectivity and makes it so painful for him to realize that he is someone else for the others. Eloquently she writes, "Words, universal, eternal, presence of all to each, are the only transcendent I recognize and which moves me; they vibrate in my mouth and through them I communicate with humanity. They tear from the instant and its contingency the tears, the night, even death, and transfigure them." [36]

The novel is the literary form most suited to expressing the original thrust of existence, Beauvoir explains in *L'existentialisme et la sagesse des nations.* For the novelist-philosopher concerned with subjectivity and temporality this literary genre above all others approximates the ambiguity of man's condition. A unique and irreducible mode of communication, the novel becomes the testing ground where philosophical hypotheses are concretized in

[33] *La force de l'âge,* 109.   [34] *La force des choses,* 681.
[35] *Ibid.,* 684.   [36] *Ibid.,* 679.

the elaboration of character and situation. The novelist finds new problems, learns new truths along the way. "The novel will then appear," Beauvoir writes, "as genuine spiritual adventure." [37] She distinguishes between the aim of her essayistic writings and that of her novels by pointing out that in the former she writes on the basis of certainties, while the latter express the astonishment aroused in her by the totality of our human condition.[38] "An essay should provoke the reader. . . . In a novel, on the contrary, one tries to show. One must render life, people in their ambiguity. The novel must not conclude, it is written to take account of uncertainties, of fumblings . . . ." [39] But we must understand that the uncertainties of which Beauvoir speaks are not the traditional *crises du coeur* which have been the stock in trade of the novel. The existentialist novelist is above all interested in man's situation in the world. By contrast, the "bourgeois psychological novelist is not interested in the situation of his heroes: he studies the human heart in general. . . . The only reality the bourgeois writer wants to take account of is the inner life." [40]

While most accurate in assessing the technical flaws in her own novels, as we shall see later on, Beauvoir is very little concerned with form and technique in the novel. She has nowhere sketched an aesthetic of the novel, since she is interested primarily in what the novel does rather than in how it does it. As she maintained in *Pyrrhus et Cinéas*, "Techniques are modes of appropriating the world . . . ."; she is concerned primarily with the end result.[41] Her aim as a novelist has always been to confront reality "in its ambiguity, in its opacity rather than reducing it to meanings which can be expressed in words." She has been, she says, "attached primarily to life in its immediate presence . . . ." [42] Beauvoir confesses that in her earlier years as a novelist, while fleeing the old essentialism, she had not yet accepted the notion of *situation* "which alone can concretely define human ensembles without making them subservient to a nontemporal fatality." [43] She is alluding of course to the

---

[37] *L'existentialisme et la sagesse des nations* (Paris: Nagel, 1948), 111–12.
[38] *La force des choses*, 342.   [39] Chapsal, *Les ecrivains en personne*, 34.
[40] *Privilèges*, 187.   [41] *Pyrrhus et Cinéas*, 18.
[42] *La force de l'âge*, 151.   [43] *Ibid.*, 172.

difference between *L'invitée* and her subsequent novels. It is ironic that what appears to her as progress in existential appreciation of the world has been reflected in novels of inferior fictional merit (*Le sang des autres, Tous les hommes sont mortels*). Only in *Les Mandarins* did she once more approach the artistic success of her first novel.

A vigorous moral critic, if not a subtle aesthetic one, Simone de Beauvoir has always been ready to judge other writers on the basis of her overriding concern with ethics. Her critical point of departure has remained the situation of the book and its author: "A book takes on its true meaning only if one knows in what situation, in what perspective and by whom it was written . . . ." [44] Since we write in order to *be*, the work *is* the man and can be judged as expressing his ethical as well as personal commitments. For Beauvoir, Flaubert, for example, is not a man who managed to evade his era or his class: "Rather, he constitutes himself as a nineteenth century bourgeois whose fortune, leisure, and vanity mask from him his solidarity with his era." [45]

Beauvoir's most extensive work of literary criticism is her essay on Sade, "Faut-il brûler Sade?" In it she deploys all her ethical zeal to demonstrate that Sade's literary product is a prime example of the existential nature of fiction. "Sade tried to convert his psychophysiological destiny into an ethical choice; and by this act through which he assumed his separateness, he intended to make an example and an appeal: this is why his adventure assumes a large human significance." [46] Close in some ways to Malraux, who interpreted Sade's obsession with eroticism as a cerebral effort to fully experience himself, Beauvoir interprets the overwhelming minuteness of Sade's fictional evocation of erotic pleasures as an adventure in "the imaginary." But she finds in Sade's erotic exploits a *defiance of society* as well as an individual attitude. "From his sexuality he made an ethics; he manifested this ethics in a literary work; through this reflected action of his adult life Sade mastered his true originality." [47] She also finds in Sade a reflection of the self-other dilemma which is her own personal one. In order for Sade to

[44] *Ibid.*, 10.   [45] *Pyrrhus et Cinéas*, 35.
[46] *Privilèges*, 12–13.   [47] *Ibid.*, 15.

experience himself fully as self, he needed others and he needed them free. But in bending them to his unusual sexual demands, he tended to make them into objects; thus, Sade's particular form of existence required "free slaves," a contradiction in terms.

Sade's greatest importance, according to Beauvoir, lies in the fact that in his quest for being he turned to writing. His actions and his unrealized fantasies, she wrote, became the substance of his fiction, because "writing . . . can give images the solidity of a monument . . . it resists all contestations." [48] However, she criticizes the aesthetic value of Sade's fiction for its very *necessity*; Sade was too obsessed. He lacked the distance requisite to creating a believable fictional world. But in her eyes he remains a great literary moralist because, she says, "his enterprise is truer than all the instruments it utilizes. . . . Although not a consummate artist or a coherent philosopher, thanks to this opinionated sincerity, Sade deserves to be hailed as a great moralist." [49] Sade denied the accepted morality, the benighted essentialism of his era; he also transcended its sensualism "in order to transform it into an ethics of authenticity." [50]

Beauvoir evaluates the Surrealist movement in terms of its end results. She notes that after clearing the terrain of meaningless traditions some of the Surrealists went on to "realize their freedom," to give it a content. Referring to those Surrealists who, like Aragon, went on to become Communists, she writes, "They engaged in . . . political action, in intellectual or artistic research . . . ." [51] While never herself a member of the French Communist Party, Beauvoir has sided with the Communists on most issues of the past twenty-five years because she has experienced the bad conscience which troubled many French intellectuals of bourgeois origin. She frequently used André Malraux as an illustration of rightist thought and condemned his contention that art transcends man. She and Sartre were able to admire Malraux's *L'espoir* because it described events which interested them and introduced themes which echoed some of their own concerns: "the relationship between individualistic morality and practical politics, the possibility of maintaining humanist values in the midst of war." [52]

[48] *Ibid.*, 50.   [49] *Ibid.*, 59.   [50] *Ibid.*, 87.
[51] *Pour une morale de l'ambiguïté*, 78–79.   [52] *La force de l'âge*, 330–31.

However, they deplored Malraux's glorification of the *adventurer* in his earlier novels. Beauvoir has been critically consistent, basing her valuations on the subject matter of fiction and on the author's political and social viewpoint. When these agreed with hers, she found kind things to say; when they did not, she mounted her arsenal of existentialist terminology to condemn them. She cited Drieu la Rochelle as an example of the inevitable results of nihilism. "Drieu chose . . . to refuse his condition as a man, which led him to hate all men along with himself. . . ." [53] At first dazzled by the revolutionary style of Céline's *Voyage au bout de la nuit* in 1932, Beauvoir later changed her estimation of his work because, she wrote, "*Mort à crédit* opened our eyes. There is in it a certain hateful contempt for little people which is a pre-Fascist attitude." [54] Kafka's impact on her was based in large measure on his themes rather than his style: "Kafka spoke to us about ourselves; he revealed our problems to us, facing a world without God where our salvation was nevertheless at stake." [55]

The American novelists avidly read by French intellectuals in the 1930's and 1940's—Dos Passos, Hemingway, Faulkner—occupy a privileged position in Beauvoir's critical canon. The technique of Dos Passos' *42nd Parallel* seems to have been a revelation to her and to Sartre:

Each man is conditioned by his class, no one is entirely determined by it; we were between these two truths; Dos Passos offered us on the aesthetic plane an admirable reconciliation. He had invented with respect to his heroes a distance which permitted him to present them at once in their minute individuality, and as a pure social product. . . . It was cruel to see men at once through this comedy of freedom which they play within themselves, and as the fixed reflections of their situation. We often tried, Sartre and I, to take this double point of view on others and above all on ourselves. For while we were going along in life with lively assurance, we still treated ourselves without complacency; Dos Passos furnished us with a new critical instrument . . . . [56]

Hemingway also suited Beauvoir's and Sartre's emerging philosophy because he presented a new form of realism. Traditional real-

---

[53] *Pour une morale de l'ambiguïté*, 80. [54] *La force de l'âge*, 142, 2 n.
[55] *Ibid.*, 193. [56] *Ibid.*, 143.

ism, based on erroneous postulates, had tended to describe objects in themselves. The new subjectivism of Proust and Joyce was equally unsatisfactory. In Hemingway, Beauvoir writes, "the world existed in its opaque exteriority, but always through the perspective of a singular subject; the author gave us only what the consciousness described could seize of it; he managed to give objects an enormous presence, precisely because he did not separate them from the action in which his heroes were engaged . . . ." [57] Beauvoir attempted to use the techniques learned from Dos Passos and Hemingway in her own novels. She experimented with discrete, sometimes alternating, points of view in order to express the subjectivity of her characters in their relation to one another. However, she never achieved Sartre's success in using *things* because she was always more inclined to tell than to show. Faulkner offered still another refinement on the technique of point of view. Not only did he orchestrate a plurality of points of view, she said, but he also organized "in each consciousness . . . the knowledge, the ignorance, the bad faith, the fantasies, words, silence, so as to plunge the events into a *chiaroscuro* from which they emerged with a maximum of mystery and relief." [58]

Not surprisingly, Simone de Beauvoir has reacted unfavorably to the recent rise and popularity of the *nouveau roman* in France. Inclined to judge fiction in moral terms, to be interested above all in the ethical dilemmas it narrates, she has found almost nothing favorable to say about Robbe-Grillet or Nathalie Sarraute. (Sartre, on the other hand, was one of Sarraute's most influential partisans, and wrote an introduction to one of her novels.) Beauvoir bases her criticism of the *nouveau roman* on the fact that it is impossible to deduce a viable aesthetics from fiction based on outdated psychologism which refuses to recognize the fact that the external world exists. "Collectivities, events, crowds, the relations of men with one another and with things, all these objects which are indeed real and not reducible to 'subterranean palpitations,' deserve and demand to be illumined by art. . . . There is need for techniques which can help the novelist to better reveal the world,

[57] *Ibid.*, 144–45.   [58] *Ibid.*, 192.

not for techniques to turn him away from it in order to isolate him in an insane and false subjectivism." [59] Above all, Beauvoir objects to what she calls the pessimism of the new novel, pessimism because it ignores man's movements toward progress and deprives him of his "historical dimension." She quotes Nathalie Sarraute, who said, "When I sit down at my desk, I leave politics, events, the world at the door: I become another person." In her comment on this statement, Beauvoir expresses rage at such a flagrant denial of the writer's most vital obligation, to be engaged. "How, in this action which is the most important for a writer, writing, can one avoid being totally committed?", she asks. "This mutilation of writing and of oneself, this recourse to the phantasms of the absolute testify to a defeatism justified by our moral decay. France, once a subject, is now nothing but an object of history: her novelists reflect this degradation." [60] Beauvoir wrote these words during the Algerian War, a period which saw her moral indignation reach its high water mark. The new novel appeared to her a further symptom of what had gone morally wrong with France: even her writers had abdicated their responsibility.

Beauvoir admits that she did not always believe the writer should be politically engaged. Like Mauriac, she found the experience of the Second World War and the Occupation the turning point in her thinking. She admits that her "schizophrenic attachment to happiness" made her "blind to political reality." [61] Then the war showed her to what extent she depended on the rest of the world. What is most surprising in her change of heart and development of political consciousness is the degree to which she believed herself uniquely immune to the common fortunes of men before the war. This naïveté is one of Beauvoir's most engaging and often most irritating qualities. It makes her thunderous demands for political engagement faintly suspect at times; one feels she is trying to make up for years of non-involvement, to expiate the sin of her relatively comfortable youth and superior educational advantages.

Beauvoir has stated explicitly that there is "more than one way to unify the moments one lives through: by subordinating them to

[59] *La force des choses*, 291–92.   [60] *Ibid.*, 650.
[61] *La force de l'âge*, 372.

an action . . . or by projecting them in a work." [62] She has herself tried to do both, to engage in political action and to continue writing. Much of her writing is in fact entirely devoted to "testifying" to things which concern her politically and socially. In addition to *Le deuxième sexe*, and the various philosophical essays, we find *L'Amérique au jour le jour* (1954) and *La longue marche, essai sur la Chine* (1957). In these books she adopts the stance common to leftist intellectuals in France since the early forties: pro-Marxist, she tends to sympathize with Communist countries and be critical of the United States on any and all occasions.[63] In *La morale de l'ambiguïté* she stressed the ambiguous element in engagement, the fact that there are no guarantees: "Political choice is ethical choice; it is a decision as well as a gamble; one gambles on the chances and the risks of the measure envisaged; but whether the chances and risks should or should not be assumed in the given circumstances must be decided without help . . . ." [64] In the second volume of her autobiography she describes vividly the despair which paralyzed her during the early months of the Occupation, and how she finally managed to begin writing again: "What difference did the hours vainly spent writing make, if tomorrow everything went to pieces? If ever the world, my life, literature took on meaning again, I would reproach myself with the months, the years I lost doing nothing." [65]

Retrospectively meting out praise and blame, Beauvoir summarizes the ethical positions of writers who continued to work in Paris during the Occupation. The rightist writers committed "unpardonable crimes" by their approval of the status quo and by adding fuel to the fires of hatred. On the other hand, Beauvoir explains, "the writers on our side had tacitly adopted certain rules. One must not write in the newspapers and magazines of the occupied zone nor speak on Radio-Paris; one could write in the press of the free zone and on Radio-Vichy: everything depended on the meaning of the

---

[62] *Ibid.*, 368.
[63] See George Lichtheim, "The Transformation of Marxist Theory," *Marxism in Modern France* (New York: Columbia University Press, 1966), 69–111.
[64] *Pour une morale de l'ambiguïté*, 207–208.   [65] *La force de l'âge*, 482.

articles and the broadcasts. To publish a book on the other side of the line was perfectly licit; on this side, it was a problem; finally we decided that in this matter as well, it was the content of the work which counted." [66] Thus, Sartre felt that to produce *Les mouches* during the Occupation was a legitimate form of resistance, since it urged the French to rid themselves of remorse and to stand up for their freedom. (Apparently the occupying enemy thought the play something less than dangerous. Aside from material and technical difficulties such as limitations on electricity the play was performed without any danger to its author.) The chief organization of the "intellectual Resistance" was the Comité Nationale des Écrivains which united Communists like Eluard, *sympathisants* like Sartre, firm anti-Communists like Camus at least temporarily.

On the basis of a simple ethical standard, namely whether an action aimed to "free freedom" for oneself and/or others, Beauvoir, Sartre, and Camus decided that their most crucial mission was to "furnish an ideology for after the war." [67] Sartre and Camus became the *maîtres de pensée* of an entire generation. *Les temps modernes* was founded. Simone de Beauvoir continued her own evolution toward a stronger position with respect to political responsibility. She admits that even when writing *La morale de l'ambiguïté*, she was still not sufficiently freed from the ideology of her class. She and Sartre found their former values relatively idealistic, insufficiently existential to face the postwar world. "For now I know," she writes, "that to seek reasons why one must not stamp on a man's face is to accept stamping on his face." [68] From the Liberation until the serious rift of 1952, Sartre, Camus, and Beauvoir together defined the tone of French literature and thought. Engaged literature was the fashion, and engagement meant political action. During the "settling of accounts" which followed the Liberation, Beauvoir apparently had no quarrel with the process which singled out alleged collaborators and killed or hounded them in the name of justice. Her only objection to Brasillach's trail, for example, was that the judicial apparatus seemed to transform the executioner into a victim and to make his just condemnation seem

[66] *Ibid.*, 528.   [67] *Ibid.*, 577.   [68] *La force des choses*, 81.

inhuman. Where Mauriac pleaded with the *Résistants* not to murder in the name of justice, Beauvoir tacitly approved.

Beauvoir's strongest political stand was occasioned by the lengthy Algerian war. She wrote about it, wrote prefaces to books exposing some of the French brutalities, worried about it, and stopped writing fiction until the war was ended. In her autobiography she tries to explain why this event so aroused her. "I am an intellectual, I value words and truth; I had to endure every day, infinitely repeated, the aggression of lies spit forth by every mouth." [69] Convinced that the Algerian situation was the result of bad faith on the part of the French colonial administration and the national government in Paris, she devoted her considerable energies to revealing this bad faith. A tone of discouragement pervades the pages of her autobiography devoted to this period. With the passing of years, Beauvoir seems to have realized fully what her youthful optimism had concealed from her, that political engagement does not always solve the problems it attacks. It also appears, in her case, to have detracted considerably from the creative energy requisite to writing fiction. Between *Les Mandarins* in 1954 and *Les belles images* in 1966, Beauvoir published no fiction, and the latter novel is distinctly inferior to her best. Many critics have in fact maintained that her only fully successful work of fiction was *L'invitée*, which appeared in 1943.

"At twenty," Beauvoir confessed to an interviewer, "I believed myself more or less the center of everything . . . . And then little by little I discovered that the other escapes us." [70] *L'invitée* deals with the realization of this fact by Françoise, a successful professional woman who has what she believes to be a totally honest and inseparably close relationship with Pierre, a talented theater director. When a self-centered young girl, Xavière, comes to stay with them, the illusions of Françoise's life disintegrate. She discovers first that there is no "us." She has assumed her own subjectivity to be inseparable from Pierre's while she has in fact relinquished it almost entirely. Separated from him by the presence of a third party, she realizes that she actually "has no self." Her second

[69] *Ibid.*, 387.   [70] Chapsal, *Les écrivains en personne*, 34.

principal discovery is precipitated when she attempts to annex Xavière and create a trio in order somehow to reestablish the sense of self she has lost. She then discovers that the consciousness of an other is totally closed to her: Xavière remains impenetrable to her and worst of all she remains an object for Xavière. The novel, which ends with the murder of Xavière by Françoise, is as a whole so dazzlingly ambiguous that the dénouement is hardly jarring: the metaphysical problem it poses cannot be solved; a metaphysical murder is hardly bloody.

Any simple outline of the novel fails to convey the technical skill with which it is written or the brilliance of the characterizations, particularly those of Françoise and Xavière. Beauvoir tells us elsewhere that remembering Dos Passos she deliberately used the highly special and limited viewpoint of a single character for each chapter.[71] Another device which serves her well, and which she claims to have learned from Dostoyevsky and Dashiell Hammett, relates to the use of dialogue: "Every conversation must be in action, that is it must modify the relationships of characters and the whole situation. Also, while it is taking place, something else which is important must be happening elsewhere: thus, straining toward an event from which he is separated by the printed pages, the reader experiences just as do the characters themselves the resistance and passage of time." [72] The tension Beauvoir creates by means of this device, which is in fact an effective concretization of the *ambiguity* of the human situation, endows *L'invitée* with a sustained mood of anxiety and uncertainty. She conveys the sense that as time passes, choices being made are altered by these unknown events. The density of the dialogue is due more to what is not said and what cannot be said than to the spoken words.

On the basis of the traditional triangle situation Beauvoir has created a novel subject to various interpretations. The perceptive philosopher Merleau-Ponty has rightly pointed out that the novel is a metaphysical one in which the characters and plot represent the dialectic of self and other. He is wrong, however, when he says that the novel's essential drama is not psychological but

---

[71] *La force de l'âge*, 347.   [72] *Ibid.*, 353.

metaphysical; [73] it is both. The art of the novel lies precisely in the fusion it achieves between abstract considerations on human self-identity and relationships with others on the one hand, and on the other the very real psychological dilemmas and crises these abstractions become in daily life. In a retrospective evaluation of her novel, Beauvoir admits that its weakest point is the murder of Xavière. However, she points out that there is no satisfactory *resolution* to Françoise's dilemma, that the murder is one possible if unsatisfactory *response*, a response which fascinated Beauvoir personally and which she felt compelled to work out in a literary medium. [74] The novel's greatest merit in the author's eyes is "in the successful passages . . . where one arrives at an ambiguity of meanings which corresponds to the ambiguity of reality itself." [75]

Le sang des autres (1945) and *Tous les hommes sont mortels* (1946) are distinctly inferior to *L'invitée*. In *Le sang des autres* Beauvoir extends the self-other problem to a larger context. The hero, Jean Blomart, moves from a position of neutrality toward politics to one of involvement, when he discovers that his flights and his silences had as much weight as actions and words; during the Occupation he learns to act, to accept violence, to live in anguish. He witnesses the death of Hélène, whom he loves, after hearing from her that he is not responsible for her death because he is only an instrument in someone else's destiny; she has chosen her death freely. "My second novel," Beauvoir wrote, "is composed with more art than the first; it expresses a larger and truer view of human relationships." [76] However, in answering Blanchot's criticism, that she *said* rather than *showed* what she wanted to express, Beauvoir admits that *Le sang des autres* is a *roman à thèse* and that didacticism is fatal to fiction. After 1939, she explains, she sought

reasons, formulas to justify to myself what was imposed on me. . . . I discovered solidarity, my responsibilities, and the possibility of consenting to death so that life might preserve a meaning. But I learned these truths against myself; I used words to urge myself to accept them; I reasoned with myself, I persuaded myself, I gave myself a lesson; this is

[73] See Maurice Merleau-Ponty, "Le roman et la métaphysique," in *Sens et non-sens* (Paris: Nagel, 1948), 45–71.
[74] *La force de l'âge,* 348.   [75] *Ibid.,* 352.   [76] *Ibid.,* 558.

the lesson I tried to transmit, without realizing that it did not have the same freshness for the reader as it did for me. Thus I entered what I might call the "moral period" of my literary life . . . ."[77]

Beauvoir clearsightedly explains that the novel was well received because her readers had lived through the same period as she; they read the book from the same perspective she had when writing it, that of the Occupation and the Resistance. "Then time passed: circumstances change, and our feelings; together we undid the work we had imagined together. There remains today a book whose flaws are glaring." [78]

In *Tous les hommes sont mortels* Beauvoir presents a new kind of hero, Fosca, who is immortal and therefore aspires to universality. As he moves through a panorama of history, he discovers that the world consists of individual liberties, each out of his reach. More important, he finds that he is unable to relate to others because his life does not have the same meaning as theirs: the significance of human existence is conferred by its very limitations. Death gives a shape to life and value to human choice. Even more didactic than *Le sang des autres*, *Tous les hommes sont mortels* also suffers from weakness in characterization and damaging diffuseness. In her autobiography Beauvoir accurately calls the novel "an organized digression."

Les Mandarins (1954) was Beauvoir's most widely acclaimed novel. It achieves a density and complexity lacking in *Les sang des autres* and *Tous les hommes sont mortels*. Whereas her earlier novels attempt to make concrete metaphysical and ethical concepts, *Les Mandarins* gives life a sensuous form in art and presents the author's philosophical presuppositions as discoveries rather than strictures. It reveals less an intellectual thesis than a startling emotional observation which defies the philosopher's logic. In her autobiography, Beauvoir describes her objectives in the novel: "I wanted to put all of myself into it: my relationships with life, death, time, literature, love, friendship, travel. I wanted also to paint other people and above all to tell the feverish and disappointing story of after the war." [79] She felt that "only a novel could . . .

---

[77] *Ibid.*, 561.   [78] *La force des choses*, 50.   [79] *Ibid.*, 211.

disengage the multiple and turning meanings of this changed world.
. . ." [80] She denies vehemently that *Les Mandarins* is a *roman à clé*,
although after the publicity conferred on it by the Prix Goncourt,
guessing the identity of the major characters became public sport.
(Henri Perron was identified as Camus, and Robert Dubreuilh as
Sartre; Anne was in part Beauvoir herself; and Lewis Brogan of
course was Nelson Algren.) The novel lent itself to such key-hunt-
ing, since it obviously portrayed the peculiar problems of leading
French intellectuals just after World War II. However, simple
identifications left many aspects of the characters unresolved and
obscured the novel's essential themes. Since 1954, Beauvoir has
published her autobiography, in which she reveals the complex
transpositions and changes by which she turned living models into
living fictional characters. She moved the events of the early fifties
to the years immediately following the war. She interchanegd characteristics. She created a heroine who is in many ways unlike
herself. In short, she wrote a novel on the basis of her own experience. She says regretfully in her autobiography, "I would have liked
for the book to be taken for what it is, neither an autobiography
nor a reportage, but an evocation." [81]

Les Mandarins shares the preoccupations of her earlier novels:
the relation of self to others, the ambiguities of choice and action.
It extends the emotional psychology used in *L'invitée* to a larger
cast of characters and refines it to greater complexity. *Les Mandarins* is Beauvoir's most successful fusion of her two principal concerns, sensibility and responsibility. Within its pages it poses in
fictional terms the dilemma of the twentieth century writer with
which this study deals. But it offers no simple solutions.

After the resistance years, which offered clear-cut choices and
all-absorbing action, the intellectual Left of Paris finds itself in
1945 restored to a civilian existence to which it is no longer accli-
mated. Robert Dubreuilh and Henri Perron, two influential men of
letters, meet the peace in different ways. Perron, tired of war and
temperamentally unsuited to involvement in politics, tries to enjoy
his first peacetime Christmas in many years. "If there were no

---

[80] *Ibid.*, 283.   [81] *Ibid.*, 289.

holidays, of what use would victories be?" he asks.[82] He feels himself on the verge of breaking with Paule, his mistress of ten years, who has become an emotional burden to him, and he plans a trip to Portugal. He sees the liberation as a personal one.

Perron is the editor of *L'Espoir*, a journal of the Left which he hopes to maintain in its present uncommitted position.[83] Dubreuilh, older, more firmly established as a writer and leader of opinion, is Perron's closest friend. Dubreuilh is convinced of the necessity for engagement in politics and seeks to consolidate the S.R.L., a liberal-revolutionary coalition which is attempting to work with the Communists without actually joining them. Dubreuilh feels that the S.R.L. stands a greater chance of success if it has a newspaper, and he tries to persuade Perron to commit *L'Espoir* to this movement.[84] Dubreuilh's wife, Anne, some twenty years younger than he, finds herself aged by the war years and uncertain of the meaning of her existence. As a professional psychiatrist, she can understand the mechanisms of others, but seems distinctly alienated from herself, so busy is she living the active life which her work, her husband, daughter, and friends demand of her. As she says, she had few relations with herself.[85] Her relation to her husband is one of trust and understanding, the free union of Pierre and Françoise of *L'invitée* seen at a later stage, when the relationship has been stripped of its physical side by the passage of time. Paule, Henri's mistress, clings more strongly to her prewar illusions than any character in the novel. She still sees herself as the most beautiful woman in the world, loved by the most talented writer in the world, and refuses to accept Henri's present indifference. These

[82] *Les Mandarins* (Paris: Gallimard, 1954), 16.
[83] Here Beauvoir has fused her own desire to pursue personal freedom with Camus' real dilemma as editor of *Combat*.
[84] Dubreuilh reflects Sartre's own position after the war. He does not, however, correspond in age or character to Sartre himself, who is portrayed in Beauvoir's autobiography as far from the Olympian figure she has created in the novel.
[85] Beauvoir has confessed that some of Anne's problems were her own, while Anne's total character is essentially dissimilar to hers. Anne has no creative work; she is much more mired in the "female condition" than Beauvoir. For this reason, Anne is a more universal and sympathetic character.

are the four central characters, although the portrait of Nadine, Dubreuilh's daughter, is a memorable one—a moody, sensitive, self-contradictory young girl who rages at others for their acts of bad faith (Nadine is indeed reminiscent of Sartres' Ivich).

Beauvoir alternates third-person narrative chapters with chapters in which Anne narrates directly. Thus, many events are seen from two different perspectives, revealing the subjectivity with which any one character appraises a situation. The most important function of Anne's first person narrative, however, is to permit the intimate, extraordinarily sensitive portrait of her love affair with an American writer. For these sequences, any point of view but that of the individual involved would have seemed like an intrusion of privacy. Wayland Young has voiced an objection which was common in the earlier notices of the novel, that Anne's love affair with Lewis Brogan is irrelevant to the intellectual subject matter of the novel.[86] This criticism implies that the novel has no organic unity. However, a careful reading of Les Mandarins as a coherent work, rather than as a treatise on politics, reveals that the romance of Anne and Lewis is a microcosm of the novel's entire scheme, in which responsibility and emotion are shown to be inseparable both in politics and in love.

Henri Perron is the most fully described character in the novel. In him we see the dilemmas of the intellectual magnified, we discover how the man of "good intentions" acts very frequently in bad faith, and we find, nevertheless, a man who is enormously attractive. Lacking Dubreuilh's Olympian detachment, Perron manages to come to the same conclusions earlier. Without ever experiencing the emotional holiday he dreamed of after the Liberation (it is Anne who experiences this), he continues actively to vindicate the value of physical beauty and physical pleasure which Dubreuilh seems rarely to appreciate.

The writer is the prime focus for Beauvoir's inquiry into the nature of responsibility. Her presupposition is the same one stated earlier in Pyrrhus et Cinéas, that the work of art is an object made by man for man. Perron, tired by his frenetic wartime activity,

[86] Wayland Young, "The Mandarins of Paris," Twentieth Century, CLVIII (July, 1955), 76–81.

hopes to return to literature relieved of responsibility. He will write only of himself:

"To speak of that which I loved, that which I love, of what I am". . . . Who was he? What was he uncovering after this long absence? It's difficult to define oneself and to delimit oneself from the inside. He was neither a fanatic about politics nor a fanatic about writing, nor a man of great passion; he felt himself rather as just anyone; but this did not bother him. A man like everyone, who would speak sincerely of himself, in the name of everyone, for everyone. Sincerity: this was the sole originality at which he should aim, the sole task he had to carry out. . . . It's not so easy to be sincere. . . . For the moment, above all not to burden himself with problems; set out at random, begin any way at all . . . .[87]

Beginning his new book in this way, Perron finds himself incapable of writing. He finds himself complaisant rather than sincere and is quickly disgusted with a gratuitous work in which he attempts to speak of himself unrelated to the past or the present: "The truth of his life was outside of himself, in events, in people, in things; in order to speak of oneself, one has to speak of everything else." [88] Instead he writes a play which illuminates the postwar guilt of the living over those who did not survive. The play is a stormy success and brings its author great emotional satisfaction. When speaking for the silent voices of his audience and for their hidden fears, Perron senses himself launched toward eternity. He perceives that the emotional reward he seeks from literary effort is achieved by responsible creative action. But Perron also continually discovers, in his public and private life, that there are no unmixed rewards and no clear-cut choices. His holiday in Portugal is a revelation of painful human misery. He refuses at first to ally his newspaper with the S.R.L., then sees his reasons for abstaining as meaningless. In attempting to keep his readers impartially informed, he finds that he never has quite enough knowledge of a given situation to make an accurate appraisal.

Perron arrives at last at one of Beauvoir's most crucial points about action: one acts always to some extent in ignorance, without

[87] *Les Mandarins*, 51. Here Perron voices many of Beauvoir's own feelings about literature and the relation of art to personal happiness.
[88] *Ibid.*, 255.

guarantees; one is forced to choose almost blindly, and yet one is responsible for the choice. Indirectly she asserts that most choices are blind ones, based on half-truths and an enormous element of chance; however, it is necessary to act. The view of politics presented in *Les Mandarins* is at once bitingly objective and yet veiled by the particular illusions of each character. In contradistinction to Dubreuilh's immediate and obstinate stands on unclear issues, Perron expresses the nostalgic desire of most characters in the novel when he says, "If only one could be completely for or completely against." [89]

Beauvoir's portrait of Perron is distinctly ambivalent. One senses her sympathy for his desires—"to be free and happy"—along with her ironic judgment of his life as a series of self-delusions. He is readily willing to admit guilt over things political. "When the situation is unjust, you can't live it correctly; that's why one is led to mix in politics: in order to change the situation." [90] But Perron's enormous cowardice in his relationship with his mistress is something he manages to push out of his mind by turning to politics. This relationship in bad faith is Perron's greatest fault; by refusing to make an overt gesture to rupture, Perron allows Paule to carry on the martyred role in which he had cast her years earlier and which she readily accepted. The bad faith is on both sides—Paule is as unwilling to accept the end of the affair as Henri to state it. In his next relationship with a woman, he has learned to wear guilt well enough to perjure himself for "humane reasons." And he continues his literary career because he loves to write, justifying this activity by saying, "One does not prevent a war with words; but words don't necessarily intend to change history: this is also one way of living history." [91]

The Olympian Dubreuilh seems to be glimpsed from a distance of enormous admiration, so that he is far less human a character than Perron. As an engaged writer, Dubreuilh is emotionally committed to vindicating mankind, which he intellectually equates with the working class. He never wavers from his conviction that one does not write simply to write, that literature is made for men

[89] *Ibid.*, 301.   [90] *Ibid.*, 133.   [91] *Ibid.*, 571.

and not men for literature.[92] Discouraged at first by the failure of
his *modus vivendi* with the Communists and even more when he
fully realizes the import of the slave labor camps in Russia, Dubreuilh experiences a profound depression which appears to Anne
and Perron like the symptoms of aging. His melancholy is that of
an *amour déçu*, including its irrepressible hope. Dubreuilh's hope
remains fixed on the U.S.S.R., demonstrating one of the axioms of
the novel's intellectual milieu, namely, that should the world have
to choose between the United States and Russia, the choice would
"of course be Russia." Americans will object to this assumption for
obvious reasons, while an Englishman may point out that Great
Britain has already achieved a successful socialist revolution without the cruel expedients characteristic of the Soviet march to the
future.[93]

Dubreuilh admits to Anne that should the intellectuals of the
Left succeed, the result will be a society in which he himself would
be unable to live. This is the prime instance of "the uneasiness of
the intellectual" the novel depicts.[94] In addition to a fear of being
totally ineffectual, the intellectual experiences the opposite of this
fear: should one succeed too well and too practically, the result
may be too real and not at all beautiful. One is reminded of
Malraux's hard-headed Communist tactician Garcia, of *L'espoir*,
who cautions idealists fighting by his side in the Spanish Civil War
that it is fatal to pit a dream against a political reality—it is "a
desperate game." The "beautiful equilibrium" which Dubreuilh
had achieved between aesthetic standards and revolutionary inspiration is threatened, as the anti-Communist Scriassine points out,
by the process of the revolution itself,[95] by a technical society which
will brush aside aesthetic concerns. At the end of the novel one
feels that the doubts Dubreuilh has suffered will permanently
affect his work. Only when Dubreuilh becomes disillusioned with

---

[92] For a similar statement see Jean-Paul Sartre, "Qu'est-ce que la littérature?" in *Situations* II (Paris: Gallimard, 1948), 83–84.
[93] See Young, "The Mandarins of Paris," 78–79.
[94] In this connection see Victor Brombert, "Toward a Portrait of the
French Intellectual," in *Partisan Review*, XXVII (Summer, 1960), 480–
502.   [95] *Les Mandarins*, 34.

the efficacy of writing does the reader come close enough to him to find sympathetically that he is merely a man growing old. As a character with few ambiguities in most of the novel, he is too theoretical, too inhuman.

Anne Dubreuilh, not actively interested in politics herself, experiences the emotional price of responsibility at the level of personal relations in her love affair with Lewis Brogan. Calling this romance "an emotional holiday," Hazel Barnes notes an element in it which runs counter to the existentialist theory which the novel seems for the most part to follow closely; namely, that Anne discovers she has no choice in this affair, that the commitment is as if fated.[96] "The measure of my life," Anne reasons, "is as easily a single smile as the whole universe; to choose one or the other is equally arbitrary." Then she adds, "Besides, I had no choice." [97]

Anne Dubreuilh is not the only character in *Les Mandarins* who "has no choice." Henri Perron finds that politics chooses him, rather than that he chooses politics. His innate need to be happy, famous and emotionally at ease forces upon him the choice of responsibility: when he discovers that the happiness he pursues is not to be his as long as he abstains; when he finds that the admiration of others is impossible without a work of art which will be read by others and which must therefore speak of and to them; when his painful affair with Paule makes it clear to him that emotional ease is impossible in a relationship based on bad faith. Dubreuilh is emotionally committed to life, as Anne frequently remarks, so that his perennial vindication of human values in his writings is revealed as a personal commitment which again allows no a priori choice. Even when discouraged over the possibility of being effective, Dubreuilh goes on writing—as Anne goes on loving when her affair is ended by Brogan. Paule is only able to take on a role other than that of victim when she is desensitized by psychoanalysis. The somnabulistic figure of Anne at the novel's beginning finally takes on dimension when she becomes involuntarily involved in an emotional experience. Paule, with her insane inability to accept the truth of Henri's indifference, is far more vivid a

[96] Hazel Barnes, *The Literature of Possibility* (Lincoln: University of Nebraska Press, 1959), 233–34.   [97] *Les Mandarins*, 509.

character. The roles are finally reversed when Paule is "cured" and Anne finds herself without power to remain detached. It is important to note that it is not Anne who undertakes Paule's psychoanalysis. In fact, Anne becomes more and more skeptical of the value of Freudian analysis, which, as Hazel Barnes points out, "is made to serve as a device in bad faith to help the subject evade self-responsibility" in the works of Sartre and Beauvoir.[98] Anne senses that Paule had to betray her past in order to be cured; she had to deny a love which was the meaning of her existence for ten years. Watching Paule totally struck down by Henri's first clear statement of his feelings in a telegram, Anne says aloud, "You'll get well, you must get well. Love is not everything . . . ." and thinks to herself, "Knowing very well that in her place I would never want to get well and bury my love with my own hands." [99]

When Paule is "cured" she becomes a fat, lifeless woman. In a moment of nostalgia for her days of obsession and suspicion, she says to Anne, "You can't imagine how the world was rich, before; the least thing had ten thousand nuances." [100] Anne thinks, "Yes, in order to deliver Paule it was necessary to ruin her love even in the past; I was thinking of those microbes which one can exterminate only by destroying the organism they devour." [101] Even in her unhappiness over the break with Brogan, Anne is unwilling to alleviate her pain by reasoning away her feelings for him; she is convinced that her feelings "are not a sickness." She also doubts the value of liberating her patients from their obsessions. A man's past is his substance. To deny one is to deny the other. The sole alternative to obsession and involuntary engagement is the suspension of life, death, whether in the form of Paule's "cure" or of Anne's momentary consideration of suicide.

The heroes and heroines of *Les Mandarins* are not anonymous creatures with no center and no past, who take on life only in the moment or in projections for the future and in strict accord with existentialist theory.[102] The fundamental choice for Beauvoir's he-

[98] Barnes, *The Literature of Possibility*, 303.
[99] *Les Mandarins*, 413.   [100] *Ibid.*, 494.   [101] *Ibid.*, 496.
[102] For an example of such an interpretation, see Hanna Charney, "Le héros anonyme: De Monsieur Teste aux *Mandarins*," *Romanic Review*, L (December, 1959), 273.

roes in the novel is between life and death, and it is a specious
choice except for deliberate suicide. At the novel's end Anne turns
from suicide, thinking, "Either one falls into indifference, or the
earth becomes inhabited again; I have not fallen. Since my heart
continues to beat, it will have to beat for something, for
someone." [103] Beauvoir seems to say that man may be a useless
passion, but he is an inevitable one.

Les belles images (1966) is Beauvoir's most recent novel. In it,
she examines a problem which is a corollary to her former preoccupation with the self-other dilemma: *who* lives behind the images of
ourselves we see in mirrors and in the eyes of others? Laurence, a
married professional woman of comfortable circumstances, discovers that her life is inauthentic because it is lived in bad faith with
respect to herself and to the world at large. She learns this when
her young daughter Catherine asks crucial questions which are
unanswerable in the context of their milieu: Why do we exist?
What can we do for those less fortunate than ourselves? Why is
there misfortune in the world?

Laurence is prone to spells of ennui, during which she realizes
that her existence has been empty, that she feels neither hope nor
despair. She is only "a waiting without a beginning or an end." [104]
Her ennui is a twentieth century version of that moral malady dear
to Baudelaire and his successors in the nineteenth century. Laurence's career is in advertising, a perfect and too-obvious foil for
Beauvoir's message. When Laurence sees her mother Dominique
abandoned by her wealthy lover, she is "seized by horror, by the
horror of what is going on inside Dominique . . . . All the images
have broken into little pieces, and it will never be possible to put
them back together." [105] Laurence also becomes disillusioned with
her husband, who is unwilling to accept any image of her but the
one he has created for his own comfort.

The novel is written primarily in the first person indirect point
of view, with awkward parenthetical insertions by the author to
indicate the universality of Laurence's situation. For example,

[103] *Les Mandarins,* 579.
[104] *Les belles images* (Paris: Gallimard, 1966), 177.   [105] *Ibid.,* 174.

"(Another young woman, hundreds of young women are asking themselves at this very moment: why him rather than an other?)" [106] Laurence finally experiences a major emotional crisis, indicated by a persistent nausea reflecting her inability to any longer accept the false images of her imposed by those around her. The idea of the novel is interesting, but it fails as fiction because it lacks indirection and subtlety. Beauvoir tells us, rather than showing us, that we are mutilated by living as others would have us live. *Les belles images* lacks the rich ambiguity of *L'invitée* and the scope of *Les Mandarins*.

Maurice Cranston is correct in pointing out that Beauvoir's main interest is in ethics rather than in metaphysics.[107] Her fiction and nonfiction center around the ethics of ambiguity. Sartre's fiction attempts to reveal the metaphysical experience of freedom and contingency, and the acts in bad faith by which men attempt to evade their freedom. Beauvoir is more concerned with the relationship between the self and others, the self as a subject who needs others in order to experience his existence and his freedom. In the best of her novels she evokes an emotional, sensible universe, where responsibility is *felt* rather than demonstrated. She is both easier to read and less profound than Sartre, her technique less radical, her characters either far more vivid than his or, when unsuccessfully created, totally wooden. In existentialist fiction, Simone de Beauvoir occupies a domain which is uniquely her own. In her concern with the relationship between sensibility and responsibility, best expressed in *L'invitée* and *Les Mandarins*, she has achieved an imaginative recreation of the human situation in mid-century.

[106] *Ibid.*, 192.
[107] Maurice Cranston, "Simone de Beauvoir," in *The Novelist as Philosopher*, ed. John Cruickshank (London: Oxford University Press, 1962), 166–82.

Georges Bernanos

EXILE AND THE
EARTHLY WAY

The fame of Georges Bernanos will most likely rest on just those writings which cost him the least time and the greatest anguish, some eight novels and a play. One of France's major novelists in this century, Bernanos did not publish his first novel until he was thirty-eight. Practical considerations—the support of a large family by work as an insurance inspector, frequent moving all over the world in search of an inexpensive habitat, several near-fatal illnesses, psychological problems, an impulsive willingness to engage in a political or polemical enterprise on the spur of the moment, coupled with a totally uncompromising artistic integrity where creative writing was concerned—these factors shaped the life of a temperamental, irrascible genius.

Bernanos never elaborated a consistent theory of the novel and its relation to political and social responsibility. An examination of his critical judgments reveals a great deal of passion and very little critical method. For example, his review in 1932 of Céline's *Voyage au bout de la nuit* records Bernanos' ironic satisfaction that Céline did *not* win the Prix Goncourt, since such recognition would have in fact meant that a true artist, one with a unique voice, would have been crowned by the hypocrites who exemplify the falsest elements of French society. One feels that Bernanos would almost have been disappointed had Céline been named— the latter's unique and "true" voice would have been weakened or insulted by recognition from the "enemy." Instead, Bernanos writes:

We shall tell another day, or leave to others more qualified than ourselves, the task of stating what an artist can think of an extraordinary work, comparable to the inundation of a flood in the depths of night, when with each simultaneous palpitation of the wind and the sea the livid edge of the foam appears and disappears. It matters not at all to me whether this great surge of poetry passes unnoticed by my contemporaries. . . . I try simply to calculate his power and his scope, already measurable by a certain muffled grumbling and by the undermining of several usurped glories.[1]

Bernanos goes on to admire the essential verity of Céline's depiction of man's misery. He supports Céline's observations by pages of his own, on factory workers, prostitutes, the French Revolution, and continues, "For us the question is not if M. Céline's picture is atrocious; we ask if it is true. It is." [2] Aside from a few telling comments on Céline's language, in which Bernanos astutely recognizes not an accurate recording of the speech of the poor but rather an artful deformation of that speech, the review is almost entirely a polemic on man's earthly misery and on the falsity and cowardice of French society.

Bernanos was not a critic of literature; he was a perennial critic of everything else. The largest part of his writings consists of tracts, speeches, and letters. The few early short stories, the eight novels, and a play constitute a very small portion of the total work. But their content is shaped by Bernanos' polemical spirit, and their value must be judged by those few standards which the other writings provide. Bernanos' standards are personal ones, shaped by a view of literature as an individual struggle with the metaphysical and temporal forces of darkness and deceit which drag human lives into obscure despair. His Catholic viewpoint is an integral part of his understanding of literature and a shaping force in his imaginative works. Bernanos' personal vision is most clearly expressed in his letters, which constitute a document of intense

---

[1] Georges Bernanos, "Au bout de la nuit," *Le crépuscule des vieux* (Paris: Gallimard, 1956), 343.   [2] *Ibid.*, 345.

passion filled with unusually perceptive insights into the private ways of artistic creation.

Standing behind the literary product, showing its origins and its meaning, illuminating the life and ideas, is Bernanos' voluminous correspondence, written from many countries and during all but the earliest years of the writer's life. In this correspondence and in a few prefaces and lectures, Georges Bernanos reveals his conception of his vocation, his creative method, the origins of his literary themes. In all these letters one discerns a sense of childlike awe. This sense of awe is evident not only in the poignantly personal matters of his life, but also in the vehement moments when he excoriates those abuses of man's inherent greatness which he particularly detested, hypocrisy, sin, and political viewpoints different from his own. "God, how I love life," wrote Bernanos from Majorca in 1937. "I am truly alone. And not as unhappy as one might think, however, because of that talent I have from childhood of hoping every morning for I don't know what." [3]

A tone of awe permeates the letters which describe Bernanos' discovery of his own talent and creative power. He sees the writer's enterprise as "the other face of a priestly vocation." To an aspiring author he writes, "Either you will be an original writer, or nothing at all. If God really wants a testimony from you, you must expect to work a great deal, to suffer a great deal, to doubt yourself endlessly, in success as in failure. For taken in this spirit, the writer's craft is no longer a craft, it's an adventure, above all a spiritual adventure. All spiritual adventures are Calvaries." [4]

The thirty-eight years preceding his first novel are described as a period of collection, of ripening, but not in the sense of gathering material for his art. The material is present at the beginning. Bernanos reveals time and again his essential conviction of what one might call a limited determinism. When he says, "I had to reach the age of thirty-eight to have the power to exploit an inner experience," he is referring to an inner experience which was his

[3] *Bernanos par lui-même*, ed. Albert Béguin (Paris: Editions du Seuil, 1954), 125.
[4] *Bulletin de la Société des Amis de Georges Bernanos*, Nos. 2–3 (March, 1950), 24.

during those thirty-eight years, not attained at their end.[5] He describes the lineaments of his experience in these words: "I am beginning to dominate this accumulation of dreams, images, characters whose superabundance was choking me." [6]

Bernanos seems certain of the stature of his creative imagination. "I am conscious of having spent twenty years creating in my mind an imaginary world of singular grandeur. I am impatient to reveal it to those who deserve to know it. I know that its realization would put me on a level with the greatest . . . ." [7] In a man whose early life, while revealing a monumental temperament, did not reveal a great writer (the early short stories and polemic pieces show very little of the power to come), it is surprising to find such certainty of greatness. Yet this assurance is present in almost all the letters dealing with Bernanos' fictional undertakings in the period preceding the publication of his first novel, *Sous le soleil de Satan* (1926), and continuing up to the time of his death. However, the sources of this strength of conviction do not lie in arrogance. Bernanos reserved that failing for his political proclamations. Rather, the greatness of his subject matter buttressed him against the discouragements natural to a penurious writer. As he put it, "It is not my song which is immortal, it is that which I sing." [8] The novelist's subject matter, his themes are the source of his pride. Before examining some of these themes, let us consider their origin.

In the letters dealing with his creative process, Bernanos describes a method essentially based on inspiration. In answer to an inquiry about the original model for a character in the *Journal d'un curé de campagne*, he writes:

I began the *Journal* one evening last winter, absolutely without knowing where I was going. . . . As soon as I take up my pen, what rises up at once in me is my childhood, my so ordinary childhood, which resembles all others, and from which, nevertheless, I draw all I write as from an inexhaustible fountain of dreams. The faces and landscapes of my

[5] Cited in Georges Bernanos, *Un mauvais rêve*, édition critique établie par Albert Béguin (Paris: Plon, 1950), 323.   [6] *Ibid.*
[7] *Georges Bernanos. Essais et témoignages*, ed. Albert Béguin (Neuchâtel and Paris: Collection des Cahiers du Rhône, 1949), 38. Hereinafter cited as *Cahiers du Rhône*.   [8] *Ibid.*, cited on plate X.

childhood, all mixed together, blended, stirred up by this kind of unconscious memory which makes me what I am, a novelist, and, if it please God, also a poet. . . . Beginning with a certain moment I invent nothing, I tell what I see. Beings I have loved pass on the screen, and I only recognize them much later, when they have stopped acting and speaking. . . . Perhaps I never recognize them at all, because they have been transformed, bit by bit, mixed together [into] an imaginary creature, more real to me than a living one . . . .[9]

The unique source of Bernanos' fictional world was his childhood. He revealed that try as he would, he could imagine only one setting for his characters, the landscape of his early years. One cannot help thinking of Proust's Combray on reading Bernanos' words, "There is a mystery of childhood, a sacred part in childhood, a lost paradise of childhood to which we always return in our dreams." [10]

Bernanos described early visions of his characters, visions of Mouchette and Donissan, Cénabre, Chantal, and the "cher curé d'un Ambricourt imaginaire," revealing that these figures were with him long before they appeared in his novels. Apparently they were the imaginary companions of his childhood. For Bernanos childhood was the source of *characters* as well as of *setting*. Still a third, perhaps the most important aspect of this return to one's origins, hinted at in the words "a sacred part in childhood," is referred to by Bernanos as "language." "One does not speak in the name of childhood, one would have to speak its language. And it is this forgotten language, this language I seek from book to book. Imbecile! As if such a language could be written, was ever written. No matter! Once in a while I happen to rediscover some accent of it . . . ." [11] At the end of the preface just quoted, Bernanos indicates that the language to which he refers unlocks a special domain with other-worldly accesses. "My profound certainty is that that segment of the world still susceptible to redemption belongs only to children, heroes and martyrs." [12] These same terms appear fre-

[9] *Bulletin*, No. 1 (December, 1949), 5.
[10] *Bulletin*, No. 4 (June, 1950), 8.
[11] Georges Bernanos, *Grands cimetières sous la lune* (Paris: Plon, 1938), v of Préface.   [12] *Ibid.*

quently in his polemical writings. They denote the forces of good which the corrupt world of his contemporaries, especially in France, is trying to destroy. The imagery of Bernanos' fictional theories, that of saints, martyrs, and children, is the same as that of his polemical writings; it also constitutes the framework for his occasional efforts at literary criticism. These facts only serve to support his contention that everything is present in the writer from the very beginning; his earliest nonfiction predates the first novels.

For Bernanos, fiction and the incantatory quality of language seem capable of reversing the process of falling away from grace which comes with growing up. The strongest characteristic common to the martyrs in his novels is their childlike simplicity. Very few of his children, however, seem to retain for very long that susceptibility to redemption of which he speaks. Too soon they are corrupted by the growing up, the growing away from innocence which colors the world in which they live. The forces which martyr innocence in the world force them to the brink of despair, frequently to suicide. But for the writer, the return to childhood is, if not wholly attainable, at least desirable as a direction. All this Bernanos seems to have realized instinctively, before grasping it intellectually.

The true writer is not one by choice. None of the literary hacks who people Bernanos' novels are treated with anything but contempt. He made a strong distinction between the artist, or "poet," to use his preferred word, and the professional writer, that is, the man who chooses to make his living by putting words on paper. "I believe that a true writer is but the overseer and dispenser of goods which do not belong to him . . . ." [13] The other kind of writer, the literary craftsman who deliberately chooses writing as a profession, appears in Bernanos' novels as the "scribbler," a half-human figure, a social and intellectual parasite who merits Bernanos' wrath because he has nothing to say, because his ideas are second- or third-hand. In short, he is not the vessel of any message greater than himself. There is a fine distinction between a *profession* and a

[13] *Bulletin*, No. 5 (Christmas, 1950), 8.

vocation. "As I grow older, I understand better and better that my modest vocation is truly a vocation—*vocatus.* The Good Lord has to call me each time he needs me. . . . Then, I get up grumbling and as soon as the task is finished, I return to my very ordinary life . . . ." [14] Bernanos affirmed frequently that the literary craft did not tempt him. Rather, he felt that it was imposed on him by a force outside of himself. He had nothing but contempt for the art for art's sake frame of mind which colored the lives and work of some contemporaries. Pointing to the fact that he had waited until nearly the age of forty to publish his first book, Bernanos repeated that he was not a "writer"—a writer writes books at the age of twenty. No, he was forced to write, called to write. And write he did—on trains, in cafés, laboriously, painfully, in a kind of blind agony, feeling that the act of writing was cutting him off from the human world.

I am not a writer. The mere sight of a piece of blank paper fatigues my soul. The kind of physical introversion which such work imposes is so distasteful to me that I avoid it as much as I can. I write in cafés at the risk of passing for a drunkard. . . . All year long I swallow those sweetish *cafés-crèmes*, with a fly inside. I write on cafe tables because I can't for very long do without the human face and voice of which I have tried to speak nobly. Let the rogues say that I "observe." I observe nothing at all. Observation doesn't lead to anything. . . . I write in cafés as once I used to write in railroad carriages, so as not to be the dupe of imaginary creatures, in order to find, in a glance at an unknown man passing, the true measure of joy or of sorrow.[15]

If the novelist gains nothing from "observation," what is the relationship between his life and his work? Bernanos repeats that all of it somehow comes from childhood. If this is taken literally, then the persons and places the child saw would be those which appear, somewhat changed by time and the erosion of memory, in the adult work. Bernanos explains that this is not precisely what happens. There occurs instead what he calls a fictional sublimation, which he describes thus: "The artist's work is never the sum of his disappointments, his sufferings, his doubts, of the evil and the

---

[14] *Ibid.,* 6.   [15] *Grands cimetières,* ii–iii.

good of his whole life—it is rather his life itself, transfigured, illuminated, reconciled." [16]

Another term crucial to Bernanos' view of artistic memory is the word *rêver*, to dream. He defines the true novelist as one who has "really dreamed his book . . . has drawn most of his situations or characters from that foundation of subconscious experience . . . the precious, irreplaceable and incommunicable experience of childhood, which the crisis of adolescence almost always thrusts back into the night . . . ." [17]

Unlike Proust, whom he resembles in his emphasis on the unique function of childhood as a key to the adult experience, Bernanos seems to have found no *method* for drawing the past out of oblivion. One might of course speculate that Bernanos was simply not clever enough to have invented a so-called method after the fact. In any case, the correspondence reveals no set order of procedure for the beginning, continuation, or completion of the novels. A character seems to spring up out of nowhere:

I still see myself, one September evening, my window open on an immense twilight sky. . . . Then little Mouchette rose up . . . and suddenly she signalled to me, with that avid, anxious look.—Oh! how the birth of a sincere book is a fragile thing, furtive and difficult to recount. . . . I saw the mysterious little girl between her father, a brewer, and her mother. I imagined her story little by little. I followed behind her, I let her go. I sensed her fearless heart. . . . Then little by little, around her, like a shadow thrown on a wall, the very image of her crime was dimly drawn. . . . The first stage was over, she was free.[18]

The face of a character, with what that face conveys of anguish, loss, sin, or divine illumination, seems to have been the starting point of several of Bernanos' novels. Then followed intense periods of activity. However, any period which produced an unusual amount of pages was followed by a time of relative sterility, as if the novelist's tired faculties demanded a temporary truce in this battle, this unnatural state which was his creativity.

Occasionally, Bernanos determined to write a novel "to order," that is, one which he hoped to complete quickly, in order to be able

[16] *Cahiers du Rhône*, 50.   [17] *Bulletin*, Nos. 7–8 (October, 1951), 2.
[18] *Bulletin*, Nos. 12–13 (Christmas, 1952), 25–26.

to support his family in a more regular fashion. Such was the case of *Un crime* (1935), intended originally as a brief and facile *roman policier*. The end result was actually two novels, *Un crime* and *Un mauvais rêve*, the latter published posthumously. *Un crime* itself expanded beyond the originally intended crime novel, assumed metaphysical overtones, while the second novel is in many ways one of Bernanos' best. The letters of this period reveal that Bernanos found himself incapable of deliberately and objectively shaping the structure and direction of his work. He wrote of the first draft of *Un crime* which he was sending to a friend: "[This section] . . . permitted me to trace the portrait of my heroine (a criminal one) in my own manner—that is, in the manner I believe good, in short, in the Bernanos manner. The *roman policier* takes on stature." [19] A few weeks later he became aware that the novel had gone its own way, or rather the predetermined way of its author. "I began by wanting to write a *roman policier*, but one is what one is. The Maison Bernanos does not work for the five-and-dime." [20]

By contrast with the freedom his characters had in relation to their creator, Bernanos' personal lack of freedom to pursue his art is striking. We have already noted some of the limiting factors, the predetermination of the work from early childhood, the essentially unnatural state requisite to the act of writing, the discouragement of seeing the newborn works misunderstood or even ignored. None of these seems to have weighed as strongly in the life of Georges Bernanos as financial need. Thinking of moving to Paraguay and of making some kind of permanent page-by-page arrangement with his publisher, he wrote, "Whatever happens . . . [I'll move] before winter, which is summer there. To miss this departure would slow me down a full year. For ten years now I should have freed myself, saved my intelligence, my heart, my work, all of which the stubborn work of the *salauds* will eventually reduce to a little heap of ashes. Yes, I'll leave whatever happens." [21] Though seldom able to resist an invitation to lecture or write a polemical piece in his youth, as Bernanos grew older he became aware of the limitations of time. He weighed the 120 pages necessary to a series of three

[19] *Bernanos par lui-même*, 170.   [20] *Ibid.*
[21] *Bulletin*, Nos. 2–3, p. 19.

lectures against 120 pages of a novel, and admitted that the artistic work would take scarcely any more time, and would, as he put it, be far less likely to give the public the impression of "some literary clown." [22] His early alliance with the Action Française group seemed far less important to him later on.[23] The author's judgments on the secular preoccupations of some of his characters reflect his changing valuations on purely temporal matters.

One extra-artistic consideration, however, continued to dog Bernanos, even during his periods of greatest creativity: the relation of his Catholicism to his fiction. Writing of the free choice of evil by his character Mouchette, Bernanos said:

Around the miserable revolted child, no road open, no way out. No end possible to this frenetic surge toward an illusory deliverance except death or nothingness. . . . The Catholic dogma of original sin and of redemption arose here, not out of a text, but out of the facts, the circumstances and conjectures. Once the problem was stated, no solution was possible but that one. At the limits of a certain degradation, of a certain sacreligious dissipation of the human soul, the idea of redemption imposes itself on the mind.[24]

Bernanos consistently denied writing novels designed to prove a Catholic point of view. In his judgment, the term Catholic novelist was unjust, since it implied that a man is first of all a Catholic, and that his art is in the service of his religion. It would no longer be art if this were the case.

I have already written, on this subject, that I refused the name of Catholic novelist, that I was a Catholic who writes novels, nothing more, nothing less. What would be the value tomorrow, for unbelievers, of our feeble testimony, if it were proved that a Christian is never Christian enough to be one naturally, as if in spite of himself, in his work? If you cannot without effort and grimaces reconcile your faith

---

[22] *Ibid.,* 21.
[23] For an interpretation of Bernanos' political involvements and thoughts, see Thomas Molnar, *Bernanos, His Political Thought and Philosophy* (New York: Sheed and Ward, 1960). Documents relating to Bernanos' involvement with Charles Maurras and the Action Française group may be found in the following: *Bulletin de la Société des amis de Georges Bernanos,* Nos. 17–20 (Christmas, 1953); No. 43 (October, 1961).   [24] *Bulletin,* Nos. 12–13, pp. 25–26.

and your art, don't force it, keep silent. . . . All the gold in the world cannot buy the testimony of a free man.[25]

Man is endowed with free will and Bernanos' novels vividly describe its exercise. The same freedom is a condition for artistic creation: only a novelist who is free can speak to the human condition.

Georges Bernanos' novels revolve about two central themes, sin and death. It appears that the choice of themes was not a conscious one. To Claude-Edmonde Magny, one of the few critics to understand the novel M. *Ouine* when it first appeared, Bernanos wrote, "I am a novelist, that is, a man who lives his dreams, or who relives them without knowing it. Therefore I have no intentions . . . you make intelligible to me this world in which I advanced once, page by page, in the darkness, guided by a kind of instinct like that of the navigation of birds . . . ." [26] Mme. Magny had made explicit to Bernanos the structure and themes of an immense and puzzling novel in which Bernanos had tried to render physical and visual his obsession with sin and the metaphysical revolt which is its origin. But Bernanos had accomplished this task intuitively. His novel said what he wanted to express, but *as novel*, not as intellectual statement. In fact, in the correspondence Bernanos spoke very lamely of the ideas which underlay his novels. The reason is evident. As abstractions these ideas meant nothing to him. To speak of sin, of the temptation of evil, Bernanos put characters into situations. Indeed, according to the creative method revealed by the correspondence, it would be more accurate to say that Bernanos' characters lived out these themes, each in his own way, as the novelist recorded the resultant spiritual adventures. However, one does find in the correspondence revealing statements on the nature and meaning of Bernanos' key themes.

"The hatred of man against himself," "this contradiction in man," these are the phrases used to describe the phenomenon of sin.[27] Almost naïvely Bernanos wrote to a friend that man is simply

[25] *Bulletin*, Nos. 15–16 (August, 1953), 13–14.
[26] *Bulletin*, No. 4 (June, 1950), 7.
[27] "Lettre—préface" to Paul Fronville, *Hors de l'intelligence pas de salut* (Paris: Éditions Renée Lacoste, 1949), 9.

not reasonable—if he were, would sin exist? "The world is dying for lack of childhood," and he concluded that only saints and poets could save it.[28] While not always certain of his methods, Bernanos occasionally saw his own preoccupations reflected in other authors. One such was Léon Bloy, whom he greatly admired. On an application form he filled out for his publisher, under the heading, "Principal idea or aim pursued by the author, for this book and those to follow," Bernanos supplied the following quotation from Bloy: "A horrible lament over sin, without bitterness or solemnity, rather, grave, orthodox and of an inexhaustible veracity." [29] On another occasion, in reply to a questionnaire entitled "Have you seen the Devil?", Bernanos wrote for a newspaper:

I would say rather that evil is a fact of experience which is not easy to deny. Now, to claim that man sins only to escape from restraint and that he draws only a negative satisfaction from his sin seems to me a useless statement. There is a joy in evil. . . . At the bottom of this dark motivation, there is rather a cruelty against oneself, a grinding and painful pleasure. . . . Who is the director of this absurd and fierce tragedy? I cannot believe that we find within ourselves a wickedness so black and so futile. Thus I arrive, in the oldest human tradition, at the existence of demons . . . .[30]

Notice that Bernanos here uses the word demons in the plural. It might appear that he is dodging the question which prompted his statement, that is, whether he had seen the Devil. In this instance he does avoid meeting the problem directly. However, he mentions the devil quite frequently in connection with an author he greatly admired, Racine. "Jean Racine," he wrote, "believed in the Devil as I do." [31] When confronted with the self-destruction which possessed Racine's characters, Bernanos called it the Devil. In his first novel, *Sous le soleil de Satan*, the Devil appears to one of his characters, and at this point the three apparently disparate sections of the book are united. Once again, the visual, the concrete illustration serves to convey Bernanos' thought while the abstract idea seems to elude him.

[28] Preface to Raymond Christofleur, *Louis le Cardonnel, pèlerin de l'invisible* (Paris: Plon, 1938), iv.   [29] *Bulletin*, No. 1, p. 8.
[30] *Bulletin*, No. 6 (June, 1951), 13.   [31] *Bulletin*, Nos. 12–13, p. 25.

Evil finds other concretizations in Bernanos' novels. The curé in the *Journal* is slowly killed by a tumor, which appears almost a physical manifestation of evil in the world. In this connection it is interesting to cite a letter Bernanos wrote when his father was dying. "My poor papa is stricken by one of those ignoble tumors which have always seemed to me, more than any other illness, the figuration of Satan, the symbol of his monstrous fertility in souls." [32]

Most frequently, Bernanos treats sins as a form of revolt: "This kind of lucid madness, the voluntary and deliberate search for evil, for evil loved for itself, in short, total, absolute Revolt, for which no exercise of our reason can furnish a satisfactory definition. . . ." [33] In Bernanos' novels sin is best expressed by the solitude which inevitably accompanies it. As his characters plunge further into sin they are more completely cut off from the human world. "Misery . . . closes in upon itself. It is walled in, like Hell." [34] In *M. Ouine*, which is in fact a novel about Hell on earth, the characters are unable to experience anything resembling love. Bernanos clarifies this situation in a letter: "Hell is not to love. . . . Hell hates itself because it is no longer capable of loving. There is no other damnation but that one." [35]

If most of Bernanos' characters appear lost from the outset, if sin covers the world like a fine rain of dust, from where is hope to come? Of *M. Ouine*, the darkest of his novels, Bernanos wrote, "I want hope to spring from the depths of anguish as once the light sprang from the depths of chaos." [36] Hope must come from the very bottom, the very absence of hope, as if called forth by a vacuum.

Death, the other major theme in Bernanos' work, is also the answer to some of the questions arising out of his preoccupation with sin and evil. From his earliest years Bernanos appears to have

[32] Cited in Guy Gaucher, *Le thème de la mort dans les romans de Bernanos* (Paris: Lettres Modernes, 1955), 111.
[33] *Bulletin*, Nos. 12–13, pp. 24–26.   [34] *Bulletin*, No. 6, p. 2.
[35] *Bulletin*, Nos. 37–38 (June, 1960), 4.
[36] Cited in *M. Ouine, Notes et variantes* (Paris: Club des Librairies de France, 1955), [11].

been obsessed with death, fearing it and dreaming of filling his life with activity and glory so as to lessen death's importance. Then, as he described it, "at the moment of my first communion, an illumination came to me. And I said to myself that it was not life above all which one should try to make happy and good, but death, which is the conclusion of everything . . . ."[37] Once this realization had taken place, he began to look on death as the highest, most mysterious and most personal form of human experience. The death of his characters is often their only instant of self-realization; frequently they discover it was the goal of their existence, a goal of which they were unaware. Mocking those who believe that the essence of adventure lies in travel, Bernanos once addressed an audience thus:

There is always an adventure which you will have in spite of yourself, which perhaps you will have tomorrow. . . . The most sedentary of men will have it, and it is a greater and more marvelous adventure than any of those you have read in books. Yes, death, your death, yours, all yours —private . . . [At the moment of death] the commonest bed seems to me a miraculous little ship which weighs anchor and goes off. . . . Thus begins the great adventure.[38]

While he learned not to fear death, Bernanos above all loved this world, which he called "a universe streaming with beauty." He was moved by the ugliness of sin and the beauty of the human soul. All these passions he transformed into the stuff of novels. He once wrote, "When I shall be dead, tell the sweet Kingdom of Earth that I loved it, more than I ever dared say . . . ."[39] This love encompassed the tormented Mouchette and the fallen Abbé Cénabre in a vision of anguish and possible redemption, set on a planet which is the stage for dramas greater than itself.

Writing from Brazil, where he spent the last years of his life, Bernanos expressed the conviction which made him an artist, perhaps a greater one than he himself realized: "My music comes to you from the end of the world. When you no longer hear it, it will not be my fault, I shall have bravely finished my career as a singer of streets in a country with neither streets nor roads—unless you

[37] *Cahiers du Rhône*, 19.   [38] *Bulletin*, Nos. 12–13, p. 24.
[39] Epigraph of the *Bulletin*.

believed you still heard it. For it is not my song which is immortal, it is that which I sing." [40]

Bernanos' personal art of the novel was, as we have already pointed out, fundamentally untheoretical and provides few critical criteria for judging his own work. Some of the scattered comments he made in his lifetime on other writers, however, do provide certain negative criteria valuable to an understanding of the form his own novels took. Among the novelists he most frequently criticized was Marcel Proust, of whom he wrote, "If Monsieur Marcel Proust displeases many honest folk to the point of horror, it is because he symbolizes perfectly the most subtle and most serious forms of our decadence; the diversity of his ingenious vices is such that one finds in them not only a deterministic evil, but also a series of ills tied the ones to the others by a causal relationship!" [41] However, it should be noted that Bernanos himself portrays at least as many vices as did Proust. Bernanos' novels include pure evil, transvestitism, suicide, torture, mendacity, theomania, pyromania, lesbianism, religious hypocrisy, etc. His objection to Proust's gallery of evil stems from a qualitative rather than a quantitative reaction: Proust's vices seem to Bernanos inevitable, at times almost pleasurable; they seem to define man as a network of vices, the relationships between men as a working out of evil according to a preestablished pattern with no theological basis. The ontology of evil which he found in Proust disturbed Bernanos because there seemed to be no room for "hope to spring from the depths of anguish as once light sprang from the depths of chaos." Undoubtedly Bernanos tended to misread Proust, who was not as detached and delighted an observer of evil as Bernanos made him out to be. But Bernanos' objection to what he calls deterministic evil is a consistent one in his comments on other novelists. In André Gide he found another attitude toward evil which in some ways infuriated him even more. He described it as a deliberate flaunting of perversion for pure sensationalism, a sensationalism which devolved, among the lesser disciples of Gide, to a swarm of "little immoralists" actually afraid of life itself. Gide was a corruptor of

[40] *Cahiers du Rhône*, plate X.
[41] *Bulletin*, No. 14 (February, 1953), 5.

youth, a shaper of souls who himself remained ambiguous toward evil, as toward everything, by a combination of intelligence and sensuality. For his lack of clear commitments, for his detachment, Gide earned Bernanos' powerful anger.[42]

Another literary fashion which irritated Bernanos was what he called "pure verbal logomachy." Writing in 1939 of styles in contemporary poetry, he said:

I adore the clarity of Racine, I detest the verses of M. Cocteau as, for example, I detest a certain kind of pious and episcopal poetry, falsely Catholic and strictly for clerical usage. . . . I love the poetry of mystery, which is quite another thing from the incomprehensible poetry of many of our contemporary poets, a poetry reduced to a pure verbal logomachy. In short, I detest the poetry called irrationalist, hermetic or metaidiomatic. I do not accept nor admit of an absolutist poetry which seeks to isolate itself from literature . . . .[43]

His favorite example of "whole poetry" was Whitman. For Bernanos the ideal poetry was one which "seizes us with its eternal, torrential and generous wave. All the great poets of the world have been thus. It is only today that poetry fragments itself into little compositions, cold verbiage. . . . The poetry of Whitman . . . is massive and gigantic, never a fragment of poetry . . . ." Bernanos sought in poetry as in fiction the voice of the inner man. This is the sound literature must try to capture. "There is in the expression of the inner man . . . an oceanic agitation, an anguish for perfection, which is an endless road, the road of creation aimed at eternity. . . . The inner man only makes sounds so that his cries may shake the world . . . ."[44]

The same polemic spirit which inspired Bernanos' pamphlets and speeches underlay the inception of his novels. The quality of the contemporary world which most enraged him was mediocrity, and his impatience with mediocrity nourished his gallery of strange saints and grotesque sinners. In an abandoned preface written in 1947, Bernanos expressed succinctly the threat to modern civilization he saw all around him. "The mediocre man cannot construct

[42] See *Le crépuscule des vieux*, 31, 33, 35, 37, 42–43.
[43] *Bulletin*, Nos. 15–16, p. 15.   [44] *Ibid.*, 16–17.

any kind of civilization, even a mediocre one: he is capable only of destroying. In a vigorous, hierarchical society each mediocre man remains more or less isolated, in his particular mediocrity. But as society falls apart, the mediocre ones succeed in clumping together, the mediocre man becomes the man of the mass, the mass of average men submerges the elite, stifles its creativity." [45] Bernanos found this same rampant mediocrity among Catholics. He described the "Catholic Bookshop" in Reims as "a pious drugstore for pale souls," and saw the majority of Catholic novels as still another form of pulp fiction.

In describing how the man of genius fights the tide of mediocrity, Bernanos explained that the genius does not know his own aim when he undertakes the struggle. All he can do is grope toward it "at the cost of a great, painful and decisive effort." [46] His own work methods apparently inspired the adjectives he chose. In a letter to Robert Valléry-Radot on the difficulties of writing, he wrote:

Whether I remain at home or run like a madman here and there, the results, in the final analysis, are the same. If I write two pages a day for a week, the next week deducts the advance benefit, and at the end of the month I must consider myself lucky if I can salvage from a mess of paper the substance of thirty miserable pages, where I have to keep from subtracting anything when my conscience—or my scruples, or my mania, or that I don't know what which eats at me night and day—invites me to cut a third, or a half, or the whole thing.[47]

But the creative struggle was unavoidable because, "the artist can keep still, but he cannot give himself by halves . . . [the] sensual imagination . . . is the very sign of the gift of creativity." [48]

For Bernanos creation was a kind of exorcism of personal demons, an involuntary testimony to the realities of life. "Having been born a novelist, I naturally had the desire to depict the passions, but I would have liked to seize them, surprise them in their rapports and their movement; in short, I wanted them alive.

[45] Bulletin, No. 50 (July, 1963), 4.   [46] Ibid., 6.
[47] Cited by Béguin in his notes to the first integral edition of M. Ouine (Paris: Club des Librairies de France, 1955), 292.
[48] Bulletin, Nos. 51–52 (Christmas, 1963), 12.

Then I realized the need to put them back into a plan which was on their own scale, in this spiritual universe whose entry the melancholy peons had barred to us. . . . And once I had stepped into this invisible world where lie the roots of these mysterious forces, I met there the Devil and God." Going on to explain why pure Evil is so seldom treated in fiction, Bernanos wrote, "There is too great a disproportion between the visible verifiable ravages of this fearful phenomenon, and the puerile explanations people make of it." [49]

Bernanos' ideal of literary drama, of the perfect equilibrium the treatment of evil demands, was to be found in the poetry of Racine. "The inner drama appears in a light so pure that it threatens to dissolve. The most carnal of our poets carried his secret off with him, the miracle of an iridescent transparency where nothing seems to impede one's vision although everything appears in it, with its own form and color, right down to that 'shameful part of shadow' of which Shakespeare speaks." [50] Bernanos' own "art for the soul's sake" relies on visual, auditory imagery. The psychology is unanalytical; it is visual. His novels attempt to express, with varying degrees of success, individual encounters with evil in this world, and rely for their effect upon a unique blending of visual detail and metaphysical overtones. In some ways, the confrontation of man and the transcendent in Bernanos is not unlike the confrontation of man and nature one finds in Malraux, with this difference. Bernanos' heroes assume greatness when they confront forces beyond themselves and grapple with them, almost hand to hand. Malraux's heroes assume their ultimate stature when they refuse almost gratuitously to acknowledge the reality of such forces. The difference of course stems from the initial point of departure: a human world measured against the divine as compared with one which admits of no divinity above man. Both Bernanos and Malraux share, however, a contempt for mediocrity and a desire for an elitist society.

Bernanos' first three novels, *Sous le soleil de Satan* (1926), *L'imposture* (1927), and *La joie* (1929), form a group, as Berna-

---

[49] *Le crépuscule des vieux*, 29–30.   [50] *Bulletin*, Nos. 15–16, p. 12.

nos himself recognized.[51] He did not publish another novel for almost six years, apparently fearing that his effectiveness in fiction was declining. All three novels have in common the Bernanosian preoccupation with evil and its physical manifestations in the world of men, but the *landscape* of the metaphysical drama becomes paler with *L'imposture*, and fades almost entirely with *La joie*. Bernanos' major strength as a novelist lies in his ability to suggest meanings beyond the grasp of his characters; characterization is generally subordinate to mood, atmosphere, and visual drama. Admitting that he no longer liked his first three novels, Bernanos wrote, "The *Soleil de Satan* is a fireworks display sent up on a stormy night, in the wind and the rain. *La joie* is but a murmur, and the awaited Magnificat never bursts forth. *L'imposture* is a face of stone, but one which weeps real tears." [52] It is indeed true that no one of these novels approaches the artistic success of the *Journal d'un curé de campagne*. However, Bernanos' own judgments of them are overly harsh.

Sous le soleil de Satan is divided into three parts. The first is the tale of Germaine Malorthy, a young girl who becomes a living illustration of the power of evil in the world. The second and third parts deal with the career of the abbé Donissan, his development from an awkward young priest into the saintly curé of Lumbres. Bernanos described his objective in this novel thus: "I wanted simply . . . to fix my thought . . . on a supernatural man whose exemplary total sacrifice would restore to us each of those sacred words whose meaning we fear we have lost. I asked of my saint not esthetic emotions, but lessons." [53] Aware that the ultimate subject of his book could never be realized within the domains of a novel, Bernanos admitted, "My curé of Lumbres is no doubt a kind of saint, but it is through his temptations, through his despair that he can be made accessible to us. The lived experience of divine love is not of the domain of the novel." [54] The organization of *Sous le soleil de Satan* is intuitive rather than logical, a group of novellas having in common the physical and moral manifestations of Sa-

[51] See citation by Béguin in his edition of *La joie* (Paris: Club du Meilleur Livre, 1954), 308.   [52] *Bulletin*, No. 46 (June, 1962), 1.
[53] *Le crépuscule des vieux*, 73–74.   [54] *Ibid.*, 82.

tan's power in this world.[55] The severest flaws in the narrative arise from Bernanos' polemical tendencies, as when he editorializes on Germaine Malorthy's father as a despicable type common to decadent modern "republican" France. When deployed so openly Bernanos' royalist leanings in no way add to the effectiveness of his fiction. However, his contempt for the crafty meanness of the petit bourgeois lends piquancy to the fictional characterization: he reproduces the speech and mannerisms of Malorthy with just enough acidity of tone to make the character unpleasantly vivid. The landscape descriptions are a kind of visual mirror of confounded souls mired in evil and rarely glimpsing hope. Underlying all three parts is a strong sense of destiny or fatality, stemming less from the phenomenon of authorial intrusion than from the novel's underlying assumption that evil plays a powerful role in the world of men. Germaine (known as Mouchette) becomes less a rebel than a victim of her exercise of free will in pursuit of love, pleasure, and evil, in that order. As she tries to explain the intoxication of evil to her second lover, Germaine almost inarticulately expresses the nature of her temptation: "You've never felt . . . how to say it? It comes to you like an idea . . . like a vertigo . . . to let yourself fall, slide . . . go all the way down—all the way—right to the bottom —where the contempt of the imbeciles wouldn't even follow you . . . ." [56] This is the vertigo which has already led her to commit fornication, murder, and adultery. She falls into a period of madness and eventually, after an encounter with Donissan in the second part, she realizes her revolt to be fruitless and unoriginal, and commits suicide. Bernanos was to return to the Mouchette figure in a later work, *Nouvelle histoire de Mouchette* (1937), where his heroine seeks love in the arms of a bandit, is violated by him, and then drowns herself. But the second Mouchette is less depraved, more pathetic, and perhaps, in Bernanos' particular theology, more liable to salvation because of her good intentions.

---

[55] See Bernanos, *Oeuvres romanesques* (Paris: Bibliothèque de la Pléiade, 1961), 1,757, where Michel Estève chronicles the changes Bernanos made in the order of the novel's three parts. All citations from the novels are from this edition.

[56] *Sous le soleil de Satan*, in *Oeuvres romanesques*, 97.

Bernanos' curé of Lumbres is a sympathetic if insufficiently drawn figure precisely because, as his author admitted, "the lived experience of divine love is not of the domain of the novel." The descriptions of Donissan's experience of divine joy and love fail as fiction. The novel is most successful in those moments when the curé physically wrestles with the powers of darkness. Here, Bernanos' striking talent for creating mood and atmosphere provides a visual backdrop for the metaphysical drama. The high point of the novel's second part is a physical encounter with the devil, whom the curé meets during a dark night when he becomes lost traveling on foot. The devil appears in the shape of a journeyman worker who wrestles with and torments the curé, and is eventually defeated by his humble firmness of faith. Bernanos tells us that direct *vision* of the devil is given a man only once, but that he is always present. The style of the second and third parts is that of a fragmentary biography, with an unidentified narrator who is piecing together an account of the priest's life from anecdotes and writings. This particular narrative method is well suited to Bernanos' love of editorializing, and also makes it possible for him to present supernatural events as if they were a function of realism. However, the method permits diffuseness in presentation and except for the dramatic encounter scenes—with the devil, with Mouchette, and later with the dead child—the novel drags and limps painfully. The third part of Sous le soleil de satan deals with Donissan in his last years, centering upon two capital events, an attempted miracle which fails, and his death. The figure of Antoine Saint-Marin, an ironic portrait of Anatole France,[57] is the first of several skeptical writers whom Bernanos treats with magisterial scorn is his novels. He deliberately wanted the curé of Lumbres, his "mad, but humble and powerful hero to be a stranger to [the rationalists]."[58]

Bernanos' first three novels share the same flaw. L'imposture and La joie also alternate between lengthy authorial commentaries and striking individual scenes. L'imposture deals with the abbé Cén-

---

[57] See Albert Sonnenfeld, "The Hostile Phantoms of Georges Bernanos," L'Esprit Créateur (Winter, 1964), 210–15.
[58] Le crépuscule des vieux, 14.

abre, a priest who has lost his faith but who continues his external life without change. The heroine of *La joie* is Chantal de Clergerie, a young girl who has grace and the joy of God, and therefore stands in conflict with her world and her surroundings; she dies at the hands of a madman. These two novels, in which Bernanos uses a traditional narrative technique rather than the loose biographical method of *Sous le soleil de Satan*, are less successful. They nowhere allow for the polemical, episodic tone which was apparently most natural to Bernanos at that period in his development as a novelist. Striking scenes of physical and metaphysical intensity are again present; however, with almost no commentary to link them together, they stand as isolated and almost embarrassing signs of talent in a forest of slow-moving prose.

Un crime (1935) and the posthumously published *Un mauvais rêve* (1950) form a diptych. Bernanos composed these novels at the same time and in fact exchanged characters and sequences between them.[59] Neither is a fully successful novel, but the characters in *Un mauvais rêve* illustrate the imaginative turns Bernanos' polemic spirit took. Simone Alfieri, secretary to the aging writer Ganse, is the type of self-deluding, ennui-driven woman who is led to commit murder. Ganse himself is still another of Bernanos' cast of sterile parasitical creatures who feel little emotion and feed their quest for novelty on the flesh of others—the "professional writers" whom he held in utmost contempt. Bernanos described his intention in *Un mauvais rêve*: "I could call this novel *Au bout du rouleau*. These are not derelicts, like the creatures of [Julien] Green. They are creatures who have lost their reasons for living, and who struggle desperately in the void of their poor souls before they croak (*crever*). Castoffs of former generations, or abortive products of new ones—that's all you see, when you know how to look." [60] The novelist's strong feelings are evident in his creation of characters, a gallery of oddities with twisted psychological motives. The plot is contrived and melodramatic, the dialogues awkward and unconvincing. Bernanos is unable here to employ his talents for

---

[59] See notes to *Un mauvais rêve* in *Oeuvres romanesques*, 1,802–803.
[60] Letter to Maurice Bourdel, cited in *Oeuvres romanesques*, 1,803.

visual setting and for simple encounters with metaphysical overtones.

Un crime is Bernanos' one attempt to write a *roman policier*.
Here, as elsewhere, the resemblances with some of Dostoyevsky's
novels are striking: alternating moods of exaltation and despair, a
parade of nihilistic characters flanked by terrestrial saints, an atmosphere of great spiritual density.[61] Bernanos shows how the
existence of an unsolved murder infects a community already beset
by ennui and moral decay. The essential subject of his novel is the
mystery of evil and its existence among men. *Un crime* offers a
curious telescoping of the saint and the criminal soul in the single
figure of the curé of Mégère, a young girl in disguise. The plot is
indeed incredible but no more so than the usual *roman policier*.
What underlines the oddity of Bernanos' narrative, however, is the
fact that he never adheres to the commonly agreed upon rules of
the *roman policier*, which requires the perfection of strict causality
and determinism. Questions remain unanswered at the end of
Bernanos' novel; nothing is really solved. His prose is at its best in
descriptions of a compellingly present physical world, the savage
beauty of northern France, filled with evil and the atmosphere of a
dense and suffocating moral fog.

In one novel, the *Journal d'un curé de campagne* (1936), Bernanos achieved a perfect suitability of form to content. The novel is a
beautiful one, using the simple narrative device of a diary. The curé
of Ambricourt, young and of impoverished background yet proud
and highly intelligent, recounts his struggles with his new parish,
with himself and his church superiors; records many conversations
and several lengthy dialogues; and keeps a running record of the
undiagnosed illness which eventually kills him. The curé precipi-
tates the salvation of several of his parishioners and is generally
unaware of his effectiveness in doing God's work. He worries about

---

[61] For two treatments of the Bernanos-Dostoyevsky connection, see
Rima Drell Reck, "A Crime: Dostoyevsky and Bernanos," *Forum*, IV
(Spring–Summer, 1964), 10–13; Albert Sonnenfeld, "A Sharing of
Darkness: Bernanos and Dostoyevsky," *Renascence*, XVII (Winter,
1964), 82–88.

the petty problems of daily existence in his parish and muses on the significance of his earthly task. Under a fine rain, he sees his village

suddenly, so heaped up, so miserable under the ugly November sky. . . . How small a village is! And this village was my parish. It was my parish, but I could do nothing for it, I watched it sadly sink into the night, disappear. . . . I said to myself that the world is devoured by ennui. . . . It's a kind of dust. You come and go without seeing it, you breathe it, you eat it, you drink it, and it's so fine, so tenuous that it doesn't even crunch between your teeth. But if you stop for a minute, there it is covering your face, your hands. You have to move around all the time to shake off this rain of ashes. Hence, people move around a great deal.[62]

Bernanos loved this novel above all his others, and seemed to visualize quite clearly the form it would take when he wrote in 1935:

I've begun a fine book. . . . I decided to do the diary of a young priest, when he enters a parish. He tries to do the impossible, works like ten men, undertakes impossible projects, which will naturally fail; he lets himself be more or less duped by imbeciles, evil men and good for nothings (*salauds*), and when he finally believes everything is lost, he will have served the good Lord precisely to the extent he believed not to have served him. His naïveté will have won out over everything, and at peace he will die of cancer.[63]

In the *Journal d'un curé* Bernanos succeeds in transforming into the substance of fiction the polemic themes which elsewhere tend to mar his novels. For example, in some of the unpublished pages originally intended for inclusion in *Les grands cimetières sous la lune*, a nonfiction work, he wrote: "The mediocre priest does not grow old, he grows rancid. Rancid unction is probably, of all sad human gestures, the saddest, the most filled with sorrow. To be precise, it smells of the sepulcher."[64] The young curé of Ambricourt, thinking of a fellow seminarian who has now left the priesthood, reflects on the efficacy of bad priests among their parishioners: "We pay very dearly for the superhuman dignity of our vocation. . . . The aversion of so many poor people for the priest, their

[62] *Journal d'un curé de campagne, Oeuvres romanesques*, 1,031–1,032.
[63] *Bulletin*, Nos. 57–58 (January, 1966), 2–3.
[64] *Bulletin*, No. 30 (February, 1957), 6.

profound antipathy is not simply explained, as one would have us
believe, by a more or less conscious revolt against the Law and those
who embody it. . . . Why deny it? It's not necessary to have a very
clear idea of the Beautiful to experience a feeling of revulsion at
ugliness. The mediocre priest is ugly." [65] In his simple graphic
manner, the curé sums up countless pages of Bernanosian rhetoric.

Bernanos' lack of skill in direct fictional characterization becomes a virtue in the *Journal,* where no single figure is delineated
in incisive terms. Instead, as the curé watches, notes his observations on the members of his parish, records significant and insignifi-
cant conversations, the characters gradually assume the density of
life, a density rendered the more convincing by the apparent *art-
lessness* of the presentation. The curé's peculiar gift of combining
extreme naiveté with extraordinary insightfulness serves Bernanos
well: the central figure and his human and physical context rise
slowly out of the text like the village out of its rain and fog. The
human drama is never sacrificed to its metaphysical implications;
the two become one in the very texture of the prose. The reader is
never called upon to accept a scene of superhuman visions, as in
Sous le soleil de Satan. Instead, the day to day struggle of the
young priest becomes a subtle paradigm of a struggle which transcends it. As a self-doubting agent of higher forces, the curé stands
as one of the most vivid and sympathetic figures in the French
twentieth century novel. The *Journal* is unquestionably Bernanos'
masterpiece, and serves as a yardstick by which the successes and
failures of his other novels may be measured.

Monsieur Ouine (1943), a novel on which Bernanos labored for
nine years, is a magnificent failure. Considered by sympathetic
critics such as Albert Béguin as Bernanos' masterpiece, it suffers
from all the excesses of style and form to which he was prone.
Bernanos wrote to Jorge de Lima in 1943, "I write to thank you for
the fine article on *Monsieur Ouine.* You have described it magister-
ially: like a dream. . . . Nothing is more real nor more objective
than dream. . . . Don't people understand how logical things can
become dreamlike, logically hypnotic, in novels? This is because

[65] *Journal d'un curé de campagne,* 1,089.

nothing is as lucid as a dream. And is there anything more conscious than the drunkenness of art?" [66] The novel deals with the parish of Fenouille, mired in ennui and evil and dominated by the figure of Monsieur Ouine, a sort of teacher-devil who attempts to draw into his vision of nothingness the young man Steeny. Eventually Ouine dies, an apparent victim of his own emptiness. The blackest of Bernanos' novels in its depiction of the nothingness lying at the bottom of lost souls, *Monsieur Ouine* represents an attempt to prove the absolute necessity of God by the elaborate description of a universe from which he is totally absent, so that "hope may spring from the depths of anguish as once light sprang from the depths of chaos."

The sinister Ouine (one who says *oui* and *non* at once) is a thinly veiled caricature of Gide, the immoral teacher of the young. The character lacks fictional density; he seems rather a figure out of melodrama. The other characters serve various polemic functions, and the plot is confused and unconvincing. The novel's best moments are scenes of violence, where the visual landscape overshadows the spiritual special pleading. The text presently considered definitive was reconstructed with infinite patience from the many versions, corrections and notes left by Bernanos, and some of the novel's faults no doubt sprang from the sporadic method of its composition. It continues to be an interesting example of Bernanos' attempt to say everything he had to say within the compass of a single novel, highlighting his flaws and his undeniable talents in one huge package.

Georges Bernanos' stature as a novelist remains firm, if judged by the *Journal d'un curé de campagne*. His influence on the novel in France can not yet be assessed. The tradition he represents, the tradition of Barbey d'Aurévilly and Léon Bloy, appears to have no notable practitioners among living French Catholic novelists. Bernanos sought to make what he esteemed to be the social and moral problems of his era the substance of his fiction. Like Aragon, Céline, Sartre, Malraux, he conceived of the novel as an art responsible to the life of men.

[66] *Bulletin*, Nos. 15–16, p. 17.

Julien Green

PERSPECTIVES IN

ISOLATION

In an era generally characterized by engaged literature, Julien Green has maintained a stance of separateness which has tended to limit the audience he has reached and the critical attention he has received. Born in Paris in 1900 of American parents from the South, he has written almost entirely in French, and despite the fact that ill-informed commentators have referred to him as an American living in France, Green has considered himself inalterably French in language and culture. The author of eleven novels, three plays, a number of short stories, a lengthy journal, and four volumes of autobiography, Green has elaborated an *oeuvre* which merits serious attention, for several reasons. First, he has created a major imaginative world of haunting intensity, a world shaped by a unique view of man. Second, he has managed to isolate himself from the concerns of most of his contemporaries with deliberate application. He has refused to be caught up in social and political questions, except when world events directly bore on his personal life—he fled to the United States for four years at the fall of France in 1940. Like Camus, Green has insisted on the primacy and inviolability of art. However, he rarely experienced Camus' apparent guilt feelings over this attitude. Alone of all the novelists in this study, Green is primarily the pure artist, living intellectually in the kind of splendid isolation Flaubert strove for in the nineteenth century. Whether the work of a man like Green can survive, despite its uniquely apolitical and asocial character, will not be known for some time. Its fame will no doubt be threatened by the character of the man, not as in the case of Céline by personal unpleasantness, but rather by aloofness and an unwillingness to seek attention and acclaim which have made him go relatively unnoticed.

Green's *Journal*, begun in 1928 and recently collected in one volume, provides a running commentary on his novels. It also reveals his thoughts on questions ranging from aesthetic and religious to political. When Green says, "It is my best book," he is not far from wrong.[1] As the record of a unique sensibility in all its diversity and passion, it bears comparison with Flaubert's *Correspondance*. While Green takes issue with Flaubert on matters of technique and meaning in the novel, he resembles him in other ways. Green remarks that he is writing his *Journal* for the reader of the year 2000, not because he considers himself representative, but because this record can in some ways give an idea of what it meant to be a writer in this era.[2] He is quite right; his examinations of the differences between his own attitudes and those of his fellow writers analyze the entire range of persuasions from engaged artist to deliberate aesthete. And in his insistent refusal to take any political or social stand, Green demonstrates the pervasiveness of the attitude he refuses—he feels called upon to explain *why* he refuses.

"I cannot bring myself to talk of politics," he writes. "The truth is that I hate it."[3] He reproaches politics with exuding an "immense ennui," a kind of spiritual deadness strongly reminiscent of Baudelairean and Symbolist malaises. Politics has nothing to offer him as person or as writer. "If I were asked what party I belong to I would answer, 'Not yours.' I am one of those who are lined up against the wall in all revolutions. So much the worse. In the programs offered to us, I find nothing good for me. . . . The more I think about it, the better I understand that a free writer has no place in Europe such as it is now developing."[4] And elsewhere, answering an interviewer's questions on his hatred of politics, Green replies, "Politics . . . is the reason that what I love is in

[1] *Journal, 1928–1958* (Paris: Plon, 1961), 826.   [2] *Ibid.,* 581.
[3] *Ibid.,* 636.   [4] *Ibid.,* 91.

danger, it threatens individual freedom, it threatens happiness, it disturbs me in my work. I believe with all my heart in literature and the work of art. This faith is absolutely foreign to the preoccupations of politics. In the contemporary world, where then is my place? I don't know." [5]

Green has always been aware that his apolitical stance is an anomaly in France, where the relationship between literature and politics has been a major preoccupation of twentieth-century writers. "Everyone meddles in politics except me," writes Green. "I understand nothing about it. I live stopping up my ears, otherwise I could not write. I believe that work is an end in itself and the publication of a book something almost accidental." [6] Green's attitude toward politics stems from personal predilections rather than from a deliberate flaunting of custom. He has consistently maintained that politics has no more reality for him than a nightmare, that a canon might kill him without his ever having been convinced that the canon exists, "while a few notes of Bach seem to support the whole firmament. . . . The true remains beyond harm." [7]

However, despite his unwillingness to involve himself in politics, or to make contemporary factions, wars, movements the subject matter of his novels, Green has admitted that his books are at least in his own eyes products of his time "by the anxiety which is always present in them." [8] For example, he originally intended to give the novel *Épaves* the title *Crépuscule* (twilight), confessing that the subject of the book was probably the twilight of the bourgeoisie. Green most clearly stated his conception of the relation of literature to its era in the following comment from the *Journal:* "A book worthy of the name is always of its era by the spirit which animates it. It is not descriptions of factory chimneys and women with short hair which mark a book as being of 1928, but rather that which is the very base of the book, its anxiety, its need for revolt, etc." [9]

Green's personal reactions to the events of the years covered by his *Journal,* 1928–58, were very intense, and he has recorded them vividly. Along with other Europeans he began to worry about the impending difficulties in Germany in the early 1930's and called

[5] *Ibid.,* 66.   [6] *Ibid.,* 88.   [7] *Ibid.,* 40–41.
[8] *Ibid.,* 801.   [9] *Ibid.,* 9.

the barking of the cannon "the supreme voice of our time." When his friends treated him to predictions of political and social catastrophes he wrote, "What can I do about it? One must work as if everything were all right, work right to the end." [10] The remark is strongly reminiscent of Flaubert's desire to work furiously, so that life will not be too much of a burden. Green differs very strongly from Flaubert, however, in his valuation of daily life apart from the events of history. "I am sad to think that we are all perhaps on the verge of disappearing in a stupid war," he wrote in 1931. "Life was so beautiful, there was wheat in the fields, so many beautiful faces, so much pure air. Wasn't that sufficient?" [11] While Flaubert found life most pleasurable when he experienced it through the imaginative world of his characters, Green has always admired beauty directly. His basic objection to the real historical world in which he found himself was that it tended to sacrifice beauty to a muddle of abstractions, of power plays, which have nothing to do with the quintessence of man's existence. In this respect, Green resembles Camus, who above all criticized zealots and despots because they tended to sacrifice the fragile happiness of man's life to abstractions geared to the future. However, unlike Camus, Green has never allowed his intellectual reflections on such questions to color his fiction. We find vivid descriptions of political violence in the streets of Germany in 1932 recorded in the *Journal;* Green's novels seem to be almost timeless in their setting, the plots totally centered around individuals. Explaining his fundamental unwillingness to change the direction of his life or the nature of his fiction, he wrote, "In a world which moves too quickly, I have resolved to live slowly." [12]

At times Green has admitted that he found his writing hindered by his concern with contemporary events, that present history often surpassed the novel in interest. But unlike Mauriac, who turned away from fiction when he reached a similar realization, Green has continued to pursue his individual way. In exile in Baltimore in 1940 he wrote, "While our world is crumbling, I still have this refuge where I can find something of my former habits, a

[10] *Ibid.,* 51.   [11] *Ibid.,* 56.   [12] *Ibid.,* 84.

notebook where I record thoughts, some book over which I dream." [13] Convinced that human justice is a farce, Green has held to his belief that the only progress is individual and spiritual. The prime evidence for this progress is to be found in the world of art. Looking at a Persian manuscript during his exile, he noted, "I recognized that something passed through my hands which belonged to the real world . . . and not the illusory world in which we have been living for some years." [14] He called illness, politics, and death the plagues which poison human existence.

Born into a Protestant family, Green converted to Catholicism in his youth. In his *Journal* a great deal of space is devoted to meditations on religious questions which have always played a large role in his life. Almost nothing of this carries over into the novels. Green has often been called a Catholic novelist and classed with Bernanos and Mauriac. Considering the almost total absence of religion in his novels, this seems unjustified. Green himself was quite distressed at being called a Catholic writer because he felt that appellation debased religion. He admitted that his personal readings included a great many religious mystics, whose writings were to him what the novels of chivalry were to Don Quixote. However, he abhorred the notion of apologetic fiction. "A novel is made of sin, just as a table is made of wood. . . . I speak, of course, of the novel which is not written with the aim of edifying. The edifying novel is generally written by the devil. . . . No one will ever know the harm that type of literature has caused." [15] If religion is present in Green's fiction, it manifests itself in an obverse fashion, in the same manner as in Bernanos' *M. Ouine.* The blackness of the world depicted is so total as to suggest the possibility of its opposite.

Green admits readily that his novels could probably not have been written by an unbeliever:

I believe that . . . there is a profound anxiety in all my books which an irreligious man would never have experienced. I do not try to make of my books Catholic novels. That would horrify me. But I believe that all my books, no matter how far they may seem to be from ordinary

<hr>

[13] *Ibid.*, 361.   [14] *Ibid.*, 381.   [15] *Ibid.*, 1,047.

accepted religion, are nonetheless religious in their essence. The anguish and solitude of the characters almost always comes down to what I have called the terror of being in the world . . . .[16]

The metaphysical atmosphere of Green's fictional world is very strong. However, unlike Dostoyevsky and Bernanos whom he frequently resembles, Green does not suggest religious resolutions. His technique tends instead to pose unanswerable questions, to suggest the invisible without indicating any road to its attainment. In one of the few pieces of criticism Green ever wrote, on James Joyce's *Ulysses*, he commented on the "presence of a mystery," "the glory of Joyce, which lies in hiding things." This comment, written in 1924, revealed more about Green's own fictional predilections than about Joyce's.[17]

Green frequently questioned the spiritual implications of writing novels, which for him demand complicity between the novelist and his creatures, even an absolute identification. Thus the novelist participates in their sins; but then saints do not write novels. Green's most obviously religious novel is *Moïra*, published in 1950, and he admitted that the principal character, Joseph, was haunted by a terrible nostalgia for the absolute. "But God doesn't speak in the novel, because God is not a character for a novel and it is extremely rare for God to manifest himself in the life of a man . . . ."[18] As attractive as the spiritual life was to Green (in his youth he thought of becoming a priest), he remained a writer because, as he put it, he was in the world to write. His *Journal* reveals a sense of vocation which is overwhelming; he said that he could do nothing but write; he wished to die with the certainty that he had done *all* he could do. One is again reminded of Flaubert by comments such as, "It's a powerful distraction to write a novel," "A book is a window through which one escapes."[19]

In his *Journal* Green describes an art of fiction in which the key concepts are labor and imaginative inevitability. For Green these terms are in no way exclusive of one another. He fears above all those pages which are written too easily: "My work is interesting

[16] *Ibid.*, 791–92.
[17] Review of *Ulysses*, in *Philosophies*, No. 2 (May 15, 1924), 218–22.
[18] *Journal*, 814.   [19] *Ibid.*, 2,393.

only if it is difficult. The search for the right word always brings its recompense, the very depth of the book being ultimately enriched. To use approximate terms is to make a sort of paste of words in which the sentences become mired." [20] His attention to style is evident in his novels. However, more than any other consideration, it is the strangeness of his content that has attracted critics. The few critical studies of Green tend to stop short of analyzing the texture of his prose; stylistic considerations are generally limited to analyses of recurrent imagery. [21]

The loving labor Green describes is exercised on a base which is inspirational in origin. For him the only worthwhile novels are the ones their authors *could not help writing*, such as those of Dostoyevsky. Constantly moved by the possibility of creating still better novels, Green wrote: "There is too great a distance between what I write and what I would have wanted to write." [22] In a moment of discouragement, he revealed the close resemblance in personality between his characters and himself. "I believe that if I don't give in to the lure of an easy life, I shall one day write a great book, and I hope that one day I'll feel I have not been given more than I gave . . . but right now, I am discontented with myself. . . . Does anyone suspect . . . that each time I describe an irresolute, divided man in my novels, it's myself I am angry with?" [23] When asked the origin of his characters and themes, Green replied, as Bernanos would have, that a novelist's ways of seeing and judging are formed from childhood. New situations and characters are always, he maintained, interpreted by the child the novelist used to be. [24] Commenting on a scene in *Léviathan*, one of his best novels, he noted in his *Journal*, "It seems to me that in this page I have

[20] *Ibid.*, 39.
[21] See for example *Configuration critique de Julien Green*, ed. Brian T. Fitch (Paris: Minard, 1966); Antoine Fongaro, *L'existence dans les romans de Julien Green* (Rome: Signorelli, 1954); Samuel Stokes, *Green and the Thorn of Puritanism* (New York: King's Crown Press, 1955).
[22] *Journal*, 83.   [23] *Ibid.*, 100.
[24] From a personal interview by the author with Green in Paris, September 3, 1962.

reached the depths of all the sadness which is in me. . . . Let's transform our troubles into stories." [25]

Green admits readily that despite the voluminousness of his *Journal* and the growing number of his autobiographical works, he has managed to keep his most personal thoughts and problems silent. *These* are to be found in his novels, in what he invents. Thus he indicates that the solitude, violence, frustrations, perversions which form the canvas of his fictional world all have their roots in the novelist himself. Too complex a man and too sophisticated a writer to intend us to take this notion at its face value, Green hints at the relationship between his fictional world and his own life by emphasizing what he calls the search for truth.

There is a truth one must reach at any price, that truth at the heart of every man who comes into the world. It is not a novelistic truth, it is not that air of verisimilitude which brings cries of admiration from devotees. No, to find the truth one must work against oneself, counter to one's inclination, against the facilities of habit, against success, against the public; one must suppress all pages directed only toward the entertainment of the reader. Words form a kind of current against which one must always swim; he who cedes to their pressure is doomed to failure, for it is impossible, after having abused words for a long time, to make them speak the truth.[26]

The truth his novels seek is the one locked in the contours of the human heart, which he examines in all its marvelous perversities and contradictions. To those readers and critics who have called Green a scribe of darkness, a writer who exaggerates the negative aspects of man, Green has replied in his *Journal*: "Life in its darkest moments still gives us nothing but melodrama; the writer must attenuate the contrasts and soften the violences." [27] Not only does he contend that life's raw materials are even darker (and certainly less artistically arranged) than the situations in his novels, he conceives man as a multifaceted complex of inclinations, vices, and hopes. In Green's novels we find not man the double, but man the many. The soul-body conflict which haunted Green is the

[25] *Journal*, 1.   [26] *Ibid.*, 34.   [27] *Ibid.*, 1,025.

source of infinite possibilities in his fictional creations. He dissects a character's vices with infinite care in order to elaborate these possibilities: "One reaches the soul through the body and the body through the soul, that is the whole drama of the human condition, that which makes us such profoundly mysterious beings." [28]

Green is a widely read man whose tastes in fiction, as Henri Peyre has pointed out, have run to nineteenth century novelists such as Balzac, Dickens, Hawthorne, Blake, Charlotte Brontë.[29] In his readings as well as his writings, he has sought intensity of vision rather than novelty of technique. From the multitude of critical judgments to be found in Green's *Journal* indirectly emerges a critical canon which reveals a great deal about his own work. Green's primary criticism of writers he does not favor is that they tend to be too intellectual, and for this reason he finds himself ill disposed to reading the novels of his own era. "Too many novelists of our time create their books with their brains, to the detriment and in spite of their instinct." [30] He apparently never read the novels of Camus and Sartre, although he greatly admired Sartre's play *Huis Clos*. Among his contemporaries Green tended to favor Mauriac and Bernanos and, in inconsistent fashion, Gide as well. Even when he found Chateaubriand over-eloquent and pompous, Green confessed that he preferred this rhetoric "to books where the words give the impression of having been drawn from the author's brain, one by one, like coins from a miser's purse." [31]

Green's unflagging admiration of Racine and Baudelaire reflects his own predilection for moral and spiritual issues. In a note on a production of Racine he had just seen, he marveled, "Once again I admired that the gentle Racine could say such violent things in such a guarded language . . . ." [32] Baudelaire also seems to have been a source of inspiration to Green, who apparently intended to use some Baudelairean verses as epigraph to the darkest of his novels, *Épaves*. And always Green preferred the portrayal of evil to the portrayal of good, because he felt that novelists rarely succeed

[28] *Ibid.*, 722.
[29] Henri Peyre, *French Novelists of Today* (New York: Oxford University Press, 1967), 199.
[30] *Journal*, 714–15.   [31] *Ibid.*, 8.   [32] *Ibid.*, 30–31.

when they try to paint a picture which is "all white"; "they are much more skillful with black . . . ."[33]

In Chekhov Green found great themes: ennui, pity, disgust with a society which is sinking with a yawn into despair. In Bernanos, Green discerned a writer of enormous talent, a man he called the novelist of the invisible. He also noted that Bernanos had done precisely what he himself so assiduously avoided; Bernanos had let the era destroy him by dispersing his talents in extraliterary activities. It is logical to wonder about the influence of Dostoyevsky on Green, so much do Green's scenes exude the Russian novelist's curious amalgam of intense ugly realism and intangible metaphysical implications. Green says he avoided reading Dostoyevsky for many years in order not to be discouraged or influenced by him. "A novel, a poem, a simple letter, appear to me as a kind of compromise between the expressible and the inexpressible," he wrote in his *Journal*. "Words can only make allusion to that which remains eternally beyond the reach of our language . . . ."[34] One is reminded of the atmosphere Dostoyevsky created, the dense spirituality which surrounds his characters crucified by the burden of free will.

Green conceives of the novel as a form of the most intense commitment, an overwhelming experience for the novelist. One of his strongest statements of this conception is found in the *Journal*:

The true novelist does not dominate his novel, he becomes his novel, he drowns in it. Between him and his characters there is an even deeper complicity than he believes, and if they sin, he also sins in some way. He is everything his book is, if he believes in it, if he lets himself be caught; and if he doesn't let himself be caught, if he doesn't himself experience the spell of this monstrous thing which springs from his brain—for the novel is a monster—he no longer writes novels, he fabricates them.[35]

Elsewhere he compares the novelist to a scout charged with exploring the depths of the soul, whose black recesses are his true subject matter. The novelist should not *think* in his novel, he says. He should report what he sees in the inner consciousness. Rather than using debate or intellectual display, the novelist must strive to

[33] *Ibid.*, 508.   [34] *Ibid.*, 311.   [35] *Ibid.*, 588.

embody, to make as concrete as he can what is essentially wordless and beyond the reach of the intellect. In a barely veiled criticism of some of his contemporaries, Green wrote, "The gesture must reveal what lies within the soul; that is its role; sentences are merely amplification. One sees that in almost all the novels being written today. What a wordy, rationalizing era ours is." [36] Green's own novels are filled with the overwhelming passions which twist men's lives, the unfulfilled longings which drive them to desperate acts.

According to Green, the starting point for each of his novels was an *object*, for *Mont-Cinère* a photo of the interior of a house in Savannah, for *Adrienne Mesurat* a mental image of "the cemetery," a group of family photos on the wall of a provincial living room. Related to these objects and forming the total initial vision was a character or a group of characters. Green has always been far less concerned with plot and structure than with characterization; characterization developed indirectly as he followed his creatures in their inexorable movement toward self-destruction. He recognized the differences in quality between his best and his worst novels, and attributed these differences to what he called intensity of vision, his term for imaginative immediacy.

There is in me someone or something which makes me see my characters and makes me see them acting. The intensity of vision was never greater, in my case, than when I wrote my first three novels. It became less intense in *Épaves* (influence of milieu and incomprehensible desire to go against success). Once again, this gift was returned to me in *Minuit* and *Le visionnaire*, almost completely failed me in *Varouna* and *Si j'étais vous*. . . . In the novel I am now writing [*Moïra*], the vision is so clear it prevents any explanation of a psychological order, and that is much better.[37]

In choosing the characters and situations of his novels, Green seems to have limited himself to a very dark spectrum, except for occasional glimpses by his characters of the natural beauty which surrounds them; at such moments, the characters are rendered even more unhappy, because they see beauty as a promise of happiness which will never be fulfilled. Green admits that he would have wanted to write a novel of beauty, but the era did not favor it. This

[36] *Ibid.*, 769.   [37] *Ibid.*, 785.

is one of his few stated admissions that he was in any way influenced in his fiction by the trend of contemporary events. The anxiety he felt to be characteristic of his time is translated into the vague but crushing anxiety his characters experience. However, their dilemmas are always personal and atemporal; they do not participate in the active political or social life of their time any more than does their creator. Unlike Bernanos, who fused timely concerns with ultimate metaphysical questions in his novels, Green has chosen to limit his fictional world to a realm which seems vividly to exist in a timeless setting. The source of Green's strangeness and of his unique power as a novelist is his persistent questioning of reality. "I often ask myself the meaning of life," he says, "if it has one, and above all, to what extent the external world exists. . . . I often have the fleeting impression of living in a world which does not exist, or which doesn't exist in the way we think. Perhaps the material world has only the value of a symbol." [38]

Questioning the nature of reality, insisting that to write is to allude to what cannot be expressed, Green has created a fictional universe which is curiously romantic and strongly reminiscent of earlier styles in fiction, of Hawthorne, Poe, Dickens. He once suggested that the last sentence of *Bleak House* could have served as an epigraph to all his own work: "I have purposely dwelt upon the romantic side of familiar things." However, the absence of religion and of any sense of community or social order combine with the characteristic mood of anxiety to give Green's novels a peculiarly modern flavor. While his characters do not think of themselves in relation to their social and historical world, the reader senses that this world determines that which drives them. Green criticizes Flaubert's insistence on factual accuracy in the novel because he believes that such limitations tend to strangle inventiveness or "divination." The true novelist follows an inner voice; he records and guesses, always seeking some special inner truth which constitutes his own signature.

Green's attitude toward reality is at the base of all his writing. "Life," he says, "is never so beautiful as when it moves away from

[38] *Ibid.*, 124.

what is called life. What do the *Putsch* of Hitler, the mutinies aboard English cruisers, the fall of the pound sterling mean in eternity? Everything is elsewhere. Nothing is as true as the swinging of a branch against the sky." [39] Like his characters Green has always sought a "lost country," but he has managed to fill the time of his search with creative work, whereas his characters destroy any possibility of personal peace by pursuing it frenetically. Green's admission that life has never appeared to him as something quite real is true of his creatures as well. However—and this is what makes his novels succeed—his depiction of the details of reality is intense, vivid, perfectly seen.

One of the secrets of real talent is to see everything *for the first time*, to look at a leaf as if you have never seen one, for only then can it appear to you in all its *newness*. The faculty of astonishment constitutes the genius of childhood, so rapidly worn away by habit and education, and no one will ever be able to assemble words in an acceptable order if he doesn't know how to see creation with the eyes of Adam. In art, truth lies in surprise.

When one looks at a stone like a mountain in miniature, one begins to see it such as it is. [40]

Henri Peyre is quite accurate in remarking that Green is the closest counterpart to Kafka in the French literature of this century. [41] Green's fictional world has the appalling sense of detail of a nightmare, along with its incomprehensibility; it arouses an uneasy and unwilling feeling of identification in the reader. One would like to deny that the inner nature of man is as perverse as Green presents it or that we are as guilty as Kafka would have us be. However, the fictional intensity of vision, the imaginative power of such novelists makes their special views of reality frighteningly persuasive. Kafka has had his conscious imitators in France, most notably Albert Camus, who was drawn to the parable form in his desire to give his ideas simple symbolic forms. Green appears to have imitated no one. His obsessed world seems to have sprung from prerational personal concerns. Opposed to filling novels with ideas or making ideas the impetus for novels, he has in his own unfashionable way

[39] *Ibid.*, 50.   [40] *Ibid.*, 373.
[41] Peyre, *French Novelists of Today*, 208.

created at least three novels which rank among the best of this century in Fance.

As Brian Fitch has pointed out, despite their frequent resemblance to nineteenth-century fiction, Green's novels belong intimately to the special metaphysical climate of the twentieth century.[42] Green himself has used the term *angoisse* to denote this mark his era has left on his writings in spite of his desire to remain as distant as possible from it. He may well be, as Fitch maintains, one of the precursors of existentialist literature along with Malraux and Bernanos. There are striking correspondences between certain of Green's early works and well-known scenes in the novels of Sartre and Camus.[43] But Green's place in the metaphysical trend is unique, for of all the novelists discussed here, he alone depicts characters whose questioning of the meaning of life finds absolutely no answer. Malraux elliptically offers the world of art as a sign that man's life is neither futile nor eternally lost. Bernanos offers the world of heaven. Green's characters, confronted with the unacceptability of life as it is, with a dread of death, cut off from any religious vision, are supreme embodiments of unrelieved anguish. Green is darker and less encouraging than Sartre, whose naturalistic-moral fictional world is designed to suggest a mode of action which will relieve or at least palliate its horror.

Mont-Cinère, Green's first novel, appeared in 1926. Set in a Virginia mansion, the novel is a melodramatic tale of an avaricious woman and her daughter which recalls some of the less subtle merits of Balzac and Dickens and is essentially an artistic failure. However, many of Green's major thematic threads are already present. He presents restrained existences struggling to conceal overwhelming destructive passions. The body of a dead person is an object of paralyzing terror to one of the characters. The real world exudes an air of unreality which heightens the psychological oddity of the characters. The novel suggests the problem of events which will haunt Green's subsequent work, as the characters desire to

---

[42] Brian T. Fitch, "Résonances," in *Configuration critique de Julien Green*, 13–31.   [43] See *Ibid.*, 15–20.

undo what is done. These characters, like their successors, are attracted by beauty at the same time that they fear it. And most notable, *objects* play a significant role in the narrative, standing as unique entities which seem to conceal lives of their own, while also serving as symbolic devices for the novelist.

In *Adrienne Mesurat* (1927) Green began to bring his gifts under stricter control. This is the story of a repressed and vengeful young girl who causes the death of her father and eventually falls into madness when she discovers that her crime did not cut through the solitude which surrounded her. The novel has a good deal of dramatic unity and almost unbearable suspense. In Green's only full-length book in English, *Memories of Happy Days*, written during his exile, he describes the initial conception of the novel in a revealing passage:

> Having written about twenty lines, I laid down my pen and thought, "What can happen to such a character as Adrienne? I must try to think of something exciting."
> But I could think of nothing, and yet, the more I concentrated my attention on this girl, the more real she seemed to me. I suddenly became aware that, commonplace though she might appear at first glance, this person was just as mysterious as any human being, and just as much alone. . . . I was too young then to realize that most of us never quite succeed in breaking down the barriers that separate us from the rest of humanity. To be sure, the contacts are manifold and the exchange of thought almost incessant, but no one who is in the least reflective and sensitive can fail to remark how very imperfect this communication between human beings can be. So much is unexpressed, so little can be said. When we are about to speak and reveal something of our inner life, who is in the mood to listen? And should someone be near and ready to heed our words, can we be sure that he understands what we really mean? Words are so clumsy and create such confusion. How many times, having tried to explain, have we sadly given it up and once more retired within ourselves!
> Such is the real theme of *Adrienne Mesurat*, and for that matter, the theme of most of the stories I have written since.[44]

In *Adrienne Mesurat* the purely melodramatic fright of Green's first novel has begun to expand into a sense of *horreur*. (Peyre has called Green the supreme master of this dread among the mod-

[44] *Memories of Happy Days* (London: Dent, 1944) 206–207.

erns.) Adrienne experiences a fear of the night which will reappear in almost all of Green's later major characters: "There is indeed something calm and reassuring in the first hours of darkness, but as the night advances and all the sounds of the earth are still, shadow and silence assume a different character. A sort of supernatural immobility weighs on everything and there is no word more eloquent than that of *horror* to describe the moments which precede the coming of dawn." [45]

Green's depiction of provincial life and of family life are unmatched in desolation. The Gidian "Familles, je vous hais!" is pale by comparison with the unstated criticism of the monstrous deeds members of a family inflict on one another. In *Adrienne Mesurat* and in Green's next novel, *Léviathan* (1929), *la vie de province* is painted as a concrete symbol of the ennui and despair which characterize human life. At the end of a chapter of *Adrienne Mesurat*, Green writes, "There is something terrible in these provincial existences where nothing seems to change, where everything keeps the same face, whatever the hidden modifications of the soul. Nothing can be seen from the outside of anguish, of hope and love, and the heart beats mysteriously till death without one's having dared one time to pick geraniums on Friday instead of Saturday or to take a walk at eleven in the morning instead of at five in the evening." [46] In her desperation Adrienne imagines that she has known happiness in the past, in childhood, but in weeping for an illusory past she is actually mourning an endless present leading one day only to death.

Léviathan (1929) is one of Green's best novels. The story of Guéret, a man driven by passion for Angèle, a beautiful but immoral girl, and of several other characters in a small provincial town in France, *Léviathan* successfully combines subtle characterization with visual effects of haunting proportions. The mystery at the heart of man is set against symbolic scenes—the coalyard, the Restaurant Londe, the banks of the river Sommeillante—which are difficult to forget. The novel presents clearly in the thwarted passions of its several characters that curious ambiguity which is at the

---

[45] *Adrienne Mesurat* (Paris: Plon, 1927), 45–46.   [46] *Ibid.*, 79.

heart of most of Green's novels: a belief in free will standing side by side with an almost Greek sense of tragic inevitability. Green reveals that he began to meditate on the strangeness of others while a boy in the Pension Mouton in Paris in 1915: "I felt that we were all surrounded by something horrible and mysterious, and that we were spared or crushed at random like insects on a road. Yet, in spite of this fear there was in me the growing belief that each destiny followed its course to the end, and that chance did not exist." [47] The mood and atmosphere of *Léviathan* are successfully maintained, and characterization is vivid in the peculiarly Greenian way—the mystery of intense passions is presented intact, with no effort on the author's part to explain it away. Green achieves a *density* of characterization which strongly recalls that quality Gide admired in Dostoyevsky, the ability to endow his characters with three dimensions, so that they retain "a part of shadow" which renders them intensely human.

Épaves, published in 1932, is the darkest of Green's novels. Set in a Baudelairean Paris, its principal character is Philippe, a young man of the middle class who is loved by his sister-in-law Elaine (this love is of course repressed). The novel's chief merit is its depiction of the night world of a large city, of the "cast-offs" of human life who give the novel its title. In 1941 Green wrote in his *Journal*:

Épaves . . . is my best book, my most "grown up" book, the hardest to write, the most worked-over, the richest, also the hardest to read. . . . What spoils this novel in my eyes is that while writing it I didn't see all I should have seen and that I was on the verge of seeing. Philippe is a character of catastrophe; he is the bourgeois who no longer believes in anything, not even what he himself stands for. He should have . . . foreseen the events of February, 1934 . . . his fear could have and ought to have made him a prophet. I could have written this, I didn't do so, and for this reason alone, the book does not satisfy me; in spite of everything it is the one I prefer above all my other novels.[48]

Green later attributed the critical failure of *Épaves* to the fact that "nothing happens in it." However, the atmosphere of the novel is

---

[47] *Memories of Happy Days*, 98.   [48] *Journal*, 396–97.

memorable. In one of Philippe's night wanderings, the "other face" of his world is evoked:

All big cities have sections which only take on their true faces in the shadows. By day, they hide, wear a banal pleasant face . . . but at dusk the same spot wakes to a life which is like a parody of death. What was smiling grows pale, what was dark lightens and shines with a funereal glow, glad to exist at last. The gas lamp effects this transformation. At the first ray of this sun, the night country puts on all its shadows, and matter begins its sinister and marvelous grimaces . . . .[49]

Philippe is riddled by guilt (he makes no effort to save a drowning woman from the Seine) and loneliness. His situation epitomizes that of most of Green's characters: "Each man is king in a desert." [50] Green went on to write other novels, some worse and some far better than *Épaves*. However, the atmosphere of *Épaves* is equaled in intensity only by that of *Léviathan*.

Le visionnaire (1934) and *Minuit* (1936) are inferior to Green's earlier novels. The theme of the former is summed up in the words of Manuel, the young man who lives the intense imaginary life which gives the novel its title: "If there be on this earth a man crushed as I am by the horrible weight of days, he will guess the innermost desire of my heart when he learns that in order to feel, to change my destiny, I was ready to run anywhere, and that any road suited me which led out of this world . . . ." [51] Manuel is one of those few men who "look at the world more acutely than we do . . . and in a world bathed in the invisible, the power of desire and of death do not have as much meaning as our illusory realities." [52] *Minuit* (1936) is a highly melodramatic novel whose central character experiences the conflict between spirituality and sensuality which is present to some degree in all of Green's novels. A nineteenth century quality in the physical descriptions of some of the characters is reminiscent of the slightly grotesque realism of Dickens; they are very thin, pale, frightened, bluish under the fingernails, or curly-haired, pot-bellied, red-nosed, monocled.

Varouna (1940) and *Si j'étais vous* (1947) were written during a period when Green was deeply immersed in Buddhist thought.

[49] *Épaves* (Paris: Plon, 1932), 21–22. [50] *Ibid.*, 39.
[51] *Le visionnaire* (Paris: Plon, 1934), 153. [52] *Ibid.*, 273.

They both deal in different forms with the notion of transmigration of souls. The novels lack dramatic unity and are obvious instances of failure of that "intensity of vision" Green recognized as essential in his own work. *Le malfaiteur*, begun in 1937 and completed and published in 1956, also seems disjointed and confused in its structure and objectives.

Moïra (1950) is generally considered Green's finest novel. Set in a Southern university in the United States, it centers around Joseph Day, a passionately religious young man from the hills who has come to study Greek in order to be able to read the books of the New Testament in the original. Strongly intolerant of any form of vice as he understands it, Joseph meets his fate in the person of his landlady's adopted daughter, Moïra, who shatters his resistance to sin and with it his entire personality. He murders the girl and surrenders to the police. Joseph's attraction to Moïra is only one of the forbidden desires which charge the atmosphere of the novel with uneasiness and conflict. Several homosexual attractions are present, although never expressed patently. The atmosphere of the Southern landscape and climate, the sense of fatality combine to endow this very brief novel with a unity of tone and inevitability of movement which mark it as a total artistic success. Green apparently worked very hard at achieving the narrative's apparent smoothness and changed the point of view of the narrative several times. In September, 1948, he wrote in his *Journal*, "I think the character to whom I've given the task of telling the story (Joseph) is not capable of writing a book. If he were, he would not be such as I saw him, at dawn on August 23, he would not be that some-what rough and fanatical young man, obsessed at once with religion and desire, who appeared to me. Impossible to imagine that he could, for example, come out of himself to the point of describing a room, observing the movement of a friend. I shall begin again then tomorrow, this time in the third person." [53] Rough, fanatical, more lewd in his condemnation of sin than those he condemns, Joseph Day is the ideal hero of this tragedy: his sin is his unwillingness to accept the human condition.

[53] *Journal*, 727.

One senses that in *Moïra* and in his latest novel, *Chaque homme dans sa nuit* (1960), Green has reached the mature point of his own reflections on the mystery of man. Wilfred Ingram, the hero of *Chaque homme dans sa nuit*, is, like Joseph Day, a living battleground for God and the Devil. Unlike Joseph, and perhaps to the detriment of the novel's verisimilitude, Wilfred ultimately achieves through death the purity whose sign he has borne even in debauchery. Without falling completely into melodrama, *Chaque homme dans sa nuit* manages to be too violent and lacks unity. Green noted while writing the novel, "The whole problem of the central character is that of faith. Faith which does not provoke contradiction is a sickly and dying faith." [54] With good and evil struggling within each character, from the saintly Mr. Knight to the infernal Max, the moral density of the narrative sometimes overwhelms its fictional effectiveness. The title, from a verse by Victor Hugo which continues, "s'en va vers sa lumière," indicates the comparatively hopeful nature of this novel compared with Green's earlier successes such as *Moïra* or *Léviathan*. In *Chaque homme dans sa nuit*, Green has attempted as nowhere else in his work to suggest that the substructure of sin may well be an urge to salvation.

Among contemporary French novelists, Julien Green is isolated and apolitical. Unmindful of fashions in fiction or techniques for personal publicity, he has consistently pursued the art of the novel for its own sake. In this way Green has voiced his own response to the problem of literature and responsibility.

[54] *Ibid.*, 1,157.

François Mauriac

THE NOVELIST AND THE
MORAL LANDSCAPE

"For the author who has turned in his copy," wrote François Mauriac in 1959, "there remains still the possibility of serving with the pen, if he has certainties other than aesthetic ones. The older I get, the less I find contradictions in the life of a writer between the literary work to be created and the side to be taken. If it is given to him to outlive his fictions, it is time for him to choose—either the retirement each man has a right to . . . or struggle, if he believes truth exists and that it demands of him that he defend it at every level and in every realm, as mixed with impurities as it may appear to him." [1] Mauriac presents a unique case in the relationship between literature and responsibility. He became involved in both literary and political-social activities, but at different times. Born in 1885, Mauriac published his finest novels during the 1920's and 1930's. After that time he has increasingly occupied himself with politics, history, journalism, and the publication of voluminous memoirs and *examens de conscience*. Elected to the Académie Française in 1933, recipient of the Nobel Prize in 1952, he is one of France's oldest living men of letters. He has not had actively to defend his literary reputation against newcomers, secure as he is in the literary histories and anthologies. However, the serious attention he receives as a novelist unquestionably was damaged by the

[1] *Mémoires intérieures* (Paris: Flammarion, 1959), 109.

now famous pronouncement of Jean-Paul Sartre to the effect that God is not a novelist and neither is François Mauriac. Sartre's judgment of Mauriac no doubt indicates personal resentment of a noted predecessor and rival. More important, it is symptomatic of changing tastes in moral issues and novelistic techniques.

Sartre condemns Mauriac's fiction for its narrative technique and for its religious essentialism. He does not like the problems to which Mauriac, a firm Catholic, addresses himself in his novels. For Sartre, distinctions between good and evil are less valid than distinctions between commitment and non-commitment. Mauriac's fictional world is innately metaphysical in a manner which irritates Sartre. Mauriac tends to intervene with authorial comments and spiritual predictions in his novels, while Sartre prefers to debate political issues through the words and actions of his characters. Fashions in fiction change, and only sufficient time will make clear those fashions which will have contributed something lasting to the history of the novel. In combining the heritage of the *roman d'analyse* with a personal predilection for poetry, Mauriac has exemplified a fictional tradition which continues to retain an audience, limited though it may be. The Sartrean novel has adopted the mood and atmosphere of the naturalistic tradition; Mauriac has rejected this tradition, and so he has appeared old-fashioned and ignorant of contemporary trends. However, Mauriac's theoretical writings and memoirs reveal that he has always been sensitive to fashions in fiction and aware of the damage he was doing his popularity by refusing to follow them. His major characters resemble nineteenth century fictional heroes in their proportions and in their psychological density and complexity. They are human *monsters* born to the scale of human life conceived as infinitely significant.

Like Camus, Mauriac believes that "each time . . . [the novelist] begins a new book, [he] feels himself facing an unknown world, without any link with what came before; it is that benevolent illusion of having produced up to this point only sketches of the masterpiece he is now going to produce." [2] The result of Mauriac's

---

[2] *Journal I* in *Oeuvres complètes*, XI (Paris: Grasset, 1952), 95.

quest for the ideal novel has been over twenty novels, uneven in quality, but including in their number five or six which rank among the finest of this century in France, as well as four volumes of poetry, five plays, and countless book-length essays, journals, and collections of newspaper articles. Mauriac's fiction has displayed a consistent tone which he himself explains in one of his journals: "I am a metaphysician who works in the concrete. Thanks to a certain gift of atmosphere, I attempt to render sensible, tangible, fragrant, the Catholic universe of evil. That sinner of whom the theologicans give us an abstract idea, I incarnate him." [3]

Mauriac has consistently deplored recent developments in the novel, attributing the overemphasis on technique, as in the *nouveau roman*, to the presence of a negative idea of man. His own work, that of a Christian novelist, conceives man as "in the process of becoming and of going to pieces." In this sense he distinguishes his work from the traditional psychological novel, which was based on a fixed notion of human personality, as well as from writers such as Malraux, Camus, and Sartre, whom he calls "the philosopher novelists . . . with a system of thought." [4] Mauriac recognizes the importance of Sartre, who gave "a justification and a style" to the despair of a generation, but insists that the very despair which characterized Sartre's novels contributed to the decline of the form it assumed. "The crisis of the novel comes down to this infinite insignificance of the world you describe and from which God has withdrawn, where the human adventure no longer has any meaning." [5]

Mauriac attributes the decline of the novel to the loss of the essential starting point, the knowledge of good and evil. "The human being as I conceive him in the novel is a creature engaged in the drama of salvation, even when he does not know it. Life, each life, has an aim from which it may stray infinitely . . . ." [6] In Mauriac's best novels, his Catholicism is expressed almost nega-

---

[3] *Journal II* in *Oeuvres complètes*, XI, 154.
[4] Interview with Mauriac in Madeleine Chapsal, *Les écrivains en personne* (Paris: Julliard, 1960), 124–25.
[5] *Nouveau bloc-notes, 1958–1960* (Paris: Flammarion, 1961), 329.
[6] Chapsal, *Les écrivains en personne*, 125.

tively. His characters frenetically seek infinite fulfillments in finite sources, in material possessions (*Le noeud de vipères*), in human love (*Le désert de l'amour*), in domination over other creatures (*Génitrix*). Or, like Thérèse Desqueyroux, they fall victims to the possibilities inherent in common human emotions such as curiosity, hatred, and boredom. The Catholic "answer" is rarely stated by Mauriac; rather, he exercises much the same method as Pascal, progressively pushing the *libre penseur* to the brink of despair so that he will of himself accept God because he needs him. Mauriac's heroes and heroines seek in the world of creatures what can never be found there. The result of their search is a progressive shrinking of possibilities and of hope, so that finally they are confronted with a restricted if ambiguous fate. It is entirely possible for a non-believer to find the story of Thérèse Desqueyroux ultimately hopeless, or to interpret the apparent change of heart of the old man in *Le noeud de vipères* as an abberation born of illness and unlikely to assure his salvation. One is reminded of Bernanos' assertion that the darkest of his novels, *M. Ouine*, was intended to be spiritually the most positive, since despair would call forth hope as once light sprang from chaos. Something of this same obverse effect is demanded by certain of Mauriac's novels. A religious resolution is suggested in *Le noeud*, but in *Thérèse Desqueyroux* there is no such suggestion—the heroine is set free in the world of creatures where we suspect she will continue to drift further and further from the metaphysical insight she seeks.

Mauriac has frequently been asked if his Catholicism has exercised a limiting effect on his novels. To this question he has replied that his Catholic viewpoint has both hindered and helped his fiction. "My heart secretly nourished an insatiable curiosity about the hearts of others. On this point, never did a young Catholic feel less constrained than I by his faith," he wrote in *Écrits intimes*.[7] However, he has admitted severe compunctions about the depiction of human passions, particularly in their most graphic forms. His favorite illustration of a writer who had made a literary reputation by washing his linen in public is André Gide, one of the

[7] *Écrits intimes* (Paris: La Palatine, 1953), 83.

maîtres littéraires of Mauriac's generation. And in Proust, the novelist he ranks highest, the severest fault appears to him the disintegration of the characters and consequently of the novel itself because various perverse passions eventually occupy almost all the foreground of the narrative.

Mauriac's Catholicism has been the basis for all his writings, journalistic as well as fictional. He has not been restricted by his religious viewpoint in depicting the human being. Echoing a dictum common to the so-called existentialist novelists, Mauriac wrote that the novelist must "testify to man—And this testimony *must* be disinterested, gratuitous." [8] The same thing is true of politics: "Simple Christians must be willing to get their hands dirty in the tasks of politics. . . . Let's not succumb to that facility of situating the real country at the level of Joan of Arc, of the blessed Curé of Ars and of Péguy. . . . The real country is the one we live in . . . ." [9] As a Catholic novelist, he felt bound to describe man as contradictory, unfaithful to his divine origins, because he saw him thus. As a political journalist after the Liberation, Mauriac continued his critical appraisal of man on other levels. Both activities appeared to him natural functions of his religious viewpoint and as inevitable tasks demanded by his integrity as a Catholic.

Mauriac nowhere states the function of literature succinctly, as do Camus, Malraux, and Sartre. However, he approaches a definition of this function indirectly when he writes in his *Journal*, "Much more than history, literature is a resurrection. For history does not resurrect the depths of man, nor the secret life of the heart, or it does so only incidentally . . . ." [10] The novelist provides that element of human history which is indeed most human, the individual existence, and by doing so he depicts a society as it truly is. On this point, Mauriac is closely akin to the "humanist intellectual" stance of writers as diverse as Malraux and Aragon. More important, for Mauriac and for Céline, experience of the First World War shaped a view of man based on the realization that without the testimony of artists, the discrete individual existence

[8] *Lettres ouvertes* (Monaco: Editions du Rocher, 1952), 75.
[9] *Ibid.*, 17.   [10] *Journal II*, 115.

would be obliterated by the thrust of history. However, unlike Céline's, Mauriac's resurrection of the individual depicts him against a private backdrop, with actual historical events playing no role in the unfolding of a single destiny. Mauriac's picture is no more or less true than Céline's; it is simply different, as human lives are different one from the other. The tightly knit tragedies of individual destinies Mauriac creates have always coexisted with the cosmic catastrophes which play such a large role in Céline's fictional world.

With advancing age, Mauriac, both as creator and as reader, has been less and less patient with the novel. He has admitted that in his youth, novels were a form of escape and that he no longer finds them satisfying or even absorbing. Aware that the short, intense, poetic psychological novel of which he is a master has lost its popularity in France, Mauriac considers himself a survivor of an era which has passed. "The era, the atmosphere of the era is no longer favorable to the growth of the seeds . . . [I] bear. A novelistic work only grows and unfolds with the complicity of a generation." [11] At seventy-four, he wrote, "A writer is a man who has lost his shadow —or rather, when he survives and he is no longer anything but an old mill which grinds words, he's a shadow which has lost its man." [12] When one considers that Mauriac's life span is presently twice that of Albert Camus, the reminiscent nostalgic tone of Mauriac's more recent writings is readily understandable. He has in fact had two careers, first as poet and novelist, then as publicly consecrated man of letters and journalist.

Mauriac's chief admiration is Racine, in whom he finds the type of psychological penetration characteristic of his own work. Mauriac draws a fine distinction between *penetration* and *analysis*; in this sense he practices an art somewhat different from what is generally called the psychological novel. In *Mémoires intérieures* he writes, "What is peculiar to Racine is the rigorous continuity not of a dialogue as in Corneille—but of a passion thought, expressed, clarified, transfixed by a small number of very ordinary words which constitute a music. A music without dissonance or

[11] *Mémoires intérieures*, 251.   [12] *Ibid.*, 106.

insistent harmony—suggestive, certainly, but which prohibits
dreaming, bound as it is to a horrible reality." [13] In Mauriac's own
novels, psychological penetration is achieved by careful description
of psychological states set against a physical background, either
urban or rural, which seems to reflect and reinforce them. His
poetic gifts achieve in mood and atmosphere what Racine achieved
in the special music of his incredibly simple, almost silent, monologues and dialogues. The "horrible reality" Mauriac recognizes
behind Racine's dramas is the same one pervading his own novels,
the reality of characters transfigured by their passions into monsters
with human faces. The same fundamental belief underlies Mauriac's fiction as Racine's plays, that the human person is ultimately
significant; in this, two Catholic artists join one another.

Mauriac speaks very frequently in his journals and memoirs of
André Malraux, who interested him from Malraux's earliest emergence as a writer of note. Mauriac refers to him as a Saint-Just
marked by Indochina, a remark borne out by Walter Langlois'
recent study of Malraux's earliest adventure in the Far East. Mauriac recognized the essential characteristic of Malraux's heroes
when he wrote in 1933 that they all share "the same convulsed
face." Malraux's work, said Mauriac, "testifies to the strict alliance
this young man has made with all those forces which aim to
destroy the old world." Mauriac went on to pinpoint the motivating force of Malraux heroes by describing his conception of man as
"a prisoner of his material jail, closed into a mechanistic world,
with no window on eternity . . . [who finds] his grandeur only in
despair. . . ." [14] Behind this type of fiction, Mauriac denotes an
essential contempt for man. He attributes this contempt to the
novelist's fundamental concern with himself. Mauriac discerns a
family resemblance between writers such as Malraux and Aragon,
apparently *cousins ennemis*. They share, Mauriac states, an *imposture* which resides above all in the style. "The writers of this race
all seek effect and the most advantageous attitude, the music and
the pose, while the dialecticians who succeeded them are concerned with authenticity. . . ." [15]

[13] *Ibid.*, 162.   [14] *Journal II*, 147, 149.   [15] *Nouveau bloc-notes*, 310.

Standing counter to the literary vogues which he has seen come and go since his own time of popularity as a novelist, Mauriac has from the vantage point of age and long observation characterized these vogues incisively and critically in his numerous writings. He has seen the "dialecticians" such as Sartre and Camus succeeded by prophets of the *nouveau roman*. From the "opportunism of nothingness" of the 1950's he saw the novel move on to an overemphasis on technique. But Mauriac has refused to believe the psychological novel as he practiced it is really dead. "I do not defend a technique. In a certain sense, I am opposed to all of them. In the non-plastic arts, all techniques, as soon as they are revealed, defined, imitated consciously or not, become false. Such is the mystery of technique in the novel: it must remain the secret of its inventor and it can only be used once . . . a style . . . once it exists, is unique and irreplaceable." [16] His own style is the reflection of two aspects of his thought and character: his conception of the human person and his sensitivity to nature.

"There exists in the most degraded of creatures an indestructible childhood which can come to life again at any moment, a part of himself which has not known corruption," Mauriac wrote in *Ecrits intimes*.[17] This *enfance perpetuelle*, shining from the eyes of Maria Cross of *Le désert de l'amour*, standing behind the terrible actions of Thérèse Desqueyroux, makes Mauriac's characters sympathetic even when most degraded. The same sympathy persists in Mauriac's *Le cahier noir*, a journal written during the Occupation, in which he writes, "We must conquer the temptation to hold man in contempt. . . . Contempt for man is essential to him who wants to use and abuse him. One cannot use as an instrument for all ends a creature who is immortal and almost divine. That is why they debase their victims first." [18] The continuity of Mauriac's beliefs is evident in his journalistic writings. His persistent concern with individual destinies in the novel is transferred to a wider plain when he writes, "Men are not the product of economic and historical fatalities. . . . On the contrary, human passions create History

[16] *Mémoires intérieures*, 209.   [17] *Écrits intimes*, 29.
[18] *Le cahier noir*, under the pseudonym of Forez (Paris: Éditions de Minuit, 1943), 28.

. . . war is not divine, but human . . . ." [19] Human passions are, of
course, the substance of Mauriac's novels. In the *Journal d'un
homme de trente ans*, which predates Mauriac's emergence as a
major novelist, he noted: "Let us charge human love only with
what it is capable of bearing; it is too weak for that infinite
aspiration of which we have cheated God." [20] Here is stated the
essential error of each of Mauriac's major characters, who seek in
the love of creatures what can only be found in love of God. In a
sense they resemble Proust's lovers, who can never find an *object*
worthy of their capacity for love, with one essential difference: the
pinnacle of Proust's universe is the special domain of art. For
Mauriac, "the true night is not this visible night, interpreter and
accomplice of desire. We have turned the visible world away from
its true aim, just as we have done during our lives with every
creature who interested our hearts." [21]

Mauriac's use of nature in fiction is a striking illustration of
means appropriate to ends. His landscapes, based on personal experience of the region around his native city of Bordeaux, have two
faces, Christian and pagan. The duality of man's spirit is reflected
and expressed by the contrasts between sun and shadow which
characterize the Landes region, where one emerges from the blackness of close-set pine trees into the blinding sun of sandy stretches.
The presence of evil and temptation in *Thérèse Desqueyroux* is
made concrete by the physical world in which the heroine lives.
The alienation of Mauriac's urban characters is mirrored in the
fragmented nature of life in Paris, with its sound-carrying apartment house walls and the nervous tempo of traffic noise. Background description is not used for social purposes in Mauriac's
novels; rather, it is the externalized expression of inner personal
states. "Our social milieu does not always impose its atmosphere on
us," he wrote in *Mémoires intérieurs*. "The profound nature of
a being secretes the universe it requires." [22] Mauriac provides no
naturalistic interpretation of the effect of environment on man;

[19] *Journal du temps de l'Occupation* in *Oeuvres complètes*, XI, 352.
[20] *Journal d'un homme de trente ans* (*Extraits*) (Paris: Egloff, 1948),
57.
[21] *Journal II*, 117.   [22] *Mémoires intérieures*, 72.

rather, his settings externalize the inner world of individuals whose destiny is linked to truths beyond any distinct social reality. In this sense the human adventure is eternal. "Since man lives on the earth, lies down to sleep or to weep on it, until the time when he extinguishes himself there and returns to dust, nature has become human; it is made of the ashes of human sin . . . ." [23] His admiration for Baudelaire as the greatest poet of "reality" reveals Mauriac's conviction that the real, in its precise details, is the surest sign of what lies beyond reality: "Whatever the object, Baudelaire sees it, breathes it, touches it, and shows it to be eternal, as the kitchen chair Van Gogh painted is eternal." [24]

In fifty years of reflection Mauriac has considered carefully the sources of his novels. Like Bernanos, he finds the roots of his fiction in the world of childhood: "The artist in his youth stores up faces, silhouettes, words; an image strikes him, a statement, an anecdote. . . . All that exists in him instead of being erased as in other men; unknown to him, it ferments, lives a hidden life and will rise up at the moment when it is needed." [25] Mauriac admits that his memories and imaginings are the sources of the visual elements in his fiction. "Have I ever been able," he asks, "to describe anything without closing my eyes?" [26] He conceives the novelist as a man who sacrifices life to memory, who uses that always stirring matter of the past which is in him. Mauriac has frequently used settings familiar to him from childhood as the stage for the dramas he depicts. For example, he confesses that his grandmother "was raised in that obscure quarter of Jouanhaut which I described in *Thérèse Desqueyroux* under the name of Argelouse." Elsewhere he writes, "I see it again, the vestibule of the sad house at Langon where I set the drama of *Génitrix*, a huge, badly built dwelling which the trains on the Bordeaux-Cette line made shake at night." [27]

Despite long years of residence in Paris, Mauriac is aware that his true landscape is Bordeaux:

---

[23] *Journal I*, 21.   [24] *Mémoires intérieures*, 48.
[25] *Le romancier et ses personnages* (Paris: Editions Corrêa, 1952), 100.
[26] *Journal II*, 108.   [27] *Écrits intimes*, 21, 15.

Bordeaux knows that when we have to descend into ourselves as novelists to look for landscapes and creatures, it's not the Champs-Elysées or the boulevards that we find, nor our comrades and friends on the banks of the Seine—but the family properties, the monstrous vineyards, the dull *landes*, the darkest suburbs glimpsed through the streaked windows of the school bus—and our characters are born in the same way, not resembling the fine lady at whose house I dine here [in Paris] or the master to whose words I listen—but like my rural grandparents, my cousins from the *lande*, like that whole provincial fauna which long ago I spied on as a sickly child.[28]

Bordeaux may have been restrictive, but it molded; Paris offered absolute freedom, hence a formless solitude. For Mauriac the setting is the starting point for creating a novel. He admits, "I cannot conceive a novel without thinking, down to its obscurest recesses, of the house which will be its setting. . . . No drama can begin to live in my mind if I do not situate it in places where I have always lived." [29]

Mauriac's conception of the novel is intimately tied to his idea of character in fiction. Much like Camus he feels that each novel a writer produces is an attempt to approach an ideal. In Mauriac's case this ideal is the perfect fusion of a drama of salvation (successful or not) with the physical world which is its setting. As he said to an interviewer, "More than beings, it's an atmosphere—or at least the characters cannot be separated from a fragrant and burning world."[30] Mauriac cautions that the method which worked for him is not a technique to be followed by all. "Each novelist must reinvent his technique. Each novelistic work worthy of the name constitutes a planet, large or small, which secretes its own laws just as it produces its flora and fauna." [31] Admitting that he has gone his own often unstylish way in the novel, he insists that such unselfconscious individualism is the only road to original fiction.

For Mauriac, Proust is the greatest novelist of the twentieth century. The overwhelming success of Proust's work is due to his unique approach, one uncolored by preexisting styles or concern for immediate popularity. Proust's great practical and metaphysical difficulty, one which according to Mauriac undermined the effec-

[28] *Ibid.*, 60.   [29]*Le romancier et ses personnages*, 102–103.
[30] Chapsal, *Les écrivains en personne*, 126.   [31] *Lettres ouvertes*, 75–76.

tiveness, as fiction, of the later volumes of *À la recherche du temps perdu*, lay in his conception of the human person. He notes that Proust's later volumes, those which move away from the immediacy of the childhood memories, are overwhelmed by a deterministic view of the sexual life and that "the metal of the work becomes corroded." [32] In *Écrits intimes* Mauriac suggests the nature of Proust's problem in a telling note. Referring to the narrator's obsession with Albertine, whom he tries to hold captive, Mauriac says, "Impossible, for the loved creature is not one but multiple, and how to possess something lasting? One self indefinitely follows another in the loved one; one might as well try to immobilize a river, in order to extinguish it. Hence the futility of any such enterprise. Any profound criticism of Proust should first of all concentrate on his conception of the human person." [33]

Mauriac scrupulously avoids a realistic approach to character in the novel. The world of heroes of novels does exist, he says, but "on another planet—a planet where human beings explain themselves, confess, analyze themselves pen in hand, seek scenes rather than avoid them, outline their confused and indistinct feelings with a sharp pen, isolate them from the immense living context and observe them under the microscope." The novelist isolates and enlarges certain feelings so that they may be seen more clearly. "As alive as these heroes appear, they always have a meaning, their destiny carries a lesson, a moral arises from it which is never found in a real destiny, always contradictory and confused." [34] In a barely veiled defense of the brevity of his own novels, Mauriac insists that the *roman fleuve* is no more true to life because it depicts a great number of characters than a single volume concentrating on very few. A novel in fifteen volumes remains as distant from reality as *La Princesse de Clèves* or *Adolphe*. The qualities which will probably assure the survival of some of Mauriac's novels—while the *romans fleuves* of Romains and others are already badly faded—have little to do of course with length. Mauriac's strength lies in brevity, concentration, mood, and atmosphere, in the creation of a few very striking characters whose moral and psychological ambigu-

[32] *Écrits intimes*, 205.   [33] *Ibid.*, 221, 1 n.
[34] *Le romancier et ses personnages*, 156–57.

ity radiates an unforgettable aura. He is himself aware of these factors: "As soon as I sit down to work, everything becomes colored with my persistent colors; my most beautiful characters enter a certain sulfurous light which is characteristic of me . . . ." [35] Inseparable from this "light" is Mauriac's particular method of dealing with human passions.

In *Le romancier et ses personnages* Mauriac expressed his firm belief that an essential element of the art of the novel is the power of deformation and magnification. It may be true that the novelist has himself experienced the passions which afflict his characters: however "nothing our heroes experience is on the same scale as what we ourselves feel." From the passing irritation of the novelist with his children at the dinner table after a tiring day can come rage in fiction. "The art of the novelist is a magnifying glass, a lens powerful enough to enlarge this enervation, to make a monster out of it, with it to feed the rage of the father in *Le noeud de vipères*." [36] From a glimpse in a provincial courtroom of a young woman accused of poisoning her husband because she loved another man, Mauriac creates Thérèse, a victim of the insoluble dilemma of free will.

A fleeting personal mood or vague glimpse of some unknown human drama becomes the stuff of fiction in what Mauriac calls "this mysterious union of the artist and reality." Why the deformation works in the direction of enlarging the ugly, of exaggerating evil, can be no more easily explained in Mauriac's case than in that of Dostoyevsky or of Bernanos. Perhaps, as Gide so frequently illustrated in his fiction, the lost sheep is the only truly interesting one. Mauriac stresses the differences between life and fiction in this way:

What life furnishes to the novelist is the outline of a character, the thread of a drama which *could* have taken place, mediocre conflicts which in other circumstances might have been interesting. In short, life furnishes the novelist with a point of departure which permits him to wander in a direction different from the one life took. He renders effective what was only virtual; he realizes vague possibilities. Sometimes, simply, he takes the opposite direction from the one life took; he

[35] *Journal II*, 155.   [36] *Le romancier et ses personnages*, 114–15.

reverses roles; in a drama he knew, he seeks the victim in the tormentor and the tormentor in the victim. Accepting the data of life, he takes the opposite side.[37]

Mauriac does not explain the reasons for the differences between life and fiction. He accepts as an axiom that *fiction is not life and not a mirror of it.*

The prestige of evil in Mauriac's novels is an omnipresent evidence of Mauriac's Catholicism. As Edmond Jaloux so eloquently wrote, "Mauriac's characters, hard, or suddenly broken, tense, piercing, anxious, feverish, would be impossible if they were not above all Catholic in their essence, if they did not conceive life as a terrifyingly tragic adventure with limitless consequences, and if the act of ceding to any temptation at all did not appear very grave to them—which of course increases the attraction of the temptation." [38] The existence of a sense of sin presupposes the existence of good.

The same preoccupation with moral issues which underlay Mauriac's fiction with the passage of the time made him turn away from the novel. He presently believes that it is primarily the young who read fiction; for the young fictional heroes come alive because they embody the possibilities of their readers' futures. With advancing age Mauriac found himself less interested in reading fiction and less committed to its creation. In answer to those who speculated that the time he devoted to journalism caused his fictional output to shrink, he answered that his mind and heart were occupied by the political drama. "It is because novels no longer have any hold over me that I am very much given up to history, history in the process of being created . . . ." [39] He explained his conversion to political and social preoccupations as the result of the impact of recent history. "I began to detach myself from fiction at the time of the Spanish Civil War. . . . Up to that time I was living in a kind of dream, of fictional world . . . and then there was the Occupation, the Liberation. . . . I can no longer turn away

[37] *Ibid.*, 109.
[38] Edmond Jaloux, "François Mauriac romancier," preface to *Le romancier et ses personnages*, 11.
[39] Chapsal, *Les écrivains en personne*, 122.

from the human condition such as it is imposed on some men by others. . . . The horror of the real world has chased me away from fiction." [40] In a brief autobiography appended to the *Nouveau mémoires intérieures*, Mauriac reveals another, perhaps more important, factor in his turning from fiction to other forms of writing:

After the Liberation, my life was public. . . . Despite the Nobel Prize in 1952, I was literarily the survivor of a bygone era. At least that is what I felt from that time on. . . . The boundary line of the [Second World] War brutally marked the passage from one generation to another. Another idea of the novel, another public, is not reflected in sales figures. An old author continues to live on his momentum. But it's like a state of lost grace. More than the chill of age, it is this loss which leads us gradually to silence. From 1941, date of *La Pharisienne*, to *Le saguoin* and *L'agneau*, it's not an art in decline, but a work which subsists—a work which subsists is a work which outlives itself.[41]

Mauriac began his political writing during the Occupation. In *Le cahier noir*, published clandestinely under the pseudonym of Forez, Mauriac made clear that as a Catholic he could not disengage himself from political reality *because of his faith*. He deplored detachment from the "muddle of errors and violence" which constitutes the politics of the world. With this pamphlet Mauriac's former occasional and subdued criticisms of events turned to rage. His striking journalistic style, best exemplified by the early *Bloc-notes* (first appearing in *La Table Ronde* and then in *L'Express*), began to take form. As Mauriac asked himself during the grim period of the Occupation what influence a writer can have on politics, he became convinced that "the private work" which had appeared to him the most responsible before 1940 no longer sufficed. His earlier convictions on the personal moral level led him to broader issues in France under the Germans. He wrote in the *Journal du temps de l'Occupation* that the military unpreparedness of France stemmed from "a more basic evil, one of a spiritual order." [42]

[40] *Ibid.*, 136.
[41] *Nouveau mémoires intérieures* (Paris: Flammarion, 1965), 241–42.
[42] *Journal du temps de l'Occupation*, 308.

By the time of the Liberation, the path Mauriac was to follow was clear to him. "To write is to act. Because our acts follow us, our writings follow us." [43] Looking back in 1959 on almost twenty years of involvement in politics, Mauriac wrote, "I do not feel myself more engaged today than I was in the past. Simply, I can no longer place a fiction between myself and reality. No reading any longer diverts me from what remains of my life . . . nor from politics, where day by day the ferocity or the stupidity of men is recorded." [44]

Mauriac's political journalism has aroused some strongly partisan reactions, the most notable example being Pol Vandromme's vindictive book which judges Mauriac's political writings as a form of personal vengeance and literary exhibitionism. [45] Indeed, Mauriac has attacked outspokenly anything he judged worthy of condemnation; he has liberally praised the things he likes. Aside from a growing uncritical reverence in his old age for Charles de Gaulle, Mauriac's shifting opinions have tended to bear out his contention that he has spoken his mind freely and independently at all times. At various times he has managed to anger the Catholics, the Socialists, the Right and the Left, most of the younger politically engaged writers he brushed up against, and even his reading public.

All his nonfictional writing has shown the same concern with style and intensity as his novels. "A page of a novel has no more importance in my eyes than a chronicle," he says. "All means of expression have the same value, or rather, what they have to say is that thing which I must say in no matter what form. . . . Each written word is the stroke where the whole painter can be

---

[43] *Le bâillon dénoué* in *Oeuvres complètes*, XI, 473.

[44] *Mémoires intérieures*, 70.

[45] See Pol Vandromme, *La politique littéraire de François Mauriac* (Paris: Editions Etheel, 1957). Vandromme's attack is in part justified after the fact by a work such as Mauriac's *De Gaulle* (Paris: Grasset, 1964). However, Mauriac's recent *Mémoires politiques* (Paris: Grasset, 1967) corrects the balance by showing his sensitivity to the historically mercurial character of twentieth century French politics. From this collection of journalistic pieces on a variety of subjects, prefaced by a very moving introduction, Mauriac emerges once again as a man of principle and discernment who has lived through an extraordinary variety of national crises.

recognized." [46] As he has grown older, Mauriac has tended to define his "work" as the total shape of his life. His political involvements have thus seemed to him no less valuable in this respect than his very distinguished novels of thirty years earlier. "The older a writer becomes, the less his work should be distinguishable from his life." [47]

One of Mauriac's most admirable stands was formulated during "the settling of accounts" (l'épuration) among literary figures which succeeded the liberation of Paris. He defended the right to life of the older writers threatened by the new guard, Sartre and Camus, who pretended to speak for la conscience française. In Le bâillon dénoué he wrote, "A work of purification at a national scale is not a matter of improvisation. . . . The press conceals what is happening. . . . That is the danger of a single newspaper; for as many newspapers as we have there is really only one, that of the Resistance." [48] Mauriac excoriated Camus' attacks on Duhamel and the death of literary reputations through trial by the press. He compared the entire post-Liberation period with the Dreyfus Affair and predicted, with some justification, that the events of the mid 1940's in France would not be seen in their true light of personal vengeance and literary opportunism for many years to come. His prophecy is beginning to be borne out by current attempts to rehabilitate the literary reputations of Drieu la Rochelle, Brasillach, Céline, and others. Mauriac's special moral strength during the settling of accounts stemmed from the absolute unimpeachability of his activities during the Occupation: it was impossible to accuse the author of Le cahier noir of having been a German sympathizer or a collaborationist.

It is not the aim here to examine and evaluate in detail the mass of Mauriac's journalistic writings, though the task merits serious attention. One must agree with P.-H. Simon that Mauriac's journalism is totally consistent with his perennial preoccupation with moral issues and is a natural outgrowth of his fiction.[49] However,

[46] Chapsal, Les écrivains en personne, 131.
[47] Ibid., 142.   [48] Le bâillon dénoué, 423.
[49] See P.-H. Simon, Mauriac par lui-même (Paris: Editions du Seuil, 1953), passim.

any examination of Mauriac's thoughts on the art of literature must also take account of these numerous occasional writings which form such a large part of his work and to which he has devoted extensive time and care (as for example, in the collection and publication of the *Bloc-notes* with new prefaces and detailed indices). In the preface to his journals, written for the Grasset edition of the complete works, Mauriac expressed succinctly the place journalism occupies in his work: "I conceive journalism as a kind of quasi-intimate journal—a transposition, for the general public, of the daily emotions and thoughts aroused in me by actuality. . . . On this level, an illness or some reading may take on as much value as a revolution: it is their repercussion in our inner life which measures the importance of events." [50] The mood of the *Bloc-notes* varies, but the *tone* is consistently that of the Catholic moralist primarily concerned with individual destinies and their ultimate significance. Mauriac's comments on the death of Maurras, the trial of the Rosenbergs, the fortunes of France in Indochina, the Algerian war, television, the rise of De Gaulle—all share this essential quality. They share as well the purity of style and aptness of expression which characterize Mauriac's fiction. The Nobel Prize committee said of his fiction in 1952 that they sought to acknowledge his "penetrating analysis of the soul and the artistic intensity with which he interpreted human life within the form of the novel." The same can be said for Mauriac's journalism. "I have always attempted to give as much importance to a newspaper article as to a page of a book, and never to forget that I am first of all a writer. . . . I have taken journalism seriously: for me it is the only genre properly called 'engaged literature.' " [51]

Mauriac has made frequent reference in the tradition of Catholic polemics to Pascal's *Lettres provinciales*, which are obviously a kind of model for him. "I am engaged, in the material sense of the word, like a soldier who has signed up. Whether political passion drags me on or leads me astray, I am nevertheless engaged in the problems of this world for reasons of the world beyond." [52] In his old age, Mauriac has found history more challenging than the

[50] *Oeuvres complètes*, XI, 3.   [51] *Ibid.*, 10.
[52] *Bloc-notes, 1952–1957* (Paris: Flammarion, 1958), 69.

novel, because "history cannot be corrected like copy." His "hunger and thirst for justice" led him to prefer the realm of history, which does not pardon crimes nor offer any way of redeeming and effacing them.[53] Mauriac conceives his role as journalist to be that of a disturber of the official interpretation of events. (One of the more interesting devices of his journalism is the use of literature for contemporary political criticism.)

Mauriac's concern with style in a realm where it is most often neglected is intimately linked to his mature realization that all of a writer's books, "like the reeds in the fable, whisper to us what he is. The artist is a liar, but art is truth." [54] His defense of the need for *style* in journalism is a telling indictment of the type of sloppy thinking which underlies much newspaper writing: "The writer who remains a writer in politics introduces style into an area where it is uncommon, because there conformism reigns and the written form of conformism is the cliché. To exclude clichés, for a journalistic writer, is to force himself to discover and formulate for himself a political line of thought." [55] Mauriac dates his total commitment to journalism from the receipt of the Nobel Prize for literature. From that moment he felt responsible as an internationally recognized man of letters for all that was happening in the world.

The thought had never occurred to me that I might win the Nobel Prize. I was secretly overwhelmed by it. That is the hour when Polycratus tears the ring from his finger and looks for deep waters to throw it, so that it will not be returned. . . . I was receiving the Nobel Prize on the day and almost at the hour when, at Casablanca, a miserable crowd was falling into the trap which had been set for it. Upon my return, an irrefutable document had been brought to me like a reply to my secret prayer in the midst of the festivities at Stockholm: that I was permitted to return to the sea this too beautiful ring which fortune had placed on my finger.

Henceforth I was engaged.[56]

Mauriac's final place in the history of the French novel of this century will most probably be assured by five novels: *Le baiser au lépreux* (1922), *Génitrix* (1923), *Le désert de l'amour* (1924),

[53] *Ibid.*, 76.   [54] *Ibid.*, 369.   [55] *Ibid.*, 263.   [56] *Ibid.*, 200–201.

Thérèse Desqueyroux (1927), and *Le noeud de vipères* (1932). Intense, brief, tightly dramatic in structure, colored by the poetry of that "sulfurous light" which bathes Mauriac's most successful fiction, these novels are as vivid and absorbing today as when they first were published. Human dramas set against a natural backdrop which provides their metaphysical aura, the novels certainly do not represent what we generally call engaged fiction. However, as P.-H. Simon has acutely pointed out, the themes of alienation, the isolation and incommunicability of the self, the fact that "hell is other people"—these themes so popular in the fiction of the forties and fifties are already present, concretized and poeticized, in the novels Mauriac published during the twenties and thirties.[57]

The essential difference between Mauriac and his successors is of course due to differing basic assumptions. The alien décor this universe provides man in the novels of Camus is, in Mauriac, a sign and a beacon for something lying above and beyond it. The *ugliness* of Sartre's physical world is skillfully used to highlight *intellectual* questions; for Mauriac such ugliness is nonexistent. Mauriac's landscapes have the savage beauty of his native region, and his characters are never closed to this beauty, even when they are blind to the metaphysical truths which lie beyond it. Mauriac does not depict the thorny way of the terrestrial saint, as does Bernanos; neither does he provide us with a gallery of striking vices, such as we find in the novels of Julien Green. Instead, his principal personages are terrifyingly human. Their chief distortion is to be found at the juncture of their faults and their aspirations; they err in two directions, love and faith. With a thirst which dooms them to disappointment they seek love among creatures; the level of love they want can only be found in the creator. They sin with respect to faith, believing that strict observance of the letter is synonymous with true belief. Aside from religious suggestions which naturally arise from the texts, Mauriac's novels can be read sympathetically and with pleasure by a contemporary nonreligious reader with no loss. The fictional techniques are convincing; the characters far more interesting than those in the majority of contemporary nov-

[57] Simon, *Mauriac par lui-même*, 89–90.

els. The poetic descriptions *render* the visual world intensely enough to satisfy the most literal-minded.

Le baiser au lépreux deals with the love of dark, ugly Jean Péloueyre, son of a wealthy provincial family, for Noémi Artiailh, the beautiful daughter of a genteel family which has fallen upon hard times. A marriage between the two is arranged by the town priest, whose assiduous interpretation of the ways of God to man is more than a little tainted with pride. In this he resembles several such priests in the Mauriac gallery. The central drama of the novel lies in Noémi's inability to love or even bear the physical presence of Jean. As a dutiful young daughter, however, she has accepted the marriage without a murmur. The narrative is skillfully set against the atmosphere of the Landais summer: the hot sun like liquid metal seeping through the closed blinds, the enervating sound of millions of crickets torturing the anguished protagonists. Most characteristic of Mauriac's technique is the scene in which the two young people are left alone by the curé and the parents to get acquainted. "Like a magnolia spreading over its vase, Noémi's dress overflows her chair. .... There is nothing in the darkened room now, as in an entomological experiment, except this dark and frightened little male before the marvelous female. . . . The young virgin measures with her eyes this larva who is her destiny." Jean begins to speak in his usual wild fashion for himself alone, and when he is at last silent, Noémi is frightened "as if she were in a room where a bat has gotten in and is hiding." Finally, Noémi's parents lead her off, and we see in retreat through the partly closed shutters "her rumpled dress which will unfold no more, her bent neck, a flower less alive, a flower already cut." [58] The horror of the wedding night is rendered with equal vividness. Only when Jean is at last dying (his tuberculosis is an ingenious form of suicide, in fact) can Noémi love him. The pitiful destiny of Jean and Noémi is a monument to the ascendency of the flesh in human lives.

In *Génitrix* Mauriac's growing command of his tools becomes more apparent. It is the simple story of a possessive mother, Félicité Cazenave, her son Fernand, and the young woman Mathilde

[58] *Le baiser au lépreux,* in *Oeuvres complètes,* I (Paris: Grasset, 1950), 163–66.

whom Fernand has married against his mother's will. The novel opens as Mathilde lies dying of a miscarriage in that terrible house near the railroad station at Langon which Mauriac recreated from his own childhood. The action is developed through a flashback which reveals the inception of the marriage, the mother's determined murderous opposition, the girl's own pathetic background. The last part of the novel recounts Mathilde's death, Fernand's emotional rejection of his mother, her death, and his condemnation to a life of solitude, that "desert" without love no less harsh than the one love reveals. The drama, tragic and stark, has some of the Racinian effects Mauriac always admired: the terrible story, though told in words, is at times almost wordless. There are few strong words or dramatic gestures. Concision and elimination provide the intensity of mood and the unity of tone which characterize *Génitrix*. Like *Le baiser au lépreux*, *Génitrix* has the dimensions and scope of a classical tragedy, as well as its simplicity. Félicité Cazenave is one of Mauriac's most memorable human "monsters."

Le désert de l'amour is one of Mauriac's most popular novels, and certainly one of his best. Again using the dramatic geometry of three principal characters, Mauriac recounts through a lengthy flashback which constitutes the entire second part, the complex set of relationships which existed and still exist between Raymond Courrèges, his father Doctor Courrèges, and Maria Cross, a woman they both love. All three characters are developed with almost equal care. Raymond, who as an adolescent tried to take Maria Cross by force (she is about nine years older than he), is now a tired roué sitting in a bar in Paris when Maria enters with the man whose mistress she was and to whom she is now married. Raymond is still obsessed by her, and her rejection of him determined most of his actions in the intervening fourteen years. The character of Raymond as an adolescent trying to break out of his isolation in his own body by love for Maria is sensitively portrayed. Unable to communicate any of his affection for his father, Raymond finds he is even more intimately related to him by a mutual love for Maria than by blood. Maria Cross, the kept woman, very beautiful, at once self-indulgent and self-critical, essentially repulsed by the flesh and desiring above all a love unsoiled by the contact of bodies, is one of Mauriac's most fascinating female characters. She remains in part shadowy in the novel, as she must, because her central function as the focus of desire demands a part of mystery and some lack of clarity: she is at once human and a symbol.

The most memorable character is Dr. Courrèges, who as Maria's doctor assumes the role of friend and kindred spirit, all the while tortured by desire and on the verge of confessing his feelings. Mauriac's analysis of the doctor's imaginings, hesitations, and tortures is equal in its subtlety to his portrayal of the narrator of *Le noeud de vipères*. In several striking formulations, Mauriac epitomizes the desert to which human emotions condemn the middle-aged doctor: "Certainly, he had been mad to think that a young woman could have the sensible taste for his presence. Mad! mad! but what reasoning could preserve us from that unbearable pain, when the adored creature whose presence is necessary to our very life, resigns herself indifferently . . . to our eternal absence. We are nothing for her who is everything to us." [59] A glimpse of Maria's view of the doctor's love: "Oh! the importunity of those creatures, in whom our hearts take no interest, and who have chosen us, and whom we have not chosen!—so exterior to ourselves, about whom we wish to know nothing, whose death would be as indifferent to us as their life . . . and yet those are the ones who fill our existence." [60] *Le désert de l'amour* depends less on poetic description and atmosphere for its effect than Mauriac's other major novels. It lacks the visual and sensory details which color the other novels, but for these it substitutes a moral and psychological dialectic which creates an intense *moral atmosphere*.

From Mauriac's own comments it appears that of all his novels *Thérèse Desqueyroux* (1927) and *Le noeud de vipères* (1932) are probably his favorites. In tone and structure they are his most successful. *Thérèse Desqueyroux* is the story of a young woman from the Landes region around Bordeaux who has tried to poison her husband and is returning home to face him after he has withdrawn legal charges against her. The novel is classic in structure, with present action concentrated in a short time span, and

[59] *Le désert de l'amour*, in *Oeuvres complètes*, II (Paris: Grasset, 1950), 54.   [60] *Ibid.*, 65.

background supplied by means of flashbacks. The third person narrative prevails. The *tone* of Mauriac's Jansenism, as Louis D. Rubin has acutely pointed out, is an essential part of the story.[61] The author, viewing the story as the central character experiences it, is as much agent as he is spectator. However, contrary to what Rubin suggests, the author-agent has *no answers* to the questions he raises about the meaning of Thérèse's experience. More precisely he plays the role of another mortal creature who seeks to comprehend the dilemmas to which his species is prone. *Le noeud de vipères* is far more simple in its technique and in some ways more successful. The novel is a series of letters and notations a dying man intends to leave at first for his wife and later on for other members of his family, to explain the reasons for his hatred toward them through the years. The first person form is sustained except for a few notes by others in the epilogue, and the novel's profundity lies in the subtle analysis of self-delusion and bad faith achieved by having the old man express things he himself does not always understand. The method is much the same as that of the pastor's journal in Gide's *Symphonie pastorale*. The strictness of form does not easily allow Mauriac to intrude and in some ways the novel lacks his characteristic tone for that reason.

Thérèse and the nameless narrator of *Le noeud* are Mauriac's most striking creations. Between them they subsume the characteristics of the central characters in Mauriac's other novels. They are creatures who vividly incarnate that life which strays infinitely from its aim of which Mauriac spoke. Thérèse and the old man are human, but to a degree of intensity rarely found in life. In this sense, they are monsters. Each of them attempts to live at a level of *intensity* and *honesty* which he does not find in the world around him. Thérèse seeks love, sensation, experience beyond the limitations of the provincial milieu in which she finds herself imprisoned. The old man refuses to accept any warmth from persons less than total in their commitment to feeling and instead exacts obedience by financial means to signal his utter contempt for them. Thérèse and the old man are perfectionists; they have a metaphysical thirst

[61] Louis D. Rubin, "François Mauriac and the Freedom of the Religious Novelist," *Southern Review*, II, n.s. (Winter, 1966), 17–39.

for love, for knowledge, for a form life never assumes in reality. To their families they can only be "strange ones," defiant as they are of the forms by which human life maintains the middle road between perfection and total degradation.

Thérèse and the old man are seekers after an absolute form of human life which is of course unattainable. But their thirst raises them above the level of their families and acquaintances. They become involuntary martyrs to a metaphysical quest. Thérèse refuses to accept the definition of herself as wife to her stupid husband, mother to her unwanted child. She is lured by the intellectually facile and insincere speeches of Jean Azévédo, a young man with whom her friend Anne is in love. One finds in the conversations with Azévédo echoes of the Gidian morality which Mauriac considered particularly dangerous, not so much for its insistence on individualism as for its lack of sound presuppositions in the spiritual realm. As Thérèse approaches the time when she will gradually increase her husband Bernard's dose of arsenic-based medication, she enters a state of demi-torpor in her daily life: "Everything which came to her from Bernard touched her less than usual. . . . She didn't hear him, her body and soul oriented toward another universe where those avid creatures live who want only to know, to understand,—and, according to a phrase Jean had repeated with an air of deep satisfaction, 'to become what they are.' " [62] Her husband Bernard becomes a symbol of everything in her life which is inadequate to her vague thirst. "She noticed beings and things and her own body and even her mind like a mirage, a vapor suspended outside of herself. Alone, in this nothingness, Bernard took on a terrible reality: his corpulence, his nasal voice, and this peremptory tone, this self-satisfaction. To get out of the world . . . But how?" [63]

In the novel's final scene, Bernard brings Thérèse to Paris to leave her there, to get her out of provincial Argelouse where since the crime she is a particular source of embarrassment to the family. The couple sits at a café, attempting to spend this hour with the least possible unpleasantness. Bernard for once in his life attempts

[62] *Thérèse Desqueyroux* (Paris: Grasset, 1927; reprinted in Livre de Poche, 1960), 95–96.   [63] *Ibid.*, 114.

to understand Thérèse's motivations in the attempted poisoning and asks almost in spite of himself why she did it. For the first time in their marriage Thérèse is moved by Bernard. "I was going to tell you: 'I don't know why I did it'; but *now*, perhaps I know! Perhaps it was just to see an uneasiness, an uncertainty in your eyes,—in short, a shadow; everything I've been discovering there in the last few moments." [64] The rapport created by Bernard's accession to Thérèse's realm of uncertainty and questioning lasts only a few minutes, and they part separated once again by the distance which divides the self-satisfied from those who, like Thérèse, ask unanswerable questions. Mauriac's heroine has much in common with Goethe's Faust, "doomed to err as long as he is striving." The unquiet spirit stands as the only truly religious one in a world built on petty satisfactions and unquestioning self-righteousness.

The narrator of *Le noeud de vipères*, remembering himself as an ugly young man who feared he would never be loved, recalls the short-lived joy he experienced when a young woman of good family appeared to have fallen in love with him. He asked himself how he had come to be so cruel, "I who was not a monster?" [65] Confident of accurate insight into his own motivations, he writes in a journal, "This cleverness at fooling oneself which helps most men live has always failed me. I've never had any vile instincts which I didn't recognize in advance . . . ." [66] He describes his youth as "a long suicide" in which for fear of displeasing naturally, he anticipated by being deliberately unpleasant. Confronted with the apparent love of his future wife, he had unfolded in "a thaw of my whole being . . . springs unstopped." The crucial turning point in his character was the discovery after his marriage that his wife had been in love with another young man less than a year before she married him. He immediately assumed that her affection was feigned and in large part dictated by her family's desire to marry her off to avoid any possible malicious gossip. At this point the narrator's scrupulous honesty became the weapon with which he poisoned his own life and the lives of all his family. From the

[64] *Ibid.*, 182.   [65] *Le noeud de vipères* (Paris: Grasset, 1932), 14.
[66] *Ibid.*, 19.

reader's perspective, his attitude appears in part to be precisely a form of that self-deception he so detested in others. In addition to controlling his wife by meticulously administering his growing fortune, he flaunted the observant but (to him) insincere Catholicism of his family by ritual rebellions such as his "Friday chop" and strict non-church going. But in his deliberate antireligiosity, he unconsciously ranks himself with the highest order of religious idealists. Indirectly he hints at this in a journal entry for his wife: "Your adversaries have in secret a much more elevated notion of religion than you imagine and than they themselves believe. If not, why would they be so offended that you practice it so basely?" [67] The wealth he amasses as a defense against others becomes still another form of self-torture: he adds the mistrust of the rich man who fears being exploited to the anger and sorrow of the ugly man who knows he is never loved. His several attempts at human love—for a young daughter who dies, for an orphaned nephew killed in the war—are disappointed, and the "nest of vipers" which lies in the human heart feeds on it more and more fully.

The journal becomes most moving as the narrator's death approaches, as he realizes that his written record is becoming a testament of more than simple hatred and disappointment to be read by his wife and family. The confession has moved from the realm of explanation and self-justification to a higher plane. In its pages a man unveils the self which remains when all temporal concerns sift away. Rereading what he has written, he confesses: "Every moment, I stop myself and hide my face in my hands. Here is man, here is a man among men, here I am. You may vomit me up, I exist nonetheless." [68] Realizing he has spent sixty years composing "an old man dying of hatred," he also realizes that all his hatreds and all his calculations have been exercises in bad faith. He then *gives* his children the legacy they have been vainly trying to steal from him, because "I have always been mistaken about the object of my desires. We don't know what we want, we don't love what we think we love." [69] The *suggestion* at the novel's end that the old man finds God is merely that. Mauriac does not conclude.

[67] *Ibid.*, 68.   [68] *Ibid.*, 213.   [69] *Ibid.*, 259.

Catholic critics have found *Le noeud de vipères* the most satisfactory of Mauriac's novels, since the novel's end can easily support
a religious interpretation. In some ways, the novel's one essential
weakness lies in the suddenness of the old man's final realizations.
The extraordinary ambiguity of his character and of the actions
from which the fiction derives its force is somewhat dissipated. In
the first person narrative, where authorial intrusion is least acceptable, Mauriac seems at the end of the novel to enter and guide the
pen of the old man. However, the character stands as a monumental creation, a pilgrim of honesty who has dealt dishonestly with
himself and others for lack of tolerance. The same uncompromising nature which leads Thérèse to attempt murder causes the old
man to destroy his own life day by day. They are human in their
errors; their superiority springs from an unwillingness to accept
things as they are.

Mauriac's deformation of life, his magnification of the possibilities found in reality, creates powerful fiction. He has explained his
predilection for monsters in this way: "The hero of the *Noeud de
vipères* or Thérèse Desqueyroux the poisoner, as horrible as they
may appear, are lacking the one thing I hate most in the world and
which I cannot bear in a human being—complacency and satisfaction. They are not content with themselves, they know their
misery." [70] This same concern with complacency has shaped Mauriac's political writings, that literary journalism which became the
center of his second career.

[70] *Le romancier et ses personnages*, 133.

Louis-Ferdinand Céline

THE NOVELIST AS
ANTAGONIST

"A style is an emotion," wrote Louis-Ferdinand Céline in 1938 in *Bagatelles pour un massacre,* one of his three belligerently pacifist pamphlets.[1] Deliberately opposed to the tradition of the "bourgeois novel," Céline in his pamphlets and correspondence elaborated a conception of the novelist's relation to the world which in some ways resembles Flaubert's "impassibility." But the innate social criticism his novels contain, the savage strength of the pamphlets and the infortuitous timing of their publication on the eve of the Second World War permitted no detachment for Céline or for his readers. In a written defense designed to prevent his extradition to France from Denmark where he had fled in 1944, justly fearing persecution as a "collaborator" by the reign of terror which followed the Liberation, Céline said of his involvement in politics, "I never in my life wrote for a newspaper, spoke on the radio, or gave a lecture. Everyone in Paris knows that I am anti-journalism, anti-radio, anti-republicanism in person. I am probably the only well-known French writer who has remained strictly, fiercely, wildly a writer and nothing but a writer, with no compromise at all."[2] In a general sense this statement is true, but like all Céline ever wrote, including his novels, it is, to use Karl Epting's apt

[1] *Bagatelles pour un massacre* (Paris: Denoël, 1943), 121.
[2] Cited in Maurice Vanino, *L'affaire Céline* (Paris: Editions Créator, 1952), 15.

comparison, a blend of *Dichtung und Wahrheit*.[3] Poetry and reality are fused and transformed into one indissoluble fabric which is characteristically Céline.

Céline did in fact find himself quoted in newspapers, and he delivered *one* speech, an homage to Émile Zola in 1933. He became a *cause célèbre*, a political figure from the standpoint of others: for his anti-Semitic statements in *Bagatelles* and the other pamphlets; for his curious gift of prophecy (he foresaw the war with Hitler, the East-West split, the eventual Asian threat); for his alleged collaborationist activities during the Occupation (these were never proved, and the charges finally dropped); for his position as a literary martyr in exile in Denmark from 1945 to 1951. The Comité Nationale des Ecrivains put him on its famous *liste noire* after the Liberation, and Jean-Paul Sartre attacked him in "Portrait d'un antisémite."[4] Perhaps we are still too close to the events of the 1930's and 1940's to evaluate accurately Céline's repeated claim that his pamphlets were simply polemics urging the avoidance of another world war. "How long is the next 'last war' to last?", he wrote in *L'école des cadavres*.[5] Men of unquestioned integrity like Georges Bernanos and Henri Mondor felt that Céline had been harshly dealt with and wanted to turn the tide of public opinion in his favor. Unfortunately Bernanos left Paris and died before carrying out his plan to do *un grand article* for Céline. In spite of the controversies he inspired and the treatment he received, in his own eyes Céline remained innately and honestly a nonpolitical disengaged observer, a pure writer. "I am only a workman of a certain kind of music and that's all and all the rest is infinitely indifferent, incomprehensible, hopelessly vexing."[6]

"A style is an emotion." One might also say that a novel is an emotion, a musical transformation of life. For Céline, whom life frequently handled with an unusual degree of violence and cruelty, the creation of novels was an act of pure selflessness, a gratuitous

[3] Karl Epting, "Il ne nous aimait pas," *Louis-Ferdinand Céline, Cahiers de l'Herne*, No. 3 (Paris, 1963), 57. Hereinafter cited as *Cahiers de l'Herne, No. 3*.
[4] Jean-Paul Sartre, "Portrait d'un antisémite," *Les temps modernes* (December, 1945).   [5] *L'école des cadavres* (Paris: Denoël, 1938), 78.
[6] *Cahiers de l'Herne*, No. 3, p. 105.

transformation of the world's "cruelties into flowers." [7] If the evaluation of Céline as a man remains to be completed, there is no question of his position as a novelist. Along with Marcel Proust, he is a giant of the twentieth century French novel, a relatively ignored giant in the official canon of criticism,[8] but the strongest subterranean force in the novel of today. While Proust brought to its final perfection the analytical tradition, Céline found a new path, transforming the techniques of naturalism combined with those of poetry into an idiom which is totally of the twentieth century. Only James Joyce in *Ulysses* attempted an equally radical transformation of the methodology of the novel.

Céline's originality lay above all in the nature of his language, the spoken French of our century employed in what one might call dramatic form. His narratives read like breathless first person statements. They do not tell a story, as in the traditional first person technique. Instead, they communicate directly the impact of experience and the register of emotions of the narrator. The apparently artless scream which is the sound of Céline's novels has frequently led to the complete identification of Céline with his characters. Ferdinand Bardamu, the hero of *Voyage au bout de la nuit*, (1932), *Guignol's Band*, (1944), *Le pont de Londres*, (1964) is in a limited sense Céline himself, but transformed into a character, that is, *used* by the artist as matter for his novel, changed, with his adventures intensified and his imperfections magnified. Céline uses the bare facts of his biography as material for his art. Through a

[7] Cited in Albert Paraz, *Le gala des vaches* (Paris: Editions de l'Élan, 1948), 86.

[8] The first book-length study of Céline's work as a whole is Erika Ostrovsky's *Céline and His Vision* (New York: New York University Press, 1967). Mrs. Ostrovsky's study is a balanced analysis of the major themes of those novels she considers Céline's finest. She does not consider the *Guignol's Band* series among these, nor does she attempt to understand Céline's theory of literature or his stylistics. However, her book is one of the valuable first steps in the revaluation of Céline's place in modern letters. Milton Hindus' *The Crippled Giant* (New York: Boar's Head Books, 1950) is an interesting account of the effects of Céline's personality on a man who was one of Céline's first sympathetic critics in the United States. Hindus' visit to Céline in Denmark did not lessen the former's admiration of the novels; it did make Hindus better understand why Céline was a target for persecution.

special kind of language, a unique narrative technique, the biography becomes a poetic odyssey symbolic of the life of twentieth century man.

The dramatic technique apparently came quite naturally to Céline. He was innately a special kind of pamphleteer. In *Mea Culpa*, (1936), a work written after his disillusioned return from Russia in the 1930's, he describes the plight of modern man by personifying the "old Christian religion" and by satirically describing it as offering man an answer to his innate *néant*. He treats socialism in the same manner.[9]

The "sound" of Céline's fiction, that unique *souffle* which makes him one of the most easily identifiable of the novelists treated here, is the product of two factors. The first is the dramatic monologue. The second factor, the characteristic which completes the first, is his language. It is Céline's language which made him the most exciting and the most shocking novelist of the period between the two world wars. *Voyage au bout de la nuit* left almost no one indifferent when it appeared in 1932. In addition to the rich crudity of Bardamu's experiences and encounters, the words Bardamu uses to exteriorize his reactions were something new in the pages of a French novel. To date, no one has better analyzed the *mechanics* of Céline's style and vocabulary than Marc Hanrez, in his *Céline*.[10] Hanrez classifies the variety of neologisms, the use of *argot*, the new compound words, the puns and technical terms to be found in Céline's writings. It is not the aim here to repeat his labors. However, the *influence* of Céline's style is of concern. There is no question that Henry Miller, for example, is one of the writers the *Voyage* liberated (The *Tropic of Cancer* appeared two years after the *Voyage*.), and Miller has admitted his debt to Céline from time to time. In Denmark Schade, in France Raymond Guérin, Raymond Queneau, and Jean-Paul Sartre owe much to Céline's venture into nonliterary language. The present popularity of "dirty words" in literature in the United States is probably one of the unfortunate by-products of Céline's revolution. But many of

[9] *Mea culpa* (Paris: Denoël et Steele, 1936), 16–18, 19–20.
[10] Marc Hanrez, *Céline* (Paris: Gallimard, 1961).

the imitators patently misunderstand Céline's objective, while aping what they believe to be his method.

Céline's aim was not at all to shock the reader. In a letter to Milton Hindus, with whom he engaged in an intense if brief correspondence, Céline wrote from Denmark in 1947, "To resensitize language, so that it pulsates more than it reasons—SUCH WAS MY AIM—I am a stylist, a colorist with words, but not like Mallarmé with extremely rare words—Usual words, everyday words —Neither vulgarity nor sexuality have anything to do with it— These are merely accessories." [11] Céline felt intensely the need to renew the French language. "Our fine neoclassical, Goncourtian and Proustophile literature is nothing but an immense flowerbed of wornout tricks, a vast pile of wriggling bones." [12] But his imitators understood not at all what was needed to accomplish the renewal. They mistook crudeness for life.

"To really succeed," Céline wrote, "in the honestly vulgar, in direct emotion, it's not enough, it would be too easy to invoke *la merde* each time you get stuck . . . To succeed in the 'vulgar' it is absolutely essential that your every instinct be in the opposite direction, that everything draw you away from it . . . ." [13] Céline described himself as an innately moderate man, who never drank, smoked, who appreciated beauty above all with the eye, whose every instinct moved *away* from the kind of rawness his "new style" demanded. To a correspondent he wrote, "Don't think that my tastes attract me to *le parler vert*. I am on the contrary a great admirer of the Abbé Brémond and of Tallemant des Réaux. I learned 'direct speech' above all in thirty years of medical practice. I am a doctor, before anything else." [14] Rabelais, his chief model in the enterprise of liberating written French from the tone of "a translation," was also a doctor!

In a curious introduction to *Gargantua et Pantagruel* entitled "Rabelais, il a raté son coup," Céline describes what Rabelais tried to do: to create "a language for everyone, a real one. He wanted to

[11] Letters to Milton Hindus, *Louis-Ferdinand Céline II, Cahiers de l'Herne*, No. 5 (Paris, 1965), 75–76. The punctuation is Céline's. Hereinafter cited as *Cahiers de l'Herne*, No. 5.   [12] *Bagatelles pour un massacre*, 154.
[13] *Ibid.*   [14] *Cahiers de l'Herne*, No. 3, pp. 118–19.

democratize the language, a real battle. The Sorbonne, he was against it, the doctors and all that. All that was accepted and established, the king, the church, style, he was against." [15] However, according to Céline, Rabelais lost the fight. Amyot, the translator of Plutarch, determined the nature of written French for the centuries to come—"a stiff, frozen language," wrote Céline. "Thus, to write well today is to write like Amyot, but that, it's never anything but 'a language of translation.' " [16] Elsewhere Céline admits that not all of Rabelais suits his definition of the "new style." "He's only readable, in my opinion, in the spoken passages. The 'Tempest,' for example. Except for that, he too is dialectical, like a priest or a minister or a Prix Goncourt." [17] Above all, Céline esteems Rabelais for his verbal power, his linguistic inventiveness. The rest—imagination, creative power, the comic—doesn't interest Céline. As always, he overstates in order to make his point. In his judgments of other writers he frequently condemns a lack of *fond* as well as of *forme*. The key term of Céline's aesthetics is language. In the transition from the spoken word to the written word is to be found Céline's unique contribution to the modern novel.

"What games of vanity, all these 'literatures,' " Céline wrote to Albert Paraz, one of his most faithful defenders. "They're worthless.—What a lot of wind! There are 'styles,' just words . . . But the music of Time changes and is never the same from one century to another—death alone plays this music—*one pays dearly for it*—it's horrible and sad . . . All these stammerers of literature understand absolutely zero of all this . . . ." [18] Céline's new style was an aural style, a musical style, a kind of *anti-prose*. He considered writers like Sartre "modernized, Freudianized naturalists— more intelligent Zolas." But they did not know how to cut close to the nerve. "I hate prose—I'm a poet and musician *manqué*—what interests me is the direct message to the nervous system." [19] Surrealism seemed to Céline "a fabricated delirium," lacking the genuine

[15] *Cahiers de l'Herne*, No. 5, p. 19.   [16] *Ibid.*
[17] Cited by Henri Mondor in the "Avant-propos" to V*oyage au bout de la nuit, suivi de Mort à Crédit* (Paris: Bibliothèque de la Pléiade, 1962), xiv.
[18] *Cahiers de l'Herne*, No. 3, pp. 151–52.
[19] *Cahiers de l'Herne*, No. 5, p. 78.

emotional quality of ordinary human utterances. The most striking difference between Céline and most of his literary descendants is that while they depoeticized the speech of their characters in order to render it "authentic" and flat-sounding (like the conversations in Sartre's short story, "The Wall"), he sought instead to unearth and magnify that element of common speech which is innately poetic. Defining himself as a rhapsodist, he frequently cited the well-known line from *Thus Spake Zarathustra*: "I shall believe in a God only if he dances." It is the Dionysian element in speech and in emotion which rules the universe of Céline's creations.

No style is a good one unless it achieves the authentic *tone* of its author. "There are in this world only the passions of the convinced. One must choose one's music, that's all." [20] The brutal strident music of Céline may at times sound harsh upon the ears of readers fed upon *la prose classique*, the "translated French" which has become the standard of good style in the French novel. But Céline's "music" was too loud and too hallucinating to pass without leaving its mark on the French novel. He seemed to find his harmonies in a place somewhere between the actual experience of reality and the dreams and nightmares which reality occasions. "I am going to give myself up to exploiting . . . [all my dreams] in the years to come," he wrote in 1933, just one year after the publication of V*oyage au bout de la nuit*, his first novel. Fourteen years later, from his enforced exile in Denmark, in a letter to Hindus, he was able to describe accurately his particular contribution to literature. The passage merits extensive quotation:

In truth my contribution to French letters has been I think this, it will be recognized later, to render written French more *sensitive,* more *emotive,* to *de-academicize* it—and this by the device which consists (harder than it looks) in an intimate spoken monologue but TRANS-POSED—This immediate spontaneous transposition that's the trick— Actually, it's a return to the spontaneous poetry of the savage. The savage doesn't express himself without poetry, *he can't.* The academi-cized civilized man expresses himself as an engineer, as an architect, *as a mechanized being,* plus a feeling being—It was really a small revo-lution—In the manner of Impressionism, before Manet they painted

[20] *Cahiers de l'Herne,* No. 3, p. 99.

in "studio light," after Manet they painted *in daylight* outdoors—Great surprise—they rediscovered the song of colors—I wanted them to rediscover in words the song of the soul.[21]

The source of Céline's style is spoken language as distinguished from written language. The style is based on common speech, untainted by the academic discipline which consists in expressing one's feelings as elegantly and objectively as possible. It is perhaps difficult for an English-speaking audience to appreciate the extent to which the "classical tradition" (the one Céline traces back to Amyot) has influenced the nature of French prose style. We have no equivalent in our training of the "great prose models" which are present in the mind's eye of any French student in the process of perfecting his written style. We would no more urge a young writer to emulate the style of Shakespeare (he would indeed sound bizarre) than that of Chaucer. But to capture the clarity of Descartes, the concision of La Bruyère are obvious goals if one wishes to write good French. To these models add a bit of the irony of Voltaire, and you have the beginnings of a good "academician," that is, a writer likely to be a candidate for the Académie Française. The satirical portrait of the writer who wants "to arrive" is a common one in French novels (for example, Julius in *Les caves du Vatican* by Gide), novels themselves frequently written in "arrived" style.

But because there is a greater distance between written and spoken French than there is between written and spoken English, there is also a vast fund of imagery, sound, "poetry," to use Céline's term, in the oral language which remained untapped until he attempted to use it as a literary idiom. Certainly, many writers before Céline, Daudet and Maupassant, for example, had made use of regional dialects and idioms in their writings for local color. However, the local colorist never lets the reader forget that he is a civilized man who is *observing* what is quaint and "interesting" about the strange characters he depicts. It is really a question of distance. Zola's novels abound in speech and terminology appropriate to the various milieus his "natural and social history" examines.

---

[21] *Cahiers de l'Herne*, No. 5, p. 75.

He quotes his characters, and they sound *quoted.* There is certainly *argot* in Zola. But it is part of the quoted material. Commenting on a dictionary of *argot* in 1957, Céline expressed his fundamental objection to the notion that a glossary of this kind is possible. "*Argot* is not made with a glossary, but with images born of hatred, it is hatred which creates *argot. Argot* is made to express the real feelings of wretchedness . . . *Argot* is made to permit the worker to tell his boss he detests him: you live well and I badly, you exploit me and ride in a big fat car, *je vais te crever* . . . ." [22] And there is no question that one element of the tone of Céline's novels is *rage,* the rage of Bardamu at being offered up as cannon fodder, the rage of Robinson at having to wear out his life in the morass of Africa.

Another quality of spoken French which Céline transformed in his novels is that "poetry of savages" which he heard all around him, the repetitions, the emotional imagery, the newly created words. Many of the words in Céline have yet to appear in any dictionary, although some of them have been common currency for some time. Many of his words are his own inventions, refinements of a specific *trouvaille.* For example, from the word *blablabla,* which Céline added to the language, he also derived *blablater* and *blablafouilleux.* From the influence of English on the cavalry milieu of World War I he wrote down, perhaps for the first time, *chtir,* which he explained to Paraz as follows: " 'Chtir' means 'je tire' . . . an old term of argot meaning 'horse meat'—in a time when horse meat was meat for the poorest buyer and when the butchers (*louchebems*) passed off 'chtir' instead of beef to their clients." [23] Spoken French is highly onomatopoetic, and Céline captured this quality in words like *glouglous* to describe the sound blood makes bubbling from a corpse or *boumer* as a verb meaning to make loud sounds.

Céline's novels are meant to be read aloud or heard with the mind's ear. They are essentially *aural* novels. To the speculation that his technique resembled developments in American fiction, Céline replied that *he* had not gotten his tricks *from books.* Rather, he had learned his style of prose in the English music halls,

---

[22] *Ibid.,* 31.   [23] *Cahiers de l'Herne,* No. 3, p. 155.

in rhythm, in dance. His aim was not simply to capture spoken language, but "an inner rhythmic language," more like the *chansons de geste* than like prose.[24] In other words, Céline sought not the actual accent of common speech, but the transformation of spoken language into an *ideal spoken language,* one which conveys intensely what its original would have liked to convey. It is this quality of distortion or magnification which distinguishes Céline's aural technique from that of American naturalism. While the voice of most heroes or nonheroes in American fiction tends to be a flat, understated one (excepting perhaps in the works of Saul Bellow and company), Céline's characters seem to scream, to chant, to say *more* than they mean rather than less. Their perceptions of nature are more beautiful and more ugly, their rages wilder, their glooms infinitely darker. All of this is couched in a prose style which *sounds* like someone speaking.

"I follow emotion with words I do not leave it the time to dress itself in phrases. . . . I seize it raw or rather poetic—for the center of Man in spite of everything is poetry—reasoning is acquired—like learning to speak—the baby sings—the horse gallops—trotting is taught." [25] But the technique which gives as its end result the *sound* of speech in a novel is not one of recording; it does not transfer the spoken word to the printed page. There is a trick which Céline believed was uniquely his, a kind of impressionism. "To make the spoken language into literature—that's not stenography —You must impress on the phrases, on the sentences a certain deformation an artifice such that when you read the book it seems that someone is speaking into your ear—This is achieved by a transposition of each word which is never quite the one you expect a little surprise . . . ." Céline explains the transposition by the analogy of a stick which you plunge into water. It will appear bent. If you want it to appear straight you must bend it slightly. In the same way, actual spoken language will not sound real in fiction unless it is distorted in a special way. "This distortion is a harmonic tour de force." [26]

The odd word order of Céline's written French is also unusual for *le parler direct.* The rules of grammar are made subservient to

[24] Cited in Albert Paraz, *Valsez saucisses* (Paris: Amiot, 1950), 315.
[25] *Cahiers de l'Herne,* No. 5, p. 73.   [26] *Ibid.*

the emotive aim of the dialogue. Céline deliberately makes errors of grammar "for the rhythm." The seemingly artless chaos of his novels is in fact a conscious, deliberate, highly contrived style. "One must correct down to the last carat, savagely," he wrote to his secretary.[27] The copy editors of *Voyage au bout de la nuit*, unprepared for the torrential flow of language, thought the punctuation incorrectly typed, and broke up the sentences with commas. "They want to make me write like François Mauriac!" shouted Céline, and demanded the restitution of his original orthography.

The new style had one essential aim for Céline—to achieve his "authentic tone," that quality which he felt was lacking in the "bourgeois fiction" of his contemporaries. It is a style which sees life uncompromisingly as a systematic outrage punctuated by rare moments of lyricism. Life is a long journey with a predetermined end which can in no way be redeemed by individual self-affirmation as in the novels of Malraux, or by a measured hedonism as in those of Camus. Céline's depiction of the travails of the lower classes is not designed to point the way to social melioration, as in the novels of late nineteenth century naturalism or those of social protest characteristic of the 1930's. As he says in the epigraph to *Voyage au bout de la nuit*, "Our voyage is entirely imaginary. That's its force. It goes from life to death." He drew his characters and images from an inner realm in which the real event and the personal music had already become inextricably fused. As he described his manner of conception in a letter to Hindus, it resembles very strongly that of Bernanos, whom he called "le seule . . . de ma famille":

I never have any difficulty conceiving a novel and I always follow the same procedure—I do not construct a plan—Everything is ready-made *in the air* it seems. I have twenty castles in the air where I shall never have the time to go—But they are complete everything is there—They belong to me—*But*—There is a *serious, very serious* BUT . . . For me to approach these castles, I have to liberate them, unearth them, from a kind of gangue of fog and rubbish . . . to pick at, hack at, dig, unearth all the gangue, the kind of hard cotton which encloses them . . . everything is there . . . I clean off a buried medallion, a statue buried in the clay.[28]

[27] *Cahiers de l'Herne*, No. 3, p. 31.
[28] *Cahiers de l'Herne*, No. 5, pp. 102–103.

Compared with the way recent decades of French novelists have understood their function, Céline's idea of literature was essentially a detached one. Despite the political ramifications of his hysterical pamphlets, which he insisted to the last were above all occasional works designed to avoid war, Céline considered political engagement a waste of time. He wrote to Paraz in 1947, during the high point of the postwar recriminations, "In twenty years all that will be ashes and dust, parades and cemeteries . . . street names . . . rusty plaques . . . What a lot of wasted passion! . . . life is too short. We can do so little, to finish a book is already a miracle!" [29] He said that he never voted, never electioneered, never signed any manifestos. "I never belong." [30] Unquestionably his personality worked against him during his many years of exile. Even persons originally well disposed toward him, like Milton Hindus, found the man difficult, unpleasant, hard to like in person. But the character of the man, like the rusty plaques, will have far less to do with the case than the works; and the novels, born out of the strange soil of Céline's imagination, have a power impossible to ignore.

Céline's strength lies in a combination of personal experience and imaginative power, conditioned by a view of man which is inherently *tragicomique*. Despite the social implications someone like Léon Trotsky found in the *Voyage*, Céline cannot be grouped with the socially conscious novelists of the 1930's.[31] In his view, literature is made by individuals, and men are not really determined by their society. They are instead fated, fated to be men, curious bundles of hopes and vices which move from birth to death in a jiggling dance which would be funny were it not at the same time so sad. Céline felt that true literature could only be created out of the crucible of experience, and for that reason novelists like Gide, Maurois, Giraudoux were all imposters. They had learned life in books and had nothing to reveal. Céline's Paris rings painfully true because, as he said, he *knew* it. His use of *argot*, of sex in his novels, was not for bourgeois titillation. The *analyse prousta-*

[29] Paraz, *Le gala des vaches*, 122–23.
[30] *Bagatelles pour un massacre*, 24.
[31] Léon Trotsky, "Novelist and Politician," *Atlantic Monthly* (October, 1935).

geuse fashionable in his era turned his stomach. He found more vulgarity in that than in the *grossièreté* of the common people. Vulgarity lies, he believed, not in *what* you write about, but in your attitude toward it. Thus, the middle-class novelist displaying his pederasty with "sincerity" is far more immersed in smut than Céline describing the speech of the inhabitants of *la zone* by using the words they use. Céline sought, as he once said admiringly of a novel he liked, to "catalyze all the troubled feeling of a certain milieu." [32]

"In the history of time life is but a frenzy, the Truth is Death," Céline wrote in *La vie et l'oeuvre de Semmelweis*, his thesis for Faculté de Médecine in Paris. And he continued, "As for medicine, in the Universe, it is only a feeling, a regret, a pity more effective than others . . . ." [33] In a sense, Céline's fiction is also a form of pity, but clinical in its valuations, much like the *coup d'oeil médical de la vie* which Flaubert described as his aim. Céline saw man as independent of political systems or predictions, because such temporal forces are of minor importance compared to the one tyrant who has always ruled man, namely man himself. The "black and serene despair" of Céline before the spectacle of the world resembles the painting which he admired of the "Fête des Fous" by Brueghel in Vienna. [34] Céline was interested "in what men are, not what they say." [35] And to understand the nature of men, he dealt with the concrete. He considered the abandonment of the concrete a form of desertion by the artist. The concrete must not be abandoned; but for it to become literature it must be transmuted in a special way. Of this Céline remained firmly convinced. He no more thought of himself as a naturalist or an "ashcan painter" than as a spokesman for the established order.

Art is not reality. European naturalism and realism have forgotten this, Céline pointed out. First of all, human experience is essentially uncommunicable: "Experience is a dim lantern which illuminates only him who carries it . . . ." [36] One can no more

[32] *Cahiers de l'Herne*, No. 3, p. 85.
[33] *La vie et l'oeuvre de Semmelweis* (Paris: Denoël et Steele, 1936), 48.
[34] Abel Bonnard, "A Sigmaringen," *Cahiers de l'Herne*, No. 3, p. 68.
[35] *Cahiers de l'Herne*, No. 5, p. 83.
[36] *Cahiers de l'Herne*, No. 3, p. 189.

write autobiography than the intimate biography of another. Céline thus seems to answer those critics who consistently construct
the life of Dr. Destouches from the novels of Céline. The life does
inform the novels, providing an imaginative skeleton, as it were,
upon which dreams and music come to place their beautiful or
macabre cloaks. But it is no longer "real life." Objective existence
is unbearable, Céline admitted. "I go mad, enraged so atrocious
does it seem to me thus I transpose everything in a moving dream
. . . . I guess that's probably the general disease of the world called
poetry . . . ." [37] Thus Bardamu is in a sense Céline himself, but
Céline perfected, transformed by what he called "the lyricism of
the ignoble," blackened. Céline could say honestly, "Bardamu?—
He's not me, he's my double. But so is Robinson." [38] Lucien Reba-
tet has aptly described the whole of Céline's work as a "biographical phantasmagoria." It is true that the later works such as *Nord*
are in some ways more personal than the earlier novels. But all the
novels draw from life, from Céline's own life and that of persons he
knew, all transformed according to the principle of the "bent
stick."

In some of his letters Céline identifies certain of his characters,
indicates the human models for his more-vivid-than-life creations.
He became so involved with his creations that he said to his
secretary at one point during the writing of *Mort à crédit*, "You
know I killed my father?" [39] In this novel, Céline's pernicious
distortion of his own childhood with his parents is an excellent
example of the imaginative relation between fiction and reality.
Céline's own parents are dramatized and changed, "blackened" so
drastically that it is said he begged them *not* to read the novel. But
to accuse the novelist of "lying" about the people he knew and
about himself, as did some of his friends, because of the way they
appear in his novels, is to misunderstand the nature of fiction.
Céline sought a certain density, what he called "weight," in the
men and women he depicted. Apparently the weight of certain
human existences, like those of his parents, was too slight; one
might say too unreal. In Céline's novels they take on the density of
fiction; they look real—real enough to become legendary.

[37] *Cahiers de l'Herne*, No. 5, p. 84.
[38] *Cahiers de l'Herne*, No. 3, p. 22.   [39] *Ibid.*, 31.

In a letter to Hindus, Céline admitted that his innate taste for the fantastic, for ballets and legends, was actually much stronger than his taste for realism, but, he explained, "I bent . . . [my talent] toward realism from a spirit of hatred for the malice of men —from a spirit of combat . . . ."[40] One understands better why Ferdinand Bardamu somehow does not lie quietly among the non-heroes of contemporary fiction. He is too large, a twentieth century mythical hero, noisier than Leopold Bloom, less tranquil outwardly, but of at least equal stature. Bardamu is more than a lament for the passing of the age of heroes, as are so many of the nonheroes. He is both a condemnation and a justification of man, always in very human-centered terms. Poetry and slime, sublimity and crudeness, one might almost say more and less than human— the world of Bardamu is a paradigm of the world of twentieth century man.

Speaking of the French literary scene in 1947 viewed from the lonely distance of Denmark, Céline wrote to Lucien Descaves (one of his partisans for the Prix Goncourt in 1932, ultimately awarded to someone else): "The literary harvest indeed seems rather pathetic . . . they still don't know how to transpose the 'spoken' into the 'written.' They haven't caught the trick. . . . They mistake brutality for character and the distorted, the wild for the fantastic. All these little erratics lack a Dream. . . . Nothing carries them along . . . How can they fly?"[41] He admired Barbusse, Paul Morand, Ramuz, Malraux of *Les conquérants*, Elie Faure, and in the past, Tallemant des Réaux, Agrippa d'Aubigné, Chamfort, Rivarol. Although Céline had an excellent knowledge of English, he found most of American literature of his era quite foolish, *gratuit, tocard et camelote*, and he included Faulkner, Dos Passos, Steinbeck, Miller. The most unkind thing he could think to say of Sartre was that only *he* was as *gratuit* as the Americans.[42]

Céline's literary tastes were frequently inconsistent and sometimes self-contradictory. However, there was one criterion of judgment for the novel which for him seemed to rank before all others

---

[40] *Cahiers de l'Herne*, No. 5, p. 76.
[41] *Cahiers de l'Herne*, No. 3, p. 115.
[42] Paraz, *Le gala des vaches*, 260.

—the *tone*—what Malraux has called "the written voice of the author." In the pariahs and the moralists, in François Villon and in Rabelais, in a few novelists perhaps unlike one another but all "experimental," Céline admired the quality which he himself had in abundance, the ability to communicate an intense personal view of the world around him in a strong voice. Villon, d'Aubigné, Céline—in all of them we find poetic style and rhetorical breath used to communicate a personal vision, what Céline called "a dream."

"Everything is dust in suspension. . . . Look carefully at a cemetery. It contains all the words, all the passions, everything." [43] These are words from Céline's letter to a literary friend, and they express concisely the realization which ultimately emerges from all of Céline's novels. The statement is not, as in the case of Albert Camus, the foundation for a humanism without illusions and a plea for tolerance. Céline's statement is a statement of fact, a clinical observation on the nature of things by a man who, as a doctor to the poor, saw human life in its least distinguished, ugliest forms. Céline never concealed his contempt for writers who found "easy" solutions for the world's troubles. He considered Louis Aragon as a kind of Communist pope to the poor. Aragon and his wife, novelist Elsa Triolet, translated *Voyage au bout de la nuit* into Russian in the thirties—the attacks on colonialism and capitalism were virulent enough to make the novel appear, at least on the surface, a massive social novel. This interpretation ignored the fundamental criticism it expresses, a criticism which is human rather than social: that there is no "solution" to what is wrong with the world.

Céline is a poet of the dark side of man, of his meannesses and his misfortunes. Céline's portrait of man is almost wholly one-sided, not so much because of objective facts, though they play a role in his choice, as because of the demands of his particular talent as a black lyricist. He claimed that he hated to write, that he undertook his first novel because he was starving as a doctor. But by his own admission and from comments by friends we know too

[43] *Cahiers de l'Herne*, No. 3, p. 106.

that his gift for language and his taste for fantasy predated his venture into writing. The style of his medical dissertation, *La vie et l'oeuvre de Semmelweis*, is already the style of the novelist, and its subject, the innate stupidity of the majority of men, is the subject of the works to come.

Céline seems never to have believed that writing would change anything or that the voice of the artist could be a force for political or social change. Rather, the lyrical expression of what Baudelaire called "the canvas of vices" was for Céline a demonstration of the one redeeming quality in man, his need for poetry. In a sense, Céline's work is a contradiction in terms: the ugliness described is negated by being described in lyrical terms. This is not a new phenomenon in literature. Villon is an obvious example of the same creative contradiction. But one must understand clearly that for Céline, in contradistinction to many of his contemporaries, the act of writing was not a demonstration of artistic responsibility and engagement. He was not a Catholic moralist like Mauriac or Bernanos, not an exponent of the writer's moral commitment like Sartre or Camus, not a preacher for social melioration like Aragon. Neither was he the spokesman for a special form of individual heroism like Malraux.

One factor distinguished the genuine from the specious writer for Céline, the criterion of experience. He found in the writers he admired the mark of men who had really seen what they described, in other words, a sense of authenticity. This authenticity applied to their expressions of fantasy, to their transformations of the real into dream, as well as to their descriptions of reality. The strongest words of condemnation in Céline's vocabulary were *gratuit* and *triché*. He considered the political and social preoccupations of his contemporaries a sign of bad conscience. He wrote to Hindus:

Surely one must educate the public—Sartre serves admirably for that—but how gratuitous all his theatre is! . . . and his philosophy! He needs two years of prison—three years in the trenches to teach him real existentialism and a death sentence over his head for at least ten years . . . then he won't rave any more—he won't fabricate any more gratuitous monsters—also a vice with the Americans—Passos [*sic*], Steinbeck, etc. . . . They scare themselves—They are phony—They all stink of phoniness like Baudelaire who hurled himself at poisons opium etc. . . . **in** order to be sure to be damned—People are still wondering why Rimbaud went to Africa so soon—*I know*—he was fed up with being phony—Cervantes wasn't phony—He really worked in the galleys—Barbusse really died of the war—that's not enough of course but there is an obsession in the poet *not to be phony* from which comes their disease of Politics—Lamartine, Byron, Zola, etc. . . Proust was dying through his lungs—He ended up by speaking nicely of his grandmother. That piece is successful, the best in his work—Gide always played with everything, dodged everything, what would he have to tell us? [44]

Political responsibility and engagment are, according to Céline, the banners of bourgeois writers experiencing bad conscience. When they feel they have been *tricheurs* (phonies) long enough, when they realize that they are basically detached and remote from the life of most men, they become spokesmen for moral responsibility and accuse others of bad faith. It is interesting to note that in his excellent book, *The Intellectual Hero*, Victor Brombert finds essentially the same traits of malaise at the root of political and social engagement by French intellectuals portrayed in novels since 1880.[45] It is ironic that Céline, who considered himself the most antipolitical of novelists (see also the chapter on Julien Green), should have been one of the most personally persecuted for political reasons. The anti-Semitic pamphlets may well have been, as Céline claimed, only efforts to avert another war. In any case, the persecution of Céline was itself a perfect illustration of his belief that men are *cochons*. The persecution also served as a justification and support for Céline's role as a kind of *poète maudit*, a role one senses he rather enjoyed. He saw himself as the author of highly original novels which won him notoriety and vilification.

Voyage au bout de la nuit is perhaps the most truly *modern* novel of our century. The voice of the narrator, Ferdinand Bardamu, is loud and memorable. He speaks the language of our age. As in the works of Malraux, Camus, and Sartre, in Céline's novel death is at the center of all realizations. Céline offers no palliatives, no useful preoccupations, no heroic gestures to mask the funda-

<hr>

[44] *Cahiers de l'Herne*, No. 5, p. 79.
[45] Victor Brombert, *The Intellectual Hero* (Philadelphia and New York: Lippincott, 1961).

mental horror. Everywhere Bardamu travels he finds that man is vicious, dirty, mean, and silly, *because* he is Man. For Camus poverty provides the absurd hero with a uniquely spare and rewarding vantage point from which he can view the world; poverty is a kind of beneficial ascesis. The innate injustice of life, that it must end in death, becomes a goad to intensified tasting of life's limited good. In Céline's world, which he would have us believe is *the* world and not the invention of a bourgeois mentality, death is present from the first; it is the fundamental fact of human existence. And it is a fitting fate, a just end for a creature as contemptible as man.

Bardamu moves from Paris to the battlefields of World War One, having been foolish enough to follow a recruiting parade. Realizing he has embarked on a "colossal apocalyptic crusade" he is stripped of his illusions. He decides he would rather be in prison. "When you have no imagination, dying is nothing, when you have some, it's too much. That's my opinion. Never had I understood so many things at one time." [46] But his education is only in its primary stages. He travels to Africa, to America, back to France, never free from his "mania of getting the hell out of every place." His first-person narrative is a curious mixture of imaginative description, striking moral maxims and incessant vituperation. He recounts a physical and spiritual odyssey which, in spite of its crudeness and its incredible string of misfortunes, appears like a mirror of twentieth century human existence. Céline's story is not a clever moral tale, a *conte philosophique* in the manner of *Candide*, because fundamentally he has no lesson to teach. What happens to Bardamu happens because it happens; the *grand guignol* of his peregrinations is a sketching in of the "journey to the end of night," an illustration of interest above all for its particulars, since its total message is fated from the outset and not to be discovered or debated.

Voyage au bout de la nuit is the most traditional of Céline's novels in terms of form and structure. It has a chronology, a recountable series of events. The characters, except for the narrator, are introduced in a relatively traditional fashion. And yet the

[46] *Voyage au bout de la nuit,* 22–23.

novel was, and remains, a bombshell, primarily for its *tone.* The voice of Bardamu, his brutal and yet curiously poetic speech, his deepening realization that there is nothing to realize, are all far more important than the plot, which is as wild as that of the best picaresque novels. Bardamu is the *picaro* with the hallucinations of a Rimbaud.

André Gide once said of Céline that he describes not reality, but the hallucinations which reality provokes. Bardamu's images of Africa, as Milton Hindus has so justly pointed out, are probably the most powerful, hysterical, and expressionistic to be found.[47] The colors are brighter, the sounds are louder, the insects more voracious, the water infinitely more putrid than they are in reality. But as Céline says in the epigraph, "Our voyage is entirely imaginary. That's its force." Imagination, which for him means poetry, is the only key we have to the darkness through which we travel. Occasionally Bardamu *sees* more quietly. His visit to a deserted fair with Lola has a mood of nostalgia which recurs elsewhere in the novel. It is the basic mood of Céline's second novel, *Mort à crédit.* The lower-class suburbs of Paris, the banks of the Seine have rarely been described as vividly or as poetically as in the *Voyage.* The Seine is seen as a body of water out of which dreams and phantoms rise. Céline will later, in *D'un château l'autre,* describe a contemporary version of Charon's ferry rising from the river's fog. Images of the suburbs of Paris are in many ways particularly suited to Céline's linguistic and poetic gifts. He is able to string together dirty courtyards and smoky light, sudden vistas on emptiness, so as to suggest a country at the very edge of the world. Céline's New York is "a town standing up," with Broadway "like a running sore," a huge cavern of loneliness, with benighted specimens of mankind filling it up in ignorance and in fear.

Obsessed with temporality, Céline naturally speculates on the nature and meaning of the past and its relation to the present. Remembering his departure from Topo and the colonial agent Alcide when he decides to penetrate further into the jungle to reach his own post, Bardamu muses,

[47] Milton Hindus, "Céline: A Reappraisal," *Southern Review,* I, n.s. (January, 1965), 76–93.

Perhaps none of all that exists any more, perhaps the little Congo has licked up Topo with a swish of its muddy tongue in passing one evening of a tornado and it's finished, all finished, perhaps the name itself has disappeared from the maps, and there is no one but me in short to still remember Alcide . . . . And the forest which hovered over the dune has taken everything back at the turn of the rainy season, crushed everything under the shadow of the immense mahogany trees, everything, . . . And nothing more exists.[48]

The emphasis here is on the "nothing more," and not, in the Proustian manner, on the remembering. In fact, memory for Céline is like a vast cemetery which one carries through life, no longer quite sure *who* is buried there. As Bardamu says, "It's terrifying what one has in one's past of things and of people who no longer move. The living one misplaces in the crypts of time sleep so well with the dead that the same shadow already blurs them both." [49] Bardamu becomes aware, as the number and variety of his misadventures increase, that even memories grow old and are tainted by the rot of time, *la pourriture*. For Simone de Beauvoir *la force des choses* means the force of events; for Céline it means something quite different. Things, objects, rooms—these change and grow old, and intensify the decay of man by partaking of it. "Everything had already changed around us . . . things themselves, in depth. They are different when you go back to them things, they possess, one would say, more strength to penetrate us still more sadly, still more deeply, more subtly than before, to dissolve in this kind of death which is slowly growing in us, softly, day by day, . . ." [50]

The "resurrection" of time past is impossible for Céline—he is as anti-Proustian in his metaphysics as in his style. Man is essentially a speck of dust suspended, about to disappear. Only a variety of distractions prevents him from disappearing immediately. Distractions are of course available: love, movies, hatreds, family precepts, wars; the list goes on and on. Bardamu looks down from his room in the Laugh Calvin Hotel in New York at the crowds moving along: "Day and night they just kept moving forward men. It hides everything, life does, from men. In their own noise they hear nothing." [51]

[48] *Voyage au bout de la nuit,* 161–62.   [49] *Ibid.,* 168.
[50] *Ibid.,* 366.   [51] *Ibid.,* 209.

As dark as the novel may appear from any objective description, V*oyage au bout de la nuit* is in large measure a comic novel. Bardamu's manner of speech not only strips the clichés from traditional written language; it also revaluates the clichés of the oral tradition by using them in odd contexts. For example, on a battleground facing the Germans, he suddenly reflects, "Me first of all as for the country, I'd better say so right away, I never could stand it, I always found it sad, with its endless bogs, its houses with no people in them and roads leading nowhere. But when you add war on top of that, it's just too much." [52] He thinks the horses are luckier than the men in war—they have to be there, but they don't have to pretend they believe in it. In one of the finest comic sequences in the novel, Bardamu tries to desert and find some Germans to take him prisoner. He meets another soldier, Léon Robinson, who is doing the same thing. Together they go to a French town supposedly in German hands, only to find that they are too early. The Germans have yet to arrive and the mayor is waiting to surrender. The mayor doesn't want to spoil the surrender by having two French soldiers found there, and chases them away. Bardamu and Robinson, each regretting the other is not a German to take him prisoner, give up their pursuit of "freedom" and return to their respective regiments and the war.

The largest vein of comedy in the novel comes from the scale on which misfortunes occur—if the misfortunes were not so pathetic, they would be cosmic. The "trick" of deformation of language which Céline used to make the written sound spoken has its parallel in making the fantastic sound like a realistic account of everyday life. Nothing that happens to Bardamu is totally within the realm of fantasy, and yet the proportions of each scrape, like those of the insects in the African forest, are too immense to be real. Céline describes the circus of the world, not from the perspective of a preacher, but from that of a clown with a special talent for words. Ferdinand Bardamu is the voice of Céline, yes, but the *literary* voice. He is a style of writing, a way of seeing. Aware of the biological precariousness of human life, convinced of the essential

[52] *Ibid.*, 16–17.

lowness of human character, Bardamu plays the guide with no illusions as he continues his journey across the panorama of the early twentieth century.

Mort à crédit, published in 1936, appeared to many readers Céline's autobiographical novel. The narrator, again Ferdinand Bardamu, now a doctor, explains that he has not always practiced medicine, which he calls *cette merde*. The time shifts to the turn of the century, to his boyhood and young manhood with his parents, penurious *petits commerçants* living in the Passage Bérésinas in Paris. Céline's own youth in the Passage Choiseuil is a kind of skeleton for the novel, but so changed, blackened, artistically honed to the tone of panic and vituperation necessary for Céline's special kind of poetry, that it is distinctly an error to consider the novel a veiled autobiography. Céline *used* the material of his own life in everything he wrote, used it artistically—that is to say, changed it so that it looked like reality. And perhaps the wretched youth of Ferdinand in *Mort à crédit* was more *real* than Céline's own. After the publication of his first novels, Céline began to alter the particulars of his own biography to match those of his character. His friends began to call him Bardamu.

Mort à crédit recreates the Paris of the Exposition of 1900. It is in many ways a very successful period novel in the traditional sense, completing the other half of the picture which Proust left out—*if* one accepts Céline's idiom of the spoken language. Céline's style has moved a step further since the *Voyage*. He has become more certain of his talent and more contemptuous of his critics. There is more crudeness and more poetry in *Mort à crédit*. The painfully violent scenes of family fighting are counterbalanced by fantastic dream sequences engendered by Ferdinand's fevers. The family's trip to the country in Uncle Edouard's motorcar, a sequence of high comedy, stands in striking contrast to another Sunday afternoon when Grandmother Caroline falls fatally ill as a consequence of her bout with the plumbing of her wretched suburban tenants.

There is no simple way to describe *Mort à crédit*, woven as it is of successive incidents which lead Ferdinand to leave his parents' home under the tutelage of his uncle. Despite differences of style, the novel it most closely resembles is Thomas Wolfe's *Look Homeward Angel*. They share the same sense of nostalgia; they are both highly subjective, *personal* autobiographical novels. If one judges *Mort à crédit* by the fictional quality of individual scenes, it is Céline's finest novel. It lacks the unity of *Voyage au bout de la nuit*, but it also lacks the obvious reasoned moralizing which sometimes undermines the authenticity of characterization in the earlier work. Bardamu of the *Voyage* is too clever, too gifted with words, to be totally credible.[53] In his second novel, Céline rendered Bardamu so artistically convincing that many mistook him for his author.

Voyage au bout de la nuit remains Céline's most famous book. Judged by traditional standards, it may be his best novel. It is not his most typical work, however. *Guignol's Band* (1944), its posthumously published suite, *Le pont de Londres* (1964), and the still unpublished *Rigodon* are perhaps closer to the heart of Céline's talent and intentions. *Guignol's Band* brings us the mature novelist, finally assured of his creative power and thoroughly despaired of finding an audience in the present. The stops are out. The tradition of the novel is seen for what it is, a convention and not a definition. Céline no longer listens to the idiom of the past at all, he speaks the language of the era to come. *Guignol's Band* and *Le pont de Londres* are not Céline's easiest novels to read. Along with *Casse-pipe* (1949), *D'un chateau l'autre* (1957), and *Nord* (1960), they take us far beyond the bounds of the familiar in fiction. Panic is the primary mood of these novels.

The *Guignol's Band* sequence has a freshness and an exuberance which surpass the earlier work. In the first novel Ferdinand, after being injured on the French front during the First World War, goes to London. There he becomes involved with the panderer Cascade

---

[53] In this connection, see W. M. Frohock, *Style and Temper* (Cambridge: Harvard University Press, 1967). Professor Frohock discusses the narrational problem confronting novelists (among them Céline) who choose as central characters figures *technically* unable to express the poetic insights or epiphanies their authors wish to convey. In *Mort à crédit* Céline overcame this problem, in my opinion, by totally abandoning any semblance of traditional narrative technique.

and the entire expatriate milieu of Leicester Square during the Great War—the prostitutes and pimps, the false magus Sosthènes and his nymphomaniac wife Pépé, the whole shadow world of London. The aural quality of Céline's style completely precludes even the feeblest bow in the direction of convention. We are surrounded by *sound* from the first page; we are never *introduced* to anyone or anything. The first-person narrator immerses us in his experiences and impressions, giving the sense of life as lived by the characters. Ferdinand's sensitivity to the magic of objects is not yet haunted by the sense of *pourriture* he experienced in the V*oyage*, most of which depicts him at a later period. His lyrical description of the mountains of objects at the pawn shop is one of the finest passages in all of Céline's writings. Elsewhere the fog of London parts to reveal the crowds waiting at the London Freeborn Hospital, a processional of disease and bad faith with the clarity of a Breughel painting and the intensity of a vision by Hieronymous Bosch. Of all of Céline's novels, *Guignol's Band* most strongly shows the influence of music on his style. Not only the sequences in which Borokrom plays the piano but also the fight in the brothel are lyrical in the most fundamental sense.

Le *pont de Londres*, as a direct continuation of *Guignol's Band*, takes us to the home of Colonel O'Colloghan, inventor and British patriot, who has advertised for partners in the testing of gas masks. Ferdinand and Sosthènes present themselves; the arrangement is a simple one—the colonel advances the capital and equipment, they supply their bodies. London's streets at five o'clock, the fragile springtime, Ferdinand's wild love for the colonel's niece, the explosion in the gas mask factory are scenes of startling verbal virtuosity and poetic power.

Several of Céline's novels deal with the realities of the Second World War (among them *Féerie pour une autre fois*, 1952; *Nord*, 1960), the period which initiated his personal difficulties with politics. Céline's form of noncommitment, nonengagement remained unchanged. His novels show us Frenchmen and Germans, equally grotesque, equally *guignol*. And the narrator, whom we can in the case of the last novels assume to be an almost direct *persona* of the author, continues to speak the most anti-"literary," most innately poetic language of any of the authors treated in this study.

In novels with a structure as diverse and fluid as life itself, novels which curse every aspect of his world, Céline may well be the most original writer of his era. Ferdinand Bardamu is the mythical hero of the legend of the present, a story with no conclusion in which his highest realization is that he knows nothing and his most exalted function is to be temporary head of an asylum for the insane.

Louis Aragon

MARXISM, HISTORY, AND FICTION

Louis Aragon is best known as a poet. A firebrand of Surrealism in the twenties, he became a spokesman for the French Resistance abroad, through pamphlets and lyrical poetry published in France and translated into English.[1] More recently, in his role as cultural leader of the French Communists, whose ranks he joined in the thirties, he has continued to write poetry of consistently high quality. What is less well known about Aragon, but equally important in his own eyes, is his role as a novelist. He has admitted that one of the reasons he left the Surrealist movement was the fact that it was opposed to the novel—he felt that to write a novel would be "a deliberate, and rather dangerous enterprise."[2]

Aragon has written nine novels to date. They range from *Anicet, ou le panorama* (1921), a Surrealistic burlesque of the traditional French picaresque novel, to *Blanche ou l'oubli* (1967), a curious mixture of *roman personnel*, novel on the novel, encyclopedia of French life since the thirties and poetic tour de force. *La mise à mort* (1965) had taken Aragon's readers by surprise. They were unprepared for his shift from the style and technique of the six novels which spanned the years from 1934 to 1958. These six

[1] See, for example, *Aragon, Poet of the French Resistance*, ed. Hannah Josephson and Malcolm Cowley (New York: Duell, Sloan and Pearce, 1945).
[2] *Entretiens avec Francis Crémieux* (Paris: Gallimard, 1964), 45.

constitute the heart of his fictional opus and are essentially realistic in technique and historical in approach.

Aragon's adherence to Marxism or "socialist realism," as he usually calls it, seems to have arisen almost simultaneously with his long-term dedication to a particular conception of the novel. Indeed, his own and others' accounts of his youth indicate that his artistic tastes had very early sought a rigid doctrinal framework for their unfolding. The French Communist Party was only too glad, of course, to receive into its ranks a poet of Aragon's stature. It probably did not know it was receiving a novelist as well. Aragon's wife, Russian-born novelist Elsa Triolet, was of course important in his official conversion to Marxism. But as early as 1928, when Aragon the Surrealist wrote the *Traité du style*, the novelist of the cycle "Le monde réel" was stirring.

In the *Traité* Aragon wrote arrogantly, "The function of genius is to furnish ideas to the idiots twenty years later." [3] However, he also expressed shame at not being able to *do anything* about things happening in the world. He confessed becoming sick when reading about the Sacco and Vanzetti case. He was becoming discontented with the Surrealist revolution as a form of *useful action*. Recently, in the course of several radio interviews in 1964, Aragon has made clear where the appeal of Surrealism had lain for him. He had seen it as a form of broadening, rather than escaping, the experience of reality. Poets like himself in the twenties were trying to capture the vitality of what was currently "modern," gasoline pumps, wax heads of ladies in hair dressers' windows. They wanted to capture novelty in a form which did not, by dealing with them in outmoded language, immediately reduce these exciting objects to "poetic antiques." [4] Thus from Aragon's point of view the Surrealist experience was a preparation for the realist phase which superseded it and which has persisted into the present.

Aragon wrote in a preface to a collection of drawings by an artist he admired: "Art is a serious thing and not at all gratuitous. It is not the concern of a single man. It is everyone's concern. It plays its role not only in the direction of the artist, but in the direction of

[3] *Traité du style* (Paris: Gallimard, 1928), 4.
[4] *Entretiens avec Francis Crémieux*, 20–21.

the world. One must pay attention to every single sketch." [5] These words might well serve as an epigraph to all Aragon's writings on literature since the early 1930's. Art is a serious thing, and only the realistic artist shows full awareness of this fact. One must be careful to point out, however, that Aragon uses his terms freely. He calls any writer he admires "a realist." He uses the term realism not to denote a particular historical movement in literature, but to mark those works which belong to the total movement of history, that inevitable dialectic which is fulfilling itself at every moment. Realism, he says, is "a literature of ideas . . . ." [6]

Aragon is careful to define the difference between realism and naturalism, with which it is often confused.

Realism should be distinguished from naturalism, because it is first of all a choice, and naturalism is concerned rather with the photographic image. Realism is concerned not with the surprise photo, the snapshot, but with the type, the created type—the typical man caught in typical circumstances. Therefore, it is evident that naturalism photographs the passerby, the man of chance, the existential, while realism aims at the hero, the cynosure of millions of men, the character whose very existence has an exalting, educational value. Realism begins where begins the realm of heroes. [7]

For Aragon, then, realism is a willed creation which chooses certain types of men who are worthy of being perpetuated and emphasizes *them*; it points out the "true direction" of history. Writers are "engineers of souls." That is why they must be careful of what they say, and willing to accept the necessity for change, when change is beneficial to man. [8] This is *socialist realism*.

The socialist realist writer must not be afraid to change his ideas, "to move like sand in the wind of history." The problem of contradiction is a false problem, since a man who is developing and changing his ideas is simply experiencing "dialectical contradictions"; he has recognized the need for new positions and does not feel himself hampered by the goblin of consistency. [9] This is the

---

[5] Preface to *Dessins de Fourgeron* (Paris, le 13 épis, 1947), n.p.
[6] *Hugo, poète réaliste* (Paris: Éditions sociales, 1952), 27.
[7] *Ibid.*, 27–28.
[8] *Pour un réalisme socialiste* (Paris: Denoël and Steele, 1935), 11.
[9] *Ibid.*, 20.

mechanism which tends to trouble non-Marxists when they notice Marxist writers change their ideals as the party line shifts. Aragon himself made the several shifts necessary first for French Communists who saw the signing of the Russo-German pact before the Second World War and then Russia's declaration of war against Germany. And apparently he suffered no moments of bad conscience, since dialectical contradiction is a way of recognizing the direction in which history is moving.

Aragon finds many historical illustrations of this mechanism. For example, Victor Hugo's "Les châtiments" is a poetic instance of socialist realism. Hugo's admiration for Napoleon changed to rage when he betrayed the ideals of the Revolution. Naturally, therefore, Hugo felt it necessary to punish Napoleon. For Aragon all the poets he admires, all the great poets, were realists, "in that part of their work which is lasting. Even the symbolists themselves were realists in the matter of language . . . ." [10] According to Aragon, it was a sense of realism which informed the works of Rimbaud, Apollinaire, Jarry. Thus, for Aragon the poetic conscience is a form of social realism. Any expression counter to the status quo is realism. "Socialist realism or revolutionary romanticism: two names for the same thing, and here Zola's *Germinal* and Hugo's *Châtiments* meet." [11]

It is interesting to note that Aragon most fully develops his theory of realism when discussing poetry, for him as much a locus of realism as is prose. In *Hugo, poète réaliste*, he quotes from one of Hugo's letters to Adèle: "Poetry is in ideas, ideas come from the soul." [12] Recognizing that not every realism is revolutionary (men like Hugo, Balzac, Barrès would hardly fit the revolutionary ideal), Aragon admits that at times the flight from reality is the only revolutionary form of action. One is reminded of Albert Camus' admission, in his essay on Oscar Wilde, that the "art for art's sake" attitude of many nineteenth century writers was a form of responsibility: it was the only responsible attitude toward a society which was unacceptable. Aragon joins Camus in this view by pointing out that "the realistic artist can be a reactionary man," if he is *scientific* in his art, as was Balzac. Balzac's scientific (one should

[10] *Ibid.*, 75. [11] *Ibid.*, 67–68. [12] *Hugo, poète réaliste*, 25.

read *realistic*) approach to his time made what he wrote an instrument of change and of history in spite of his own reactionary viewpoints. The great artists, therefore, are always revolutionary by the very truth of their vision, by the incisive quality of their observations. Today, however, the "historically enlightened" writer cannot believe in art for art's sake, Aragon insists. It is no longer the time for a flight from reality; the closer we approach the goal of history, the more we must work to hasten its arrival. Camus admitted that flight from reality could no longer be a responsible artistic attitude in our own time, although he of course did not invoke the "truth of history" in the Marxist fashion. However, even from Camus' humanistic standpoint, the artist *had to be a responsible artist*. The essential difference between Aragon and Camus on this point lies in the definition of responsibility. For Aragon responsibility is predefined according to Marxist doctrine; for Camus it is an intuitive apprehension of the basic needs and desires of man which determines the avenue of responsibility.

Louis Aragon has written extensive art criticism. In this criticism he develops his conception of reality and of the artist's relationship (whether a painter or a writer) to the real. In an introduction to an edition of some of Picasso's work, Aragon points out that the crucial step forward which Picasso took over Cézanne before him lay in restoring the *real object* to its rightful place in painting. For example, where Cézanne's apple used to be, Picasso put a pack of tobacco, an object related to man in his everyday world.[13] In much the same manner as André Malraux, who in *Les voix du silence* stressed the "humanization of art" which took place in post-Greek painting and sculpture, Aragon finds in the development of Picasso's style a growing emphasis on the real, unidealized human person. Paloma, Picasso's daughter, is a symbol of his postclassical works. She is represented as a girl, flesh and color, not shaped according to the neoclassical standards which characterized Picasso's "blue period." [14]

In Aragon's text to *L'exemple de Courbet*, a lavish presentation

[13] *Picasso, deux périodes* [catalog of an exhibit] (Paris: Maison de la pensée française, 1954), 4.   [14] *Ibid.*, 6.

of Gustave Courbet's paintings and drawings, we find a pocket history of realism. For Aragon, Courbet was the first painter to proclaim "the primacy of matter, the independent existence of the object in relation to the artist, the absolute necessity of painting after nature and of *only* painting after nature, what the eye has seen and nothing but what it has been able to see." [15] Aragon invokes the criterion of realism in his analysis of the importance of Courbet's contribution to the history of painting. "The history of art, that is, true art criticism, in . . . [the nineteenth] century, is nothing other than the history of realism." [16] Courbet was important because his painting affirmed a belief in "the existence of things, independently of the man who sees them, of the artist." [17] However, despite his evident love of realism in painting, Aragon is able to understand the apparently "nonobjective" trends in modern painting. Just as he saw Surrealism as a manner of exploring reality in further depth, so he justifies the experimental characteristic of modern art, of *collage*, for example, as a desire on the part of the artist to penetrate reality beneath the level of appearance: "The artist was playing with the fire of reality." [18]

Aragon's preferences in writers are of course shaped by his predilection for realism and for responsible art. He defends Georges Duhamel, much criticized by the French Communists for his uncommitted stand during the Occupation, for his cycle, *Vie des martyrs*, a series of novels dealing with the First World War: "Monsieur Duhamel is a writer whose works count for a whole period of national life. He's not an adventurer, which is more than one can say for Monsieur André Malraux . . . ." [19] (We shall return later to Aragon's long-standing animosity toward Malraux.) For Aragon, Charles Dickens is a landmark in the history of literary realism. When little Paul Dombey asks his father, "Papa, what is money?" this is "the reflection of the transformation of the world . . . ." [20] Aragon notes that "the proletariat, which in the last analysis is the origin of little Paul's reflection, and of what is new in

[15] *L'exemple de Courbet* (Paris: Editions Cercle d'art, 1952), 15.
[16] *Ibid.*, 34. [17] *Ibid.*, 39. [18] *Pour un réalisme socialiste*, 18.
[19] *La lumière et la paix* (Paris: Les Lettres Françaises, 1950), 14–15.
[20] *L'exemple de Courbet*, 12.

Dickens' novel," already existed; Dickens took account of reality by referring to it in his novel. If we go back to writers such as Fielding and Rousseau, who were "convinced materialists" and held only to an "idealistic socialism" in their time, we must not criticize them for not furthering the dialectic of history. The proletariat was not yet born, they had no help from "scientific socialism." [21] But now, any writer who chooses to ignore the vast changes which have taken place in the structure of society, who continues to write as if the nineteenth century had not seen the development of a class which is bound to alter the nature of the world, is irresponsible and unrealistic.

History, whether of art or of world events, is not an objective set of facts which does not change in the future. According to Aragon's Marxist viewpoint, as the needs of the present change, so too does one's interpretation of the past. "The unfolding of history forces us to revise the history of art . . . ." [22] This revisionist method explains many of the apparent contradictions in Aragon's literary judgments, many of the seemingly unjustifiable statements he makes—for example, in his reference to Rimbaud's "realism." His shifting valuations of other writers are not changes of heart or lapses of consistency; they are realistic appreciations of the movement of history, attempts to understand the past in terms of the present, and, above all, to make the past serve the needs of the future. Aragon uses much the same technique in his approach to the historical novel. We shall discuss *La semaine sainte* at greater length later on. It is sufficient now to point out that the common critical reading of this work as a traditional, and therefore critically acceptable historical novel when it appeared in 1958 showed a total misapprehension on the part of the critics. The true axis of Aragon's account of the moment preceding the "hundred days" in 1815 was not Napoleon's brief return to power; it was the political situation in France in 1958.

Aragon's most difficult moments as a critic arise when he is considering a poet whom he truly loves for his poetic genius, yet whose political and social opinions cannot be justified according to Marxist theory. For example, taking issue with Pierre Emmanuel,

[21] *Ibid.,* 16.   [22] *Ibid.*

who wrote, "He who wishes to know a man must seek him less in his words than in the music they make," Aragon protests that "man is in his words as well as in the music they make." [23] If, as Aragon wrote in *Chroniques du bel canto*, a collection of poetry criticism, "Poets are events of history," then one must never ignore *the historical moment of a poet*, an important factor in his thought. One of the more interesting examples of the consequences of this position is Aragon's discussion of Mallarmé, a poet he greatly admires, but whom he finds it difficult to include in his canon of "realistic poets." Attempting to elucidate some of the obscurity of Mallarmé's imagery, Aragon suggests that much of what is obscure to us now would become clear with an inventory of Mallarmé's furniture, with an accurate reconstruction of the decor.[24] And one wonders whether this might not, indeed, clarify certain dim spots in the poems. While it is highly unlikely that anyone could ever classify Mallarmé as a realistic poet, there is no doubt that some of what seems like symbol to us might merely have been based on tangible objects and particular angles of light in a *real room*. If, as Aragon contends, all poetry is *poésie de circonstance*, we certainly need to know its circumstances in order to understand it. As a matter of fact, footnotes would be helpful. Aragon himself has published several long poems in which he has supplied footnotes; *Le fou d'Elsa* is an example.

When Aragon confronts Baudelaire in the course of his discussion of the history of realism in art in *L'exemple de Courbet*, he is forced to admit, "One must be fair; all the horrors and meannesses which Baudelaire's *Journaux intimes* contain, his shift from the republican ranks to the explanation of Napoleon III's 'providentiality,' etc. . . did not prevent him from being a very great poet, did not prevent him from having an almost unparalleled sense of the French language, from attaining an elevation of thought equal to the slime of his abysses." He continues, tacking on the inevitable dialectical explanation, "One must be fair, and know how, in Baudelaire, to extract the black gold of poetry from the infamy of his class." [25] Two aspects of Baudelaire's art save him from Aragon's

[23] *Chroniques du bel canto* (Genève: Skira, 1947), 105.
[24] *Ibid.*, 146.   [25] *L'exemple de Courbet*, 31.

blanket condemnation. First of all, his poetic genius, which Aragon is unable to ignore, even under the most anti-Marxist circumstances; and second, the importance in Baudelaire's art of the *French language*. Aragon is intensely nationalistic. In this respect, he belongs to a persistent strain of French Communist thought. As George Lichtheim has pointed out, one prevailing school of Marxist thought in France, from its inception, has been militantly nationalistic.[26]

Aragon has consistently defended the idea of a national poetry. He has written tracts calling for the restitution of the *alexandrin, le chant républicain*; he has deplored the disintegration of French verse into a nondescript mass of tuneless words. Like Céline, he despises the "tone of a translation" he finds in many modern poets.[27] Despite their extreme divergence in political viewpoints, Céline and Aragon have in common a very French "ear," a sense of the spoken language, the idiomatic. They also have in common an eye for realistic detail; however, they use their acute gift of observation to very different ends. Aragon tries to prove the historical inevitability of socialism by invoking the world around him. Céline's image of the same world demonstrates only that the world is stupid, pointless (*vache*) and man along with it. That a Communist and a misanthrope usually called a fascist, alone of all the novelists treated in this study, should be most acutely aware of the contemporary French language, gives one food for thought. Aragon waged many campaigns; one of his most intense was his *politique littéraire* in defense of a French national poetry. To this battle his fighting spirit seems ideally suited. Aragon is by nature a polemicist, in the manner of Céline and of Bernanos, and his diatribes in defense of poetry are certainly among his finest. They also reveal the extent to which his conception of the novel is colored by his poetic intuitions, those intuitions which are most naturally his and which shape the nature of his fiction.

Despite the apparent modernity of his most recent novels, Aragon is scarcely a champion of modern art forms. He finds in modern art an "internal negation," a negativism which is common

---

[26] George Lichtheim, *Marxism in Modern France* (New York: Columbia University Press, 1966).

[27] *Journal d'une poésie nationale* (Lyon: Les écrivains réunis, 1954), 33.

to poetry and prose as well as to painting. "It's not simply a question of literature. The same cancer eats at all language, disintegrates all language before our eyes. Everything happens as if the honor of man were suddenly dependent on silence, on *not speaking*. Art has known many tyrannies, it has fed on them. This was because the tyrannies were exterior to it, strangers to it. Fra Angelico painted for the Church and Rubens for Marie de Médicis: the art of these painters survives faith and the court of France." [28] But the anti-creative bent which is at the heart of many modern works of art is the sign of a lack of confidence in the efficacy of art itself, and, even more crucially, it is a symptom of lack of vision. From his surrealistic youth to his maturer Marxist period, Aragon has always conceived art as having a revolutionary purpose. The artist has an aim to achieve and needs a program for carrying out this aim. It may well be that Aragon's determined functionalism has seriously flawed his art; nevertheless it has assured its uninterrupted flow. He has never been at a loss for what to write: he has always written what has seemed to him necessary to the direction art and the world were taking. The accuracy of his divination of the movement of history has little to do with the *facts* of the works, with the continuous flow of poetry, novels, polemics consistently characterized by the individuality of his talent. In Aragon we find an instance of the power of an ideal to motivate creativity.

His criticism too has been served by his vision. Aragon is ingratiatingly frank about his vagaries as a critic. He admits that he reads what he likes, that there are books he cannot read, and that he is not necessarily right. He frequently says that he likes things which are "done well," and that *that* is his principal critical standard. But once his taste has chosen its object, his ideal of artistic responsibility intervenes and gives the criticism its *raison d'être*. He finds the sonnet by Guillevic, "À Stéphane Mallarmé," admirable "because it is a magnificent lesson in literary history, in the highest sense of the term. A testimony of profound understanding of the work and the person of a poet, taken in his time and in the light of ours . . . ." [29] Writing of Hugo's "Boöz endormi," in his eyes a great poem, Aragon confesses that its historical inexactitude does

[28] Preface to *Dessins de Fourgeron*, n.p.
[29] *Journal d'une poésie nationale*, 71.

not bother him, because "historical truth is secondary to poetic creation." [30] This may seem to contradict his insistence upon the importance of history to art; it does not, because for Aragon poetic truth is the highest form of historical truth. "The strength, the profundity of art . . . stems from something which goes beyond the individual and which attains a kind of collective value." [31] The artistic testimony of a man is a testimony for all men.

In general, Aragon's approach to literature remains historical. In a speech at Medan, for the annual pilgrimage of the "Amis de Zola" in 1946 (where Céline spoke some years earlier), Aragon addressed himself to the custom of discussing literature by "movements." He admitted that such divisions are artificial. "However," he said, "for the mind they seem to have something inevitable in them, they impose themselves. Apparently, even those men who believe that literature, thought, and art are independent of events, detached from circumstances, recognize by this custom of chronological conception that history stands above literary history, that in reality nothing is written, sung, thought or painted completely detached from the brute history which is common to all men." [32]

Aragon tends to judge contemporary writers by their awareness of the stage of history in which they live. He calls Mauriac, Bernanos, and Malraux writers of "contemporary reactionary novels." He recognizes them as heritors of Barrès, whom he himself admired in his youth, although he presently disagrees with all Barrès stood for except French nationalism. But to continue the tradition of Barrès in this time as do these novelists, with the advent of such radical changes as the existence of the Soviet Union and "the growth and maturity of the French proletariat," is to work counter to the movement of history.[33]

Stendhal is Aragon's favorite example of the realistic novelist. For Aragon, Stendhal was a realist in the socialist sense. He stresses that despite Stendhal's insistence that there was *nothing political*

---

[30] En étrange pays dans mon pays lui-même (Monaco: Les Livres Merveilleux, 1945), 10.
[31] Louis Aragon and Jean Cocteau, Entretiens sur le musée de Dresde (Paris: Editions Cercle d'Art, 1957), 19.
[32] La lumière de Stendhal (Paris: Denoël, 1955), 245–46.
[33] Ibid., 267.

in his writings, "The Stendhalian spirit appears to us like that of a hunted, bullied man, who had something quite different to tell us and who, behind the prison bars of his era, makes the knowing, mute gestures of the human drama, of liberty, in our direction." [34] In *La lumière de Stendhal*, one of Aragon's most characteristic and successful works of criticism, he expands the theory of social realism in the novel. "The greatness of Stendhal . . . is the greatness of the political view." [35] Aragon feels that in order to understand how Julien Sorel becomes "the indictment of a century," the hypocrite created by his era, we must think of Stendhal the novelist as "the man, the man socially and chronologically defined." [36] Stendhal forms part of a long tradition in the French novel, a tradition which includes *Gil Blas,* for example. But the qualities which unite Stendhal with the past are those "serious things" which supersede the quality of "melodrama" in *Le rouge et le noir.* We notice here Aragon's tendency to minimize comic elements to the advantage of political and social factors. This same seriousness frequently bogs his own novels down in thesis and demonstration, when a touch of comic relief would be refreshing.

Everyone is familiar with Stendhal's statement that the novel is "a mirror along a roadway." Aragon is unable to accept this statement at its face value, and perhaps he is right. He sees this dictum as a defense against the police and the authorities of Stendhal's time, not as a sincere statement of Stendhal's theory of the novel. Aragon cannot believe this profession of authorial objectivity, because he senses that "in this novel, everything is politics. Just as in life." [37]

In a lengthy series of textual explications, Aragon compares Molière's *Tartuffe,* the closest parallel he can find, to *Le rouge,* and discovers striking similarities. His conclusion to this comparison is categorical: "Stendhal shows himself to be a historian and a critical realist." [38] *La chartreuse de Parme* and the *Chroniques italiennes* are similar efforts, works in which Stendhal uses another era to disguise the historical and critical realism which is his signature.

---

[34] Preface to Louis Delluc, *La guerre est morte* (Paris. Éditeurs français réunis, 1952), x–xi. [35] *La lumière de Stendhal*, 13. [36] *Ibid.* [37] *Ibid.,* 54. [38] *Ibid.,* 69.

We know that despite the favorable critical reaction to Aragon's own *La semaine sainte*, because it seemed to be a historical novel and not a Communist apology, it is no less political and socialist-realist than any of Aragon's other works. In some ways, in fact, *La semaine sainte* is the most political of his novels, since its art and skill make it a more powerful weapon of propaganda than the obvious homilies of *Les Communistes*. Aragon recognizes Stendhal's method quite easily: it is his own. And in Stendhal he denotes a key phase in the development of "this democratic, or if you prefer, socialist, realism." [39]

The term "lumière" in the title of this critical essay means, quite simply, historical example. Stendhal showed the way in an era even less enlightened than our own. He created the political novel when it was even more dangerous to do so than now. But Stendhal had to find defenses; his chief one was the stance of objectivity. "The real lie of Stendhal," Aragon wrote, "is that . . . [he is] not a naturalist; he pretends, precisely in order to fight against the milieu, the police, the hypocrites. And his novels are *deliberate* (*voulus*), not at all innocent, in no way disinterested mirrors; they are arms against a social milieu which must be undermined, changed, transformed from top to bottom. That is not naturalism, it's realism." [40]

Literary value in the novel is a changing taste, and for Louis Aragon the changes are determined primarily by historical change. It is not surprising that *War and Peace* is the occasion for one of his most incisive pronouncements on the criteria of literary judgment. Tolstoy's immense realistic panorama, laid over a substratum of belief in the dialectic and aim of historical movement, is in many ways a model for several of Aragon's own novels, most significantly *Les Communistes* and *La semaine sainte*. In a book on Soviet literature, Aragon speaks of *War and Peace*: "A book is not written once for all time: when it is a truly great book, the history of men adds its own passion. One reads and rereads the book: each time it changes meaning, it takes on our personal experience." [41] In

[39] *Ibid.*, 160.   [40] *Ibid.*, 64.
[41] *Littératures soviétiques* (Paris: Denoël, 1955), 16.

some ways, Aragon's theory of historical relevancy resembles Malraux's concept of "the voices of silence." Malraux maintains that certain eras of art in the past have more relevance to contemporary experience than others; that each era reads the past in its own light, and finds some moments of art more telling than others. The moments which find no present understanding and interest remain "silent," voices which make no sound because there is no one to hear them. For Aragon, this sweeping interpretation of man's culture is no doubt too broad and too eclectic, since it admits of meaning and value in *any* era of the past, whether it pointed the way to socialist realism or not. But with respect to the nineteenth century, Aragon and Malraux unwittingly join hands. They both esteem Tolstoy very highly; they both find in his writings an image of man which speaks to their contemporary experience. And in Tolstoy's image of man in history they both seek support for their theories on the relationship between culture and men.

After the end of the Second World War, UNESCO held a series of conferences at which leading European intellectuals and artists spoke on the problems of culture and civilization which confronted the West in the wake of the holocaust. Chief among these speakers was Malraux, who in November, 1946, delivered an address entitled "L'Homme et la culture artistique," subsequently published by the *Revue Fontaine* in 1947. In that speech Malraux elaborated his notion of *tragic humanism,* an attitude which accepts the fact that all secure notions of the purpose and destiny of man are no longer meaningful and which proceeds to place its hope in the role of art as the one thing which can affirm and perpetuate man's continuity. By art, Malraux meant those special products produced by a few men of genius, the creations which affirm man's higher nature and assert his identity with himself through all of recorded history. Malraux drew a firm distinction between mass culture and the history of art, and pointed out that the art of a few served to create the history of the many, and *was* the true image of man. He could find no meaning in history as generally understood. Only in the history of art did Malraux discern what he was seeking—the image of "fundamental man." Found in works of art, this image subsumes the individual obscure existences of nonartists living in a day-to-day world. (The ideas Malraux expressed at UNESCO are those which shaped his last novel, *Les noyers de l'Altenburg*.)

Louis Aragon was invited, at the same conference, to speak on the same general topic, the culture of the masses, and after some hesitation, he delivered a diatribe which he called "La culture des masses ou Le titre refusé," in which he sought to answer and refute Malraux, whose every word, it seems, enraged him. He objected to the key words in Malraux's speech, *l'homme* and *l'Europe*. He found Malraux's notion of cultural pluralism an affront to his own innate nationalism and Malraux's image of fundamental man a denial of his own Marxist interest in the amelioration of the daily lot of each man. Aragon called Malraux's key words "the passwords of the new 'happy few,' of those who are going to save the world in their fashion in a language no one but themselves will understand." [42] He then addressed himself to the notion of cultural pluralism. "We hear affirmed, as a discovery of the highest importance, that pluralism is born and that the concept of the plurality of cultures replaces the old idea of civilization, which is worn out." [43] Aragon deplored the Spenglerian basis of Malraux's affirmations, and found it ironic that in order to launch the "phantom of Western man" Malraux should use the same terminology with which Spengler predicted the decline of the West. For Aragon, Malraux's "fundamental man" was simply "the man of jargon." Aragon explained himself: "The man of jargon is not a peasant, a banker, a soldier. He does not belong to this or that society. He has no class, thus no political party. He's a marble statue who braves the intemperances of his nakedness, who is made for eternity, and who stands in contrast to the common perishable matter of the masses. The man of jargon is the negation of the masses." [44]

Aragon believed that the question on which Malraux based his speech, how to re-create man, or is man dead, was a false issue. "These are not real problems, these are *evasions* of reality." [45] In the late twenties and early thirties—when Malraux was reading and discussing Nietzsche and germinating a refutation of Spengler—Aragon, beginning to tire of his surrealistic venture, was turning to

[42] *La culture et les hommes* (Paris: Éditions Sociales, 1947), 15.
[43] *Ibid.*   [44] *Ibid.*, 17.   [45] *Ibid.*, 18.

Marxism. The conflict between the two in 1946 arose quite naturally out of their diverging preoccupations and outlooks. It seems that their very vocabulary differed, that they were destined to misunderstand one another. Malraux's approach to the problems of postwar Europe was shaped by his essentially elitist view of man and his faith in the primacy of art, art not for art's sake but for man's sake. Aragon, on the other hand, firm in his Communist beliefs and his strong sense of French nationalism, could not understand the term "culture" used chronologically. The very distinction between popular and elite culture was an anathema to him. He said, "Culture at the level of a country, which is one and indivisible in the sense that there is no culture of the elite and culture of the masses, takes on life and value in a national form. . . ."[46] Aragon was so opposed to the notion that art belongs to the world that he called for the immediate return of French art treasures then on German soil.[47] He was furious that Karl Jaspers, a *German*, was invited to participate in the colloquia at Geneva, a year after the taking of Berlin, at which the participants attempted to define "the European spirit," while there were no Russians present. Finally, he stated his position on culture: "The nation is precisely the ensemble in which the elite and the masses are united. . . . The great human culture . . . is not made by amputating these [national] cultures, but out of their coexistence, their harmony . . . ."[48]

Aragon's insistence that there is no separation between the culture of the elite and the culture of the masses stems in great measure from a phenomenon peculiar to the Communist community of France: the artistic products of the elite are consumed by the masses on command. Whether or not each buyer reads the books he purchases, a Communist novelist like Aragon is assured a healthy sale of all his works to Party members. The end result of this assured audience is twofold. First, Aragon writes in the certainty that he will be widely read, whether it be fiction or criticism. Second, he tends often to create specifically for that audience,

[46] *Ibid.*, 27.
[47] See for example, *L'enseigne de Gersaint* (Neuchâtel et Paris: Ides et Calendes, 1946), 23–24.   [48] *La culture et les hommes*, 27.

which leads to certain limitations in the products and certain unquestioned assumptions underlying them which are not always acceptable or even clear to outsiders. Thus, to a non-Communist reader, a novel like *Les Communistes* (published by Les Éditeurs Français Réunis, a Communist house) suffers severely from want of persuasiveness, lacking as it does structure, unity, and psychological characterization. But the audience for which it was intended found the novel totally satisfactory, reinforcing as it did truths common to the milieu.

However, Aragon gains one tremendous advantage in his official position as writer for the French Communists. He enjoys a sense of rapport with his audience. For this reason, he is the only writer treated in this study whose critical writings have the ring of complete self-assurance. For example, in a speech before the Congress of the French Communist Party in 1954, he reported with pride that in the previous four years he had published seven books.[49] On another occasion, he urged his readers to read some of his earlier works, dating from his pre-Communist phase, with a kind of coy conviction that his recommendation would be followed: "By the way, have you read *Anicet*? Imagine that after thirty-nine years, it's funny to look at it again, in 1959; and if your bookseller tells you it's out of print, he's lying through his teeth. There are 3,800 copies lying idle at Gallimard, I'll bring fifty or so to my booth at the Vel d'Hiver [annual sale by Communist writers], just to satisfy the curious. . . . The preceding an unpaid commercial." [50]

In his articles for the communist literary weekly, *Les lettres françaises*, Aragon exhibits his characteristic tone as a critic. He is personal, self-indulgent, full of unjustified enthusiasms, and above all, he writes as a writer who knows he has an audience. There is a great deal which is journalistic here, certainly, but also a sense of community so obviously lacking in the majority of modern French writers. Aragon can afford to be himself, capricious, at times pontifical, but always very human. He does not have to be stony and impassive. He senses his mission as an arbiter of taste for his readers. He warns them against "a vulgar realism," "a populist art,"

[49] *J'abats mon jeu* (Paris: Éditeurs français réunis, 1959), 198.
[50] *Ibid.,* 120.

what Pierre Daix has called "paternalistic books." Aragon's innate literary good sense leads him to warn his readers against some bad literature masquerading under the guise of social realism, since, to be genuine, he says, social realism must take its reality "from a world of contradictions, from the coexistence of men and women in disaccord. . . . There is no light without shadow. A book without shadow has no meaning and is not worth the trouble of opening." [51] He shows his readers how a novel by a non-Communist can still have value for them: "The author's class point of view can give rise to values which will be recognized beyond the limits of his class . . . ." [52] As we have noted, Aragon's own analyses of Hugo, of Mallarmé were justified by the same reasoning. Above all, Aragon the critic functions as a guide to taste, rather than as an analyst of texts or historian of literature. As he admits, "I believe, for my part, that taste is an essentially positive thing. That criticism should, on the subject of literature, be a sort of pedagogy of enthusiasm." [53]

Aragon has given us many insights into his theory and practice of the novel. Most of them date from the late fifties. It would appear that his thinking on fiction reached its clearest point and its maturity during and after the publication of *La semaine sainte*, his most ambitious and in many ways most successful novel to date. Speaking with an interviewer, he indicated that he had used the historical approach elsewhere. For *Le fou d'Elsa*, a long narrative poem set in fourteenth century Spain, he prepared himself by extensive research on the period. But he only really "got into the Islamic soul" by the actual act of writing. "I had to learn in order to understand. . . . I write in order to know, and thereby to communicate to another what I have learned." [54] Aragon describes writing as a kind of intuitive knowledge, based on certain simple facts of his existence; he then proceeds to the elaboration of the motives behind these facts. This he calls "the realistic method."

"Le Monde Réel" comprises six novels: *Les cloches de Bâle* (1934), *Les beaux quartiers* (1936), *Les voyageurs de l'impériale* (1942), *Aurélien* (1944), and *Les Communistes* (6 vols.,

[51] *Ibid.*, 136.   [52] *Ibid.*, 139.   [53] *Ibid.*, 107.
[54] *Entretiens avec Francis Crémieux*, 14–15.

1949–51). Each of these novels depicts a particular era, or, to use Aragon's term, a "situation" in French life in this century, and with the exception of the first, presents a large gallery of characters whose interaction underlines the theme of men in the wake of historical change.

Les cloches de Bâle is, along with *Les Communistes*, the least successful of his novels. Aragon is aware of its limitations: "It's with *Les cloches de Bâle* that I learned how to create a novel. This book is less finished than those which followed, than *Aurélien*, for example. Its construction is rather baroque, with separate parts, very different in tone." [55] This self-criticism is quite accurate. The novel deals with three women: Diane, *a demi-mondaine*; Catherine Simonidzé, a young Georgian who moves from adherence to the ideals of anarchism to those of socialism; and Clara Zetkine, the Communist "new woman." The novel ends with the famous Socialist Congress at Basel on the eve of the First World War. All the characteristics of Aragon's later novels are already present. His style is colloquial, deriving almost totally from spoken French. The narrator, a contemporary of the central characters, describes their actions and reactions. There is a great deal of reference to history, so much, in fact, that it tends to tire the reader and to make the narrative drag. Aragon writes with the same kind of historical awareness to be found in two of the novelists he admires, Stendhal and Tolstoy, with this difference: he is unable, at this point in his development as a novelist, to make the history seem an integral part of the primary narrative, so that his characters can function *while history is moving* and unwittingly *be part of it*. The easy colloquial style stops temporarily, while someone, presumably the author, fills us in on events, dates, names which are historically valid but add nothing to the fiction as fiction. The reader is inclined to agree when Aragon says, "To tell the truth, I am not very much of a novelist. . . . For me it's always a question of ideas to which I try to give a body, a face." [56]

But other facets of Aragon's characterisitc style indicate a real novelistic talent and make this "testimony of his time" into the

---

[55] *J'abats mon jeu*, 92.   [56] *Ibid.*, 92.

substance of fiction. *Les cloches* contains descriptive passages which deal with various milieus, that of the *petite noblesse*, the bourgeois, the anarchists, the strikers. In these, Aragon's poet's eye serves him well, capturing the telling visual detail which fixes his scene and characters in a moment in fiction of striking intensity. He handles dialogue with skill, and is able to sustain consistency in characterization.

One aspect of Aragon's style which reappears in his other novels with varying degrees of success is authorial intrusion. For example, justifying the last section on Clara Zetkine, he writes:

People will say that the author wanders, and that it's high time he end with a drum roll a book where they despairingly see arise suddenly, so late, this image of a woman who might have been its center, but who cannot play the role of supernumerary. People will say that the author wanders, and the author will not contradict this. The world, dear reader, is badly constructed in my opinion, as this book is in yours. Yes, both should be rebuilt, with Clara for a heroine, and not Diane or Catherine.[57]

Aragon has tried to describe what is wrong with the world by having the same things be wrong with his novel, a curious approach to fiction, one which at this stage in his career as a novelist we sense is involuntary.

Les cloches tends to deal with its heroines as types, although with Diane, and to a lesser extent with Catherine, Aragon successfully creates some density of character. However, when he comes to Clara, his admiration for what she represents completely overshadows his awareness of the needs of a novel, and he says, "She is simply, carried to a high degree of perfection, the new type of woman who has nothing in common with that doll whose subservience, prostitution and idleness have been the basis of songs and poems in all human societies, right down to our day." [58]

Les beaux quartiers is a successful novel, handling a multiplicity of characters in a unified narrative of consistent tone. The chief characters are the brothers Edmond and Armand Barbentane, the former a young medical student who attempts to climb in society

---

[57] *Les cloches de Bâle* (Paris: Denoël, 1934; reprinted in Livre de Poche, 1964), 424.   [58] *Ibid.*, 437.

by a series of advantageous love affairs, the latter a mother-dominated boy who breaks with his *petit bourgeois* milieu and runs away to Paris. Both of these characters reappear in the later novels *Aurélien* and *Les Communistes*, where the changing tide of events makes of Edmond a greedy self-satisfied capitalist and of Armand a factory laborer in the forefront of the syndicalist movement.

Les beaux quartiers is, in its earlier chapters, highly reminiscent of Stendhal's *Le rouge et le noir*. Sérianne-le-Vieux, the provincial town of Edmond's and Armand's birth, is described in the *ton du moraliste* which Stendhal adopts to introduce us to Verrières. After characterizing several of the town's important personages and the factions they represent, Aragon writes:

> But those are the small demonstrations of the striking personalities of Sérianne-le-Vieux. They would not be worth reporting, if they were not the reflection of the profound traits of a whole society, which marked the life of this society, even in those places where one would not expect to find them. For example, the way the Italians were generally treated in the town: if they were buying fruit, the fruit-seller always slipped them a rotten fig, spoiled plums, underneath. Right down to Dr. Lamberdesc who dawdled when he was called to their homes on an emergency. Let's leave them a little time to die.[59]

Aragon's Sérianne is much like Verrières, a place where the malaises of a society are best reflected and best characterized by a brief visual description followed by incisive sketches of the town's chief inhabitants. This type of social realism in the novel depends strongly upon the quality of *tone*, what Malraux has called "the written voice of the author," which conveys his attitude toward his subject matter. Although there is no direct authorial intrusion, the author is very much a part of his story: the world is seen through his eyes, and the significance of what he sees reaches the reader through his narrative technique. It is curious that Aragon, for this reason, has frequently been reproached for the lack of realism in his novels, while Stendhal is readily classified as "a realist." It would be more just to evaluate them in the same way, admitting that their type of loaded realism is an important tendency in the modern

---

[59] *Les beaux quartiers* (Paris: Denoël, 1936; reprinted in Livre de Poche, 1963), 30.

French novel, one which, while unsatisfactory to critics who prefer the novelist to be impassive in the Flaubertian tradition, is probably the more lasting trend.

In a drunken revel at *Le Panier Fleuri*, the local tavern and brothel, Aragon employs the unidentified spectator-narrator most successfully, conveying the atmosphere and actions of the principal characters in a scene filled with color, movement, and social commentary. His technique here closely parallels that of Joyce in the "Cyclops" chapter of *Ulysses*, and achieves much the same results: a satirical view of the characters at their defenseless worst, coupled with an insight into the significance of their actions for the overall meaning of the novel:

What a Sunday! The summer had outdone itself. Men, overcome, slept almost all day, despite their electoral duty. The white and powdery earth seemed to rise up into your throat. Evening was coming on, thick, full of smells. The insects in the field were singing so loudly that you could hear them in the town. The windows opened when the sun went down. . . . In the little cafés near the factory, the drinking had been serious. Music boxes were playing. The women at the fountain were gossiping, with bunches of kids trailing them. Smells of poor cuisine rose out of the houses, where infants were moaning. . . . Barbentane [father of the boys] elected! It had been official around seven-thirty. The victor appeared at the window of the city hall and spoke. There weren't many people to listen to him, but all the same. . . . "*Long live Barbentane!*" . . . "That one or another!" . . . Already the young men were beginning to head for the seat of the canton. Small carts were passing. You could hear singing a bit everywhere.[60]

This evocation of an election Sunday in the provinces is a masterful creation of atmosphere, sustained with the same lyric ease which has made Aragon an enduring poet. In such concrete views of people, places, and events sketched in simple language appealing strongly to the senses, he is able to fuse social realism with poetic vision. Similarly successful are his descriptions of the poor and downtrodden of Sérianne walking sullenly at the town fair; Armand wandering through the butchers' section of Les Halles in Paris; and the Fourteenth of July in Paris, a scene composed of snatches of dialogue, ironic glimpses of action, interspersed and

[60] *Ibid.*, 154–55.

fitted together in a total effect similar to the one Flaubert achieves in the agricultural fair scene of *Madame Bovary*.

Les beaux quartiers are those sections of Paris, the locale of the novel's second part, which symbolize the theme: the unreal way of life of those who accept the status quo unquestioningly.

> *Les beaux quartiers* . . . they're like an escape from a bad dream, in the black pleats of industry. . . . Here sleep great ambitions, higher thoughts, melancholies full of grace. These windows bathe in pure reveries, utopian meditations where goodness reigns. What idyllic images in these privileged heads, in the little salons of pink plush, where books decorate life. . . . In these decors of ease, people want so much for everything to be for the best in the best of worlds. . . . Existence is an opera in the old style, with its openings, its ensembles, its great arias, and the intoxication of violins.

Then Aragon evokes the frenzied night world of Paris, and concludes with the hours of quiet just before dawn. "The empty streets, where a car passes like a drunkard, seem with their endless streetlamps to be waiting for a traveling monarch who has changed his mind at the last moment. Dreams, dreams of stone: the statues with their white eyes dream over the squares." [61]

Aragon is far less adept in the psychological characterization of those characters who represent the future, such as Clara Zetkine in *Les cloches de Bâle*, than he is in that of members of the classes doomed by the inevitable march of social change, such as Edmond Barbentane. This flaw, barely visible in the richness of *Les beaux quartiers*, becomes an overriding fault in *Les Communistes*. One may speculate on the reason for this difference. The old order is after all the one into which Aragon was born and in which he spent his formative years; he knew the higher milieus well, while only dreaming of that utopian worker's society to come. Also, and probably of more importance, is the simple fact that creatures with flaws and vices make far better characters in novels than do men who are supposed to be perfect. The critical eye of the novelist can give life and density to the former; it can only adulate the latter. Aragon sees the upper classes as individuals, the working class as a *group*. Most of his faults of characterization stem from this differ-

[61] *Ibid.*, 190–91.

ence in initial conception. *Les beaux quartiers, Les voyageurs de l'impériale, Aurélien,* and *La semaine sainte* all deal with eras in the past, before the advent of the hoped-for millenium. They succeed as fiction, while the six-volume *Les Communistes* fails.

Aragon's class schema in *Les beaux quartiers* serves a psychological as well as thematic function. Carlotta, the beautiful young Italian girl from the poor quarter of Sérianne who becomes Edmond's mistress and helps him in his road to wealth by also becoming mistress to a rich industrialist, admits that her initial interest in Edmond was inspired by class, rather than sex. "You, you understand, were the forbidden," she says to Edmond, "the beautiful young people of the town . . . the revenge. . . . Oh! I wanted to have you right away. My lover, I said to myself . . . ." [62] While it is impossible to reduce all human motivations to class struggles (and Aragon seldom exercises such an oversimplification, except in *Les Communistes*), there is no doubt that class differences play an important role in human conduct. Aragon recognizes this fact and gives it flesh in his novel with considerable success.

While looking for work in Paris, Armand stands in a crowd which is listening to Jaurès speak. Aragon frequently uses this technique of confronting fictional characters with real historical figures in verifiable historical events. It is thoroughly integrated into the narrative in *Les beaux quartiers,* and adds significantly to the flavor of the novel. In *Les Communistes* the method is used so profusely that in many places it completely overwhelms the narrative and waters down its effectiveness as fiction. The finest example of historical realism is Aragon's masterpiece, *La semaine sainte,* where the varicolored backdrop of history is not merely an accessory to the fictional and ideological demonstration, but its very substance. Aragon uses history in still another fashion in *Les beaux quartiers*: he gives the present time of the narrative a historical future, by letting the reader know where all these events will lead, *after* the end of the novel. "In the Provençal accent there sang out something of the accent of Liebknecht, who will die like Juarès, assassinated." [63]

[62] *Ibid.,* 418. [63] *Ibid.,* 341.

One of the most effective chapters of *Les beaux quartiers* depicts the murder of the police inspector Colombin who is blackmailing the fiancée of Leroy, a minor functionary. The entire sequence is narrated in the third person by a nonexistent spectator who seems to see the events from Leroy's perspective, and who is able to supply information about the physical and psychological aspects of the murder which Leroy, in the intensity of his passion, would be quite incapable of expressing at the moment. The chapter begins, "Have you ever killed a man? It's much more complicated than you think. First of all, it defends itself. And then with a gun, for instance, I'm not talking about that. That doesn't count. It's cheating. But with your hands, with your arms, with your body." [64]

Aragon first gave a name to his novelistic cycle at the end of *Les beaux quartiers*. In the Postface, he wrote, "This book, which follows *Les cloches de Bâle*, is the second in a long testimony which I bear, from the origins of my life to this hour in the struggle when I do not feel myself separate from the millions of Frenchmen who demand *Bread, Peace, Liberty. . . .* I have to give these books a general title, and it will be in memory of the long struggle I have passed through, and of that work of dreams that I leave behind me, *Le Monde Réel.*" [65] Thus, in 1936, Aragon proclaimed definitively his rupture with his surrealistic youth, "that work of dreams," and announced his intended devotion to works of socialist realism.

Les voyageurs de l'impériale describes a period of twenty-five years around the turn of the century during which the hero, Pierre Mercadier, a teacher of history, leaves his wife and children in search of individual liberty, travels extensively, and finally returns to Paris to die, half-paralyzed, in the suburban cottage of a former madame who has fallen in love with and taken possession of him in his illness. As a story of a random existence which leads nowhere but to death, the novel is a total success. Its most effective passages deal with individual psychology, such as, for example, the flash-backs to Pierre's childhood with his grandmother, scenes of visual and sensory evocation at times worthy of Proust's account of Marcel's early years. Aragon has admitted that the evocations of

[64] *Ibid.*, 470.   [65] *Ibid.*, 499.

Pierre's childhood are largely based on his own; they do indeed have that ring of poetic nostalgia characteristic of most personal reminiscences.

Aragon analyzes with great subtlety the deteriorating relationship between Pierre and his wife, who is silly, self-centered, totally unable to understand any values or desires which are not material. He makes Pierre's decision to leave her totally comprehensible, while nevertheless showing how the abstract pursuit of individual "freedom" can destroy a man's life. Historical events of major importance such as the Dreyfus Affair take place in the background, while Pierre continues to chase the chimera of isolated fulfillment. In portraying Mme. Tavernier, the brothel-keeper, Aragon evokes the locus of her dreams, the *banlieue* of Paris where she has, with the profits of her business, secretly bought a typical cottage. His description of the *banlieue* is less scrofulous than Céline's, but no less haunting. In characteristic fashion, Aragon intervenes at several points to predict the future of some of his characters, notably the Roumanian sisters and their mother who live for a while at the *pension de famille* which Pierre's son Pascal runs in Paris in order to support his mother and sister.

The novel takes its title from Pierre's notes for an unfinished book on the Scottish economist, John Law. In them, he describes a ride across Paris on the top of *l'impériale*, a horse-drawn double-decker bus:

It was an evening when I felt anxious and sad, my head stuffed with the numbers on which my freedom depended, the current price of the stock market. . . . All of a sudden everything seemed strange to me, the cafés, the boulevards, the pharmacies. I began to look at my neighbors on the *impériale* not as companions by chance who would disperse at successive stations, but as the travelers mysteriously chosen to cross existence with me. I noticed that already, in a brief trip, bonds had formed between us, the smile of a woman, the fixed stare of a man, two old men who had engaged in conversation: a sketch of society. And I thought with a kind of horror that we were, we at that moment still strangers, equally threatened by a possible accident. So that what was going on down there, between the horses and the street, and of which we were not yet aware, risked creating between us a mortal solidarity, and an intimacy worse than the intimacy of love, that of a common grave. . . . I thought that this *impériale* was a good image of existence, or rather the whole bus. For there are two kinds of men in the world, those who like the people on the *impériale* are carried along without knowing anything about the machine they are on, and the others who understand the mechanism of the monster and who play at tinkering with it. . . . And never can the former understand anything about the latter, because from the *impériale* one can see only the cafés, the streetlamps and the stars . . . .[66]

Without laboring his point in obvious fashion, in the character of Pierre Mercadier Aragon convincingly demonstrates that a human existence without any clear social and political orientation is empty and futile. *Les voyageurs de l'impériale* ranks with *Les beaux quartiers* and *La semaine sainte* as one of Aragon's best novels. It has unity of structure and focus; it thoroughly integrates its social message into the substance of the fiction; it is highly poetic in its descriptions of places, events, and characters. The working-class section of Paris where Madame Tavernier's former brothel is located is described with haunting vividness in the setting of a sulfurous autumn afternoon. Madame Tavernier's suburban hideaway is evoked in all its touching ugliness, as she looms larger and larger at the end of the narrative. For it is Dora Tavernier, the ex-madame with a longing for a life-filling love, who ultimately becomes the symbol of *la belle époque* which is the novel's background. In her love for the dying and grotesque Pierre, she represents a foolish but touching idealism which died with the advent of World War One.

In this skeptical century where great feelings of the soul are passing away, there they all are, like picture postcards, painted in these eyes undone by an ignoble and fallen existence. Everything in which no one any longer believes in this year 1914 comes to rest in this mother pimp, who has crossed the sacred river, rediscovered the childhood of the heart. . . . There is not one of those great humbugs for which men refuse to die in this twentieth century which is at the ungrateful age of pouting cynicism, not one of those burst soap bubbles, which in this head gone adrift, doesn't retain the glow of lost paradises.[67]

Aurélien is the story of a wealthy young man who returns from military service in the First World War to find his life in Paris

[66] *Les voyageurs de l'impériale* (Paris: Gallimard, 1947; reprinted in Livre de Poche, 1964), 625–26.   [67] *Ibid.*, 673–74.

without direction and meaning. Asked after whom *Aurélien* was modeled, Aragon replied, "*Aurélien*, more than this or that man, is above all *a situation*, a man in a certain situation. He was before all else for me a veteran of a generation situated just after the armistice, in 1918, the man who has returned and who does not find his place again in the society he reenters." [68] He continued, "My characters . . . are indeed situations, but situations incarnated." [69] Aragon admits that he frequently uses his own experiences in his novels, but not in the *je* form. The experiences become those of another, different from himself. To some readers who speculated that *Aurélien* was a disguised portrait of Pierre Drieu La Rochelle, Aragon replied, "It is true that Aurélien was born out of me, and that he has some characteristics of Drieu . . . [but] Madame Bovary is neither Flaubert nor the wife of the pharmacist of Trouville." [70] He continues, "Decidedly, Aurélien is not Drieu, but a character in a novel. A real character in a novel does not permit that schematization of thought for which one would never reproach the man of flesh and blood." [71] In short, the novel is the mature fruit of the novelist's life. It includes his insights into himself and others, the telling experiences of his era, and the special moments of illumination which these insights create *at the very moment the novelist is setting them down*. Aragon calls these moments "poetry." "There is in a novel, suddenly, in the midst of daily reality, a phrase, a page, something like a window on what is not the novel, on what lies beyond it, on what in shorthand fashion we call *poetry*." [72] Aragon has consistently described the experience of writing a novel as a process of discovery, not simply a matter of technique, but "a way of thinking." He has undertaken his novels and his long poems as an enterprise of discovery.

Aurélien is a simply constructed novel, centering around a brief unconsummated love affair between the hero and Bérénice, a young married woman from the provinces who comes to visit relatives in Paris. (The relatives are Edmond Barbentane, of *Les beaux quartiers*, and his first wife.) Aurélien's inability to make a

---

[68] *Entretiens avec Francis Crémieux*, 48. [69] *Ibid.*, 49.
[70] *J'abats mon jeu*, 35. [71] *Ibid.*, 37.
[72] *Entretiens avec Francis Crémieux*, 125–26.

success of his relationship with Bérénice stems in part from his own lack of self-definition and in part from Bérénice's uncompromising desire for perfection in human beings. The epilogue jumps to a moment in 1940 when Aurélien, now married and in the army, stops with his troops in the small town in southern France where Bérénice lives. He finds her changed, devoted now to abstract social and political ideals, and their brief and difficult encounter, during which each finds that their idyll in the past was based on illusions, is terminated by Bérénice's death by stray German gunfire. The epilogue is the novel's weakest point. In his eagerness to develop the ultimate ramifications of the initial situation, Aragon sacrifices structural unity and stylistic continuity. The ending is hasty and peremptory, like the section of *Les cloches de Bâle* dealing with Clara Zetkine. Aurélien's evolution from an aimless young man to a responsible army officer is stated but not justified. Bérénice, youthful, capricious, vivid in the earlier parts of the novel, is here a wooden symbol of the "new woman" trying to be born, and incomprehensible to the reader.

The novel's chief merits are its vivid reconstructions of Paris in the twenties: the Surrealist milieu, the art show of a Futurist painter, the aimless and joyless life of the cabarets; and its evocations of Paris and the Seine, seen from the window of Aurélien's apartment on the Île Saint-Louis. Aragon's poetic gift spins out passages of powerful mood and atmosphere:

There are all kinds of grays. There's the gray full of pink which is a reflection of the two Trianons. There's the blue gray which is a nostalgia of the sky. The beige gray color of the earth after the narrow. The gray which marble wears from white to black. But there's a dirty gray, a terrible gray, a yellow gray verging on green, a grey like pitch, an opaque coating, stifling, even if light-colored, a destiny gray, an unforgiving gray, the gray which brings the sky down to earth, that gray which is the palisade of winter, the mud of clouds before the snow, that gray which makes you despair of ever seeing good days, never and nowhere as despairing as in Paris, above this luxurious landscape, which it flattens under its feet, tiny, tiny, like the vast and empty wall of an implacable sky, on a Sunday morning in December above the Avenue du Bois . . . .[73]

[73] *Aurélien* (Paris: Gallimard, 1944), 66.

The most memorable descriptive passages in *Aurélien* achieve a striking fusion of visual detail with psychological analysis, as when Aurélien sees his apartment on the Île Saint-Louis as an image of his life, a boat in the two arms of the river, adrift and aimless. Aragon's sensitivity to the moods of Paris, so well evoked in his poetry, forms in the novel a kind of unifying musical theme. In many ways, *Aurélien* is the least socially realistic of his fictional works. The tone of poetic reminiscence, the moments of high comedy as Surrealist parties are described (and comedy is indeed rare in Aragon's fiction) take precedence over the sense of men in a historical era of which they are products and playthings. The love affair is treated at great length, and rarely appears to be a demonstration of social change, as is the case with emotional relationships in the other novels.

Les Communistes, covering the period from February, 1939, to June, 1940, is the only contemporary novel of "Le Monde Réel" series. Aragon writes that it is "strongly autobiographical, despite transpositions, transferrals to other characters of episodes in my own life, notably my military life in 1939 through 1940." [74] Aragon attempted to write "scientifically" the history of the war of 1940, the *drôle de guerre* in which the French were apparently mobilized in order to prepare for possible German invasion. From Aragon's point of view, this mobilization was aimed at destroying the cohesion of the Communist movement and supplying an excuse for its suppression. He brings into play a huge cast of characters, from all milieus, Parisian and provincial, and shows how the events of 1939 and 1940 affected these characters and in turn were shaped by them.

Many characters from the earlier novels reappear, playing their appointed roles, as militant Communists, traitors, industrialists, opportunists, etc. The chief action centers around the efforts of the Communist wives of the title, those left behind who try clandestinely to continue the dispersion of information and propaganda, at great personal risk to themselves. Key historical moments, such as the declaration by the French National Assembly of the illegal-

----

[74] *J'abats mon jeu,* 149.

ity of the Communist Party, are witnessed by characters in the novel. The novel's most vivid and convincing moments are those dealing with the stupid military preparedness undertakings which ultimately left France totally unprepared for the German invasion. Much space is devoted to rationalizing the shift in Communist loyalty, from pro-German during the period of the Russo-German pact, to anti-German after the pact was broken. Each of these positions is seen as innately patriotic and pro-French, in straight party-line fashion, and Aragon views Communist leaders such as Maurice Thorez, who deserted the French army, as patriots of the highest order.

From its subject matter, it is easy to see why the novel was not a critical success. More important for our purposes, however, are its serious artistic flaws. It lacks unity, characterization, and even poetic insight. As Catharine Savage has aptly pointed out, the novel "is essentially a *roman à thèse*, an apology." [75] It sacrifices artistic value to utilitarian and ideological value, and given its particular bias, the novel was never destined to have a very wide audience. However, Mrs. Savage unjustly generalizes from *Les Communistes* to *all* of Aragon's novels, and then compares him unfavorably with Sartre as the novelist of "Les chemins de la liberté." With the possible exception of *La nausée*, Sartre has never written a novel of the power, scope, and beauty of *Les beaux quartiers* or *La semaine sainte*. It is also true, unfortunately, that almost no one has written a novel worse than *Les Communistes*.

The autobiographical germ present in most of Aragon's novels assumes a large role in *Les Communistes*. As he confessed, "Here the author exerts himself fully, he is in no way effaced, even if he does not say *je*, he speaks only of what he has seen or could have seen, what he has verified, touched, inspected first hand. He is the Saint Thomas of our era, he has put his hand into the very

---

[75] Catharine Savage, *Malraux, Sartre and Aragon as Political Novelists*, University of Florida Monographs, Humanities, No. 17 (Gainesville: University of Florida Press, 1964), 43. There is at present only one book-length study in French of Aragon as a novelist: Pierre de Lescure, *Aragon romancier* (Paris: Gallimard, 1960). Lescure finds a single key to all of Aragon's fiction in "the love of a woman." The study contributes little to any appreciation of Aragon's development as a novelist.

wound." [76] And defending himself against the accusation that, as a Communist, he is incapable of portraying non-Communist characters fairly, Aragon invokes the function of the realistic novel as he understands it: "The polemics of the realistic novel lies in its general interpretation of the era, and not in the distortion of particular images." [77] He goes so far as to claim that it took more objectivity to write *Les Communistes* than *La semaine sainte*. Aragon is suggesting that the effort involved in creating a piece of fiction is proportional to the distance necessary to gain a vantage point on it. In writing of his own time, Aragon was obliged to force this distance; in creating a novel set in the nineteenth century, the distance preexisted. *Les Communistes* lacks that sense of internal necessity which we expect of realistic fiction. He seems to have had much less success *rendering real* an era which was intimately his own.

Aragon defines socialist realism as "a new realism, which shows both the trees and the forest, and knows why it shows them, an active realism, as far away as possible from art for art's sake, a realism which aims to aid man, to enlighten him on his way, which takes account of the direction of his way, which goes ahead of him." [78] In this statement, we find what is perhaps the essential reason for the failure of *Les Communistes* and the striking success of *La semaine sainte*. In order for socialist realism to "go ahead of man," it must have a clear foreknowledge of man's direction. The dialectic of history has already revealed itself with respect to the events of 1815. At the time of writing *Les Communistes*, Aragon could scarcely move from polemics to prophecy, close as he still was to the ramifications of the events of 1940. He acknowledged the significance of the large view when he wrote, "Socialist realism is the organic conception of *facts* in literature, of the detail in art—it interprets this detail, gives it meaning and force, integrates it into the movement of humanity, beyond the individualism of writers." [79]

In his sincere concern with human and historical values Aragon is closer to the stance of Albert Camus than to any other writer

---

[76] *J'abats mon jeu*, 154.   [77] *Ibid.*, 155.   [78] *Ibid.*, 165.
[79] *Ibid.*, 173.

treated here, with the possible exception of André Malraux. However, both Aragon and Camus deplored contemporary writers who,
in their commitment to enduring values, tended to ignore the here
and now. Beneath Malraux's contemporaneity, in the subject matter of his novels lies an Olympian detachment which gives the
novels their abstract, artistic appeal and their author the stance of a
shaman. Aragon naturally disliked Camus much less than he did
Malraux, but he nevertheless found occasion to criticize him. A few
months after Camus accepted the Nobel Prize for Literature in
Stockholm, Aragon received the Lenin Peace Prize in Moscow
(April, 1959). In his acceptance speech he noted the differences
between himself and Camus. Camus, he said, confessed to an
appreciation of art for art's sake; his ultimate hope for mankind lay
in *les solitaires,* in concerned and responsible *individuals* rather
than in man in the general sense; he was firmly anti-Communist;
and he frequently invoked and defended the W*estern* heritage. In
short, Camus was a moralist in the humanistic tradition, while
Aragon saw himself as a historian and prophet of the future of
socialist realism. In this role Aragon has succeeded in creating
novels of a scope and power perhaps more lasting than the small
perfect gems of an ironic classical style for which Camus has been
much adulated in our time.

La semaine sainte, published in 1958 and very well received
critically, is the most ambitious and probably the most successful
of Aragon's novels in an artistic sense. Because of the novel's
historical setting, the week initiating Napoleon's brief return to
power in 1815, anti-Communist critics found it possible to praise it
without reservations. Classifying this vast panorama of France as a
"historical novel"—with at its center the monarchist officers who
accompanied Louis XVIII on his flight from Paris—these cautious
readers could admire Aragon's technical skill and imaginative scope
without concerning themselves with his political presuppositions.
The principal hero of the novel, the painter Théodore Géricault,
who in the course of his days as a military member of the royal
escort undergoes a development of political and historical consciousness, seemed to them simply a personage out of history
re-created in fiction. However, Aragon had warned them against

such a misinterpretation in the novel's brief prefatory notice: "This is not a historical novel. Any resemblance to persons who lived, any similarity of names, of places, of details, is only the result of pure coincidence, and the author declines responsibility for them in the name of the imprescriptible rights of the imagination." [80]

La semaine sainte is the logical successor to Aragon's earlier novels, the ultimate fusion of his dual concern with autobiography and historical dialectic. "All my novels, from *Les cloches de Bâle*, written in 1933–34, to *La semaine sainte*, written from 1955 to 1958, passing through *Les Communistes* (1940–50), spring from the same method . . . *socialist realism*, that is to say the realism of our time which takes account of the historical perspective with respect to the future or the present . . . ." [81] Aragon has stated clearly that he does not believe one can illuminate the history of the past by that of the present; on the contrary, "I find it normal to use the past . . . in order to illuminate the present; that is called experience, and science has demonstrated the value of experience." [82] *La semaine sainte* is a novel which *uses* elements from history in order to demonstrate something about the present. It resembles Tolstoy's *War and Peace*, with its multiplicity of characters and its roots in determined facts. However, where Tolstoy sought to demonstrate the superior role of Russia in the unfolding of historical inevitability, Aragon's purpose was somewhat different. While also showing the seeds of the present in the events of the past, Aragon was less concerned with proving the *rightness* of his country's role in history than with undermining any assurances that France in his own time had reached the inevitable goal implied by the progress of mankind. *La semaine sainte* serves less as a background to and reason for France in the mid-twentieth century than as a key with which to decode present ills in order ultimately to eliminate them. It is concerned with explanation rather than with predication, and for this reason, Aragon is able again and again to insist that it is *not* a historical novel.

Aware, however, that the common usage of the term evidently applies to *La semaine sainte*, Aragon tries to justify his seemingly

[80] *La semaine sainte* (Paris: Gallimard, 1958), [7].
[81] *J'abats mon jeu*, 79–80.   [82] *Ibid.*, 81.

arbitrary refusal of the term by referring us to his earlier novels: "All my novels—except for *Anicet*, and even then!—are historical, although they are not *in costume*. *La semaine sainte*, contrary to appearance, is *less* a historical novel." [83] The traditional historical novel places imaginary characters in real situations. In *La semaine sainte* Aragon gave *imaginary* traits to characters with *historical* names. He explains the procedure in the following way: "The novel here is born out of the confrontation of these men in movement and of people they had not met up to that moment, people who will be eternally lost to their sight in a few hours. . . . Linear, superficial history does not suffice to give that depth which we call the novel. Here it was necessary to invent, to create, that is to say to lie. The art of the novel is to know how to lie." [84] The central conflict of the novel resides not in Géricault's eventual decision to leave the forces of Louis XVIII, but in his nascent realization that neither Louis nor Napoleon has anything to offer the *people* of France, the people represented by the many minor characters he meets briefly along his way. Géricault's "answer" is actually a question: what can I do with my life in order to give more meaning to the lives of others? We know the answer to the question from history, from the fact that the young character of the novel went on to become a great Romantic painter. But the answer is not the aim of the novel, and it is not included within its pages. The novel's central conflict is designed as a paradigm for the present, and is endowed with meaning only in the light of the present.

La semaine sainte* achieves its peculiar prophetic and critical force with the *reader's* collaboration, from the fact that he supplies the greater part of the historical dimension stretching into the present, a dimension which bestows ultimate significance upon the casual events which are the substance of the novel. Aragon calls this process *stereoscopy*, which he defines as a fictional technique "where one seeks not merely to give the third, physical dimension, spatial depth, but also a kind of depth which is mental; I imagine two images of the same man, two images whose contours coincide, no doubt, but which were acting *in time*, in the depths of this man's life." [85] The two images are of course the one built up in the

[83] *Ibid.*, 88.   [84] *Ibid.*, 48.   [85] *Ibid.*, 49.

novel and the one we have, from our perspective in the present, of what the man was to become later on. But Aragon's Géricault is not the historical figure of the painter; he is the imaginative creation suggested by the possibilities latent in the dimness of the historical figure. Aragon points out that he added imagined characters to the ranks of real ones, changed the time sequence, played with historical personages. On a character he completely altered, he writes, "And thus, starting with a pure and simple invention, dressed up with reality after the fact, I made arise in my novel a character who was born out of the necessities of the novel itself, from the first lie at Beauvais, and who had taken on substance, shaping the hand of history just as he compelled the hand of the novelist." [86] Aragon would have us believe that historical necessity works itself out not only in the flow of real events, but in the sequence of events which *is history* within a novel. We recognize here a common tendency on the part of novelists to create characters and situations demanded by the internal necessities of their fiction. But Aragon ascribes this phenomenon to the working of history, rather than fiction, and in this departure from established terminology in connection with the novel, he once again reveals the special angle of vision which sets him apart from his non-Communist contemporaries. The practical results in a novel may indeed be the same, in terms of fictional technique, but the motivating force appears to be different.

Aragon admits that the stereoscopic device, which gives *relief* to his novel by means of added time and space, was not invented by him. "But," he suggests, "perhaps no one, before *La semaine sainte*, had applied it so knowledgeably, so consciously, I venture to say *so cynically*." [87] The wry tone of this statement reveals Aragon's awareness of the possible objections to a consistent use of extranovelistic dimensions for purely fictional aims. He apparently has hedged against such objections in his re-creation of setting, a re-creation which is minute, almost obsessively accurate, reminding one of Flaubert's archeological and historical minutiae in *Salammbô*. Why this attention to the verisimilitude of place alongside almost

[86] *Ibid.*, 51.   [87] *Ibid.*, 57.

entirely imaginative characters? Aragon's answer may well be the
answer in most cases where this apparent contradiction occurs:
"Why did I provide this minuteness in the decor, why this need to
render it as it actually was, when I played the novelist with the
characters? The décor is verifiable, one must not lie. . . . By the
exactitude of the décor the novelist makes credible the human
verity of his characters, *he makes a success of his lies.*" [88] *La semaine sainte*, therefore, is not a historical novel, "but an impudent
exploitation of history, which I have used as a stepping stone to
fiction, a passport to the novel." [89] The success of Aragon's artistic
fraud has vindicated his method. *La semaine sainte* is a novel about
the present, and not essentially historical in the usual sense. That
critics frequently praised it for the wrong reasons was less significant than that they found themselves able to praise it at all, given
their political viewpoints and their long-standing animosity toward
Aragon as a novelist. Perhaps Aragon misnamed *La semaine sainte*'s
major merit when he called it a lie. If *La semaine sainte* succeeds
where *Les Communistes* fails radically, it is because in the former
fiction has rightly taken the upper hand over history, as it should in
a novel. Beneath the cloak of verity Aragon has deployed all his
dialectical fervor and stated in concrete images his long-standing
predications—*La semaine sainte* is a major novel because ideology
has shaped fiction rather than destroyed it.

In the process of his role as law-giver in literary matters to a
faithful audience which reads the Communist newspapers in
France, Aragon has formulated a critical code which is surprisingly
tolerant and refreshingly unsophisticated. He has always been more
prone to praising what he likes than to condemning works which do
not meet the criteria of socialist realism. "For my part," he writes,
"I think that . . . a true critic is he who teaches *to love* . . . ." [90]
He is able to appreciate works which describe "a particular era of
men," like *La fin de chéri*, or those which describe a particular
man, like *Adolphe* or *À rebours*, because "a man is always the man
of a particular era." [91]

[88] *Ibid.*, 65–67.   [89] *Ibid.*, 69.   [90] *Ibid.*, 107.   [91] *Ibid.*, 122.

Aragon firmly believes that *the story* is the real backbone of fiction, even if disguised, and in this connection, he notes that while the theory of the "new novel" in France contradicts this, the actual practice does not. Discussing what is new in the novel in an article in *Les Lettres Françaises* (November, 1958), Aragon notes "this kind of extreme dispersion and this anecdotal accumulation where the author and his heroes become fused" as a hallmark of the new fiction.[92] The instances he cites are Michel Zéraffa's *Les doublures* and Claude Simon's *Le vent* and *L'herbe*. "Accumulation" manifests itself in diverse ways, by "a complex cinematographic montage" in Zéraffa, in "nature and the very matter of prose" in Simon. In these novelists and others, Aragon discerns the future direction of the novel for the twentieth century. "The novel will become no longer the affair of a few men . . . but a kind of gigantic enterprise comparable to science . . . a striking fact of the modern novel is the entry of research into the novel, up to now confined to a Balzacian *conte philosophique*."[93]

The individual experiments of Robbe-Grillet, for example, are for Aragon part of a larger work—an immense cathedral of the novel being built in this century by many unrelated artisans. The final product of this combined labor, "of descriptive details whose juxtaposition will give this century its *Summa*, will allow this century to survive in a manner heretofore unknown, just as the phonograph keeps singers from dying completely, as the cinema perpetuates actors, as photographs capture daily life."[94] Aragon states without qualification that we are in a great prose era. He believes that men are writing better, that the stream from Rabelais, Montaigne, and Saint-Simon is moving into men like Michel Butor, in whom we see the dual Apollinairian wager of tradition and adventure. Aragon himself has never stopped writing poetry, but he continues to create novels at the same time.

His own novel, *La mise à mort* (1965), is a curious melange of that "extreme dispersion" and "anecdotal accumulation" which he finds in the "new novels" he admires. The account of Anthoine, a man who has lost his image and who speaks in many voices—at times that of the author, at others as a certain Alfred—

[92] *Ibid.*, 20.   [93] *Ibid.*, 20–21.   [94] *Ibid.*

the novel appears to be an imaginative treatment of the traditional novel about a novelist. The real world serves as a phenomenological backdrop to personal questions on the meaning of creativity, of old age, and of death. *La mise à mort* represents a distinct break with the novel of socialist realism in its technique, if not in its essential content. A long step beyond the banal polemics of *Les Communistes*, it lacks the ideological and imaginative unity of *La semaine sainte*.

Aragon's most recent novel, *Blanche ou l'oubli* (1967), is in many respects one of his most interesting, if not his most successful, works of fiction. The central narrator, Geoffroy Gaiffier, is a linguist by profession. He wishes, in this moment in the present (late 1965 and early 1966) to understand the reasons why his wife Blanche deserted him some eighteen years ago, and undertakes to write a novel about Marie-Noire, a young woman of the contemporary generation, in order to penetrate the depths of feminine psychology which may provide the answer to his question. Gaiffier is the same age as Aragon and has read many of the same books, but is not a *persona* of the author. As Aragon points out in his introductory remarks on the book's cover, Gaiffier smokes (Aragon gave up smoking in 1921), is a linguist by profession, spent several years in Java, and he is *not* a Communist.

Gaiffier's central premise in undertaking to write his novel is in many ways similar to Aragon's own in *La semaine sainte*, namely, that the novel can be a means of shedding light on life itself, that the novel is *not* a form of history. "The novel," Aragon writes, "is not that which was but that which might be, that which might have been. The *reading* of a novel throws light on life." [95] Gaiffier's profession as a linguist allows Aragon to play, with obvious pleasure, with the problems of words, translations, meanings, and lack of meanings. The central *aperçu* of the book concerns the problem of *l'oubli* (forgetting, forgetfulness). Aragon explains,

The novel is a language where words say more, less, something other than the fixed meanings given in dictionaries. . . . The changes in the meaning of words always presuppose a *forgetting*, that of their original meaning. The novel is the intermediary moment when the word,

[95] *Blanche ou l'oubli* (Paris: Gallimard, 1967), cover remarks.

emptied of its first meaning, is open to the new meaning, but not yet occupied by it: this moment is the reign of availability; everything can still happen this way or that way. Until the time when a kind of hermit crab takes over the empty shell—then the new meaning makes us forget even the forgetting itself.[96]

Strange things happen in the course of Gaiffier's experiment with fiction. Marie-Noire begins to assume a reality of her own and steps out of the tale Gaiffier is constructing. She speaks to her author, contradicts him, at times begins to *narrate him*. She tries to understand Blanche and to invent a fiction which will make this woman of an earlier generation alive to her. Marie-Noire even begins to become a novelist-in-the-making, just as Blanche was at the time when she apparently first thought of leaving her husband. Woven into the various narrations are several literary works, Flaubert's *Education sentimentale*, Hölderlin's *Hyperion*, and novels by Elsa Triolet. These become paradigms of the process of "forgetting," which is also by extension the process of understanding. To further complicate the narrational technique, Aragon himself frequently steps in and comments on Gaiffier, Marie-Noire, and the literary parallels in his own voice.

The multiple points of view and their network of meanings surpass in complexity the hall of mirrors Gide created in *Les faux-monnayeurs*. *Blanche ou l'oubli* is a novel about the novel, a long poem about the poetry of language, a nest of tales related to one another by the polarity between memory and anticipation. The thesis of *La semaine sainte* is that the past can shed light on the present. In *Blanche* Aragon suggests the converse: that the present can illuminate the past. *L'oubli* is time; it is also the modifications time effects upon our understanding of events and of our relation to events. In the constant shifting between the 1920's and 1960's, Aragon has the opportunity to deploy a prose poetry of things absent from his fiction since *Anicet, ou le panorama*. Ultimately, Gaiffier is unable to evoke Blanche; he can only remember what he *understood* about her, which was in fact very little. He realizes that he cannot rescue Blanche from *l'oubli*; he also becomes aware that he is himself "only that which Blanche has definitively forgotten."

[96] *Ibid.*

The novel is thus "a lie undertaken in order to understand life in its particularity." [97]

As a work of fiction, *Blanche ou l'oubli* is marred precisely by that quality which makes it intellectually and poetically most striking, Aragon's encyclopedic memory. It is, as Robert Kanters pointed out, a novel about forgetting by a man who seems to remember everything.[98] It is above all a further indication of Aragon's continuing development, evidence that France's major Communist writer has not been content to apply endlessly the formulas which have succeeded for him in the past.

In the ambiguity of *Blanche ou l'oubli* we see Aragon reaching for a new dimension in his own fiction, attempting to add another stone to that immense cathedral of the novel he feels is being built in this century. "Ambiguity of expression," he remarked, "does not necessarily mean ambiguity of thought. I maintain, on the contrary, that ambiguity is a richer way of expressing the thing to be said." [99] It would appear that Aragon's innate artistic honesty has led him to abandon the frequently stifling confines of the theory of socialist realism. Or perhaps the richness of his imagination has so thoroughly transmuted the theory that Aragon, himself an example of the dialectic which shapes men and events, is now working on the frontiers of the novel.

[97] *Ibid.*, 350, 363.
[98] Robert Kanters, "Arlequin de mémoire," *Le Figaro Littéraire* (September 18–24, 1967), 19–20.
[99] *Entretiens avec Francis Crémieux*, 156.

André Malraux

ACTIVIST
AND AESTHETE

André Malraux is one of the most colorful literary figures of the twentieth century. With the publication in 1967 of the first volume of his *Antimémoires* he has once again demonstrated the alternation between action and art which has characterized his entire career. His last novel, *Les noyers de l'Altenburg*, appeared in 1943. Since that time he has published extensive poetic interpretations of world art: *Saturne*, an essay on Goya (1950); *Les voix du silence* (1952); *Le musée imaginaire de la sculpture mondiale* (1952–54); and *La métamorphose des dieux* (1957). He has also been Minister of State for Cultural Affairs in the De Gaulle government since 1958.

Malraux's biography remains difficult to reconstruct because of his habit of obscuring his past by blending fact and fiction into an indissoluble fabric. His life as we know it is as striking as his novels, an amalgam of verifiable historical situations and colorful myths of action.[1] Born in 1901, he was involved in marginal literary activities

---

[1] The best sources of information on Malraux's life are W. M. Frohock, *André Malraux and the Tragic Imagination* (Stanford: Stanford University Press, 1952), and Walter G. Langlois, *André Malraux, The Indochina Adventure* (New York: Frederick A. Praeger, 1966). Frohock reconstructs the "legend" of Malraux's life with considerable attention to those details which remain, as he admits, totally unverifiable. Langlois unravels the critical two-year sojourn in Indochina (1923–24), demonstrating the possibility and the difficulties of finding the real facts by extensive research. I look

in Paris in the 1920's, having already absorbed a wide knowledge of art, archaeology, and anthropology.[2] In 1923 he undertook a trip to Indochina in order to bring back some Khmer sculpture. He found the sculpture, but fell afoul of the French colonial authorities and was briefly imprisoned. In the years 1923–24 he engaged for the first time in political action with the nascent independence movement in Indochina; there he was co-editor of a short-lived newspaper of protesting opinion. He apparently also became interested in the troubled political situation in Canton and Shanghai. In 1928 he published his first novel, *Les conquérants*; this work involved him in 1931 in a brief debate with Léon Trotsky concerning the foundations of revolutionary action. He worked as an editor for the publishing house of Gallimard in Paris; he also made trips to Japan, Afghanistan and Persia during the early thirties. For his second major novel, *La condition humaine*, he won the Prix Goncourt in 1933. A year later he attempted to find the lost country of the queen of Sheba in an air expedition. Like many young French intellectuals during the thirties, Malraux became preoccupied with the rise of fascism and the emergence of Hitler Germany. He was sympathetic to the Communists, although apparently he never joined their ranks. When the Spanish Civil War broke out, he joined the Republican forces and flew several missions, during one of which he was wounded. By 1939, he became disillusioned with the Communist approach to movements of national independence and began to turn his energies in the direction of French national loyalties.

During the Second World War, Malraux was active in combat, first as a private in the tank corps at the war's beginning, later as a

---

forward to Langlois' future volumes on Malraux for the continuation of his unraveling of the legend. Also of interest are the first two volumes of Clara Malraux's autobiography: *Apprendre à vivre* (Paris: Grasset, 1963), *Nos vingt ans* (Paris: Grasset, 1966). As Malraux's first wife, Mme. Malraux noted quite early Malraux's tendency to obscure the facts of his early life and his ability "to invent a past" for himself in accordance with his imagination.

[2] For an account of Marlaux's earliest literary efforts, see André Vandegans, *La jeunesse littéraire d'André Malraux, Essai sur l'inspiration farfelu* (Paris: Jean-Jacques Pauvert, 1964).

leader of the Resistance forces under the name of Colonel Berger. His present close association with De Gaulle apparently dates from meetings during the final year of the war. When De Gaulle failed to come to power in the late forties, Malraux retired from active political life for some years, devoting himself to the writing of his art histories. When the Algerian revolt returned De Gaulle to power in 1958, Malraux resumed once again the life of action which he continues to this day. His ministry has attempted to put into practice his personal theories on French culture. His position has provided him with countless opportunities for travel and for the continuation of his restless search for answers to questions present in his writings for over forty years.

Malraux is a curious illustration of the relationship between literature and responsibility. On the one hand, of all the novelists treated in this study, he has most successfully confronted the problem of engagement in all its forms. He has participated actively in events most characteristic of the emerging political and social movements of our era. On the other hand, his conception of the *role* of literature in the life of men does not support an interpretation of his work as engaged literature. Unlike Sartre and Beauvoir, he has never written novels which illustrate a consistent theory of political and social engagement, nor has he elaborated, in his critical and theoretical writings, a definition of art as a mode of coping with quotidian reality. Malraux's novels do not even describe these problems, much less prescribe solutions. They *use* the events of his life and his time to elaborate a view which is essentially personal, poetic, a view he has himself called tragic humanism.

The ultimate touchstone for Malraux's historical world is his aesthetic one. In his aesthetic world all values are in ultimate relation not to Man, History, Progress, or any of the abstractions which usually inform theories of engaged art. As the *Antimémoires* once again demonstrates, Malraux's world is a timeless realm which depends not on a broad spectrum of humanistic values but on an elitist and limited group of men. For him, culture, history, life are formed and endowed with value by a few, those artists, creators, and heroes who are the legislators of history and the cornerstones of culture in all times and in all societies. The *Antimémoires* once again presents us with the paradox of Malraux intact. He is present as a voice, a sound, an angle of vision on the eternal themes which obsess him—death, the human condition, the universal realm of art, religion as the illustration of man's own divinity. The *Antimémoires* is the product of a unique imagination, as impersonal as a museum, as historically uninformative as a work of poetry, another facet of the legend of a life of action and of art.

Malraux's present position as Minister of Culture in the De Gaulle government is itself an interesting instance of the polarities of his life. Attempting to put into practice his conviction that experience of world art and of the French national cultural heritage can bring to the people of France a consciousness of their grandeur and a defense against absurdity, Minister Malraux has organized many reforms on the French cultural scene. He has planned and directed the cleaning of national monuments. He has revived the dusty repertoire and refurbished the productions of the national theater. He has begun a serious movement to improve the national symphonies and has fostered the proliferation of Maisons de Culture in the provincial cities. All the while he has continued to travel and speak in behalf of the De Gaulle government in many parts of the world. His speeches have stressed his dream (and De Gaulle's) of making France the symbol of non-Communist cultural and political strength in the world. His efforts in this domain are probably doomed to failure. But his obvious commitment to a notion of "destiny" with France and De Gaulle at the center reflects once again his preoccupation with the "heroes of history" and their duty to foster self-determination in underdeveloped areas through elitist leadership. He wants to make France rather than Russia or the United States the model for the emerging nations.

It is curious to find Malraux's recent political role interpreted as that of the "liberal hero." [3] The attractiveness of the man and the power of his literary creations frequently blind commentators to an

---

[3] In *Malraux, An essay in political criticism* (Cambridge: Harvard University Press, 1967) David Wilkinson attempts to interpret Malraux as the incarnation of "the liberal hero," a view colored too strongly (as is often the case with interpreters of Malraux) by the fiction rather than the facts.

aspect of his life and character which is more reminiscent of fascist theory and ideals than of anything resembling democratic values.[4] Malraux's own description of his official speeches in French Guiana leaves little doubt of the demagogic character of his present role or the elitist emphasis of his way of conceiving world politics.[5] He has become a figure in his own mythology, a *mythomane* out of his own novels and essays.

A careful analysis of Malraux's theory of literature and his conception of the artist's role reveals that his present position is consistent with his past ideals. The historical-aesthetic meditation on "man's fate" remains as always at the center of his thought. This dream unifies the pied and exciting career into that of a brilliant adventurer in the realms of action and of art.

Malraux's theory of literature, scattered through various prefaces, reviews, lectures, and interviews, is based on a conception of the novel as a mode of questioning. "One of the most profound currents of the Western novel," he writes, "is the questioning of destiny. . . . Indirect, implicit . . . [it] tends toward poetry rather than toward philosophy. . . . This is the echo which gives certain contemporary novels the grave accent of primitive poems, each time we see pass in them the eternal drift of the consciousness of men above the menace of history . . . ."[6] The fundamental dignity of art and of all human thought lies in their attempt to "accuse," to state ambiguously and yet with hope the fundamental fact that man's life and condition are rationally unjustifiable. Hence Malraux has consistently emphasized the poetic nature of literature, based on a conception of poetry as "every confrontation of the ephemeral and what we want to be eternal."[7]

The poetry of the novel lies not in its style, which is for Malraux an accessory, but in its fundamental conception. "If the novel becomes the successor . . . of the tragic poem," Malraux comments, "it is not through its words . . . nor through its ideas. It is

---

[4] A sympathetic evaluation of Malraux's recent political activities can be found in Charles D. Blend, *André Malraux, Tragic Humanist* (Columbus: Ohio State University Press, 1963).

[5] See *Antimémoires* (Paris: Gallimard, 1967), 161–85.

[6] Preface to Manès Sperber, *Qu'une larme dans l'océan* (Paris: Calmann-Lévy, 1952), xx.   [7] *Ibid.*

apparently by means of a confrontation, through the facts, of man and the universe . . . ." [8] For him this confrontation informs the genius of Aeschylus as well as that of Shakespeare; it lies at the heart of all significant art forms, plastic as well as literary. The confrontation is occasioned by one overriding question, the meaning of man's death. "Whoever seeks the *raison d'être* of human destinies cannot help being obsessed by suffering; he cannot help observing a great number of futile and lamentable lives, worthless even for those who know they are attached to life only by cowardice; . . . [they experience] in powerful and profound fashion the absolute reality of death." [9] In textual comments to Gaetan Picon's volume on him, Malraux takes issue with Heidegger's conception of man as "a being for death." "What if," he notes, "instead of 'for' we said 'against' "? [10]

The novelist at his highest is a man obsessed by a particular view of the world; he is a person in the service of a creation. Malraux's view of the writer's relation to his subject matter does not allow for the kind of deliberate impassive approach which has been a major trend in Western fiction since Flaubert and Joyce after him. The novelist does not write, Malraux insists, simply in order to express himself or to put into practice a literary theory or an intellectual speculation. "If, as some maintain, the novelist created in order to express himself, it would be quite simple. But . . . I believe that he expresses himself in order to create, like every artist. . . . As important as the *theories* of Dostoyevsky or the less profound ones of Balzac may be, in the final analysis they become simply means of creation. The image I try to achieve . . . is a trap in which I seize elements of the reality I need to express my universe . . . ." [11]

A writer's elaboration of his universe comprises two phases: the passion and the creation. And once the work of art has been made into an object, then still another passion and creation cycle comes into being, one carried out by the spectator. For Malraux the work

---

[8] *Ibid.*

[9] "*Où le coeur se partage,* par Marcel Arland," *Nouvelle revue française,* XXX (Feb. 1, 1928), 251.

[10] Cited in Gaetan Picon, *Malraux par lui-même* (Paris: Editions du Seuil, 1956), 74.   [11] *Ibid.,* 58.

of art requires creative appreciators, spectators through whom the individual obsession of the artist can once again live. Almost thirty years before the publication of *Les voix du silence*, Malraux said, "Until that time . . . [the work] will remain like a huge statue with blind eyes before which pass a cortege of blind men. . . . A work of art is an object, but it is also an encounter with time. . . ."[12] The *life* of the work of art has always concerned him deeply. He believes that for the work to be resuscitated an intelligent and cultured audience is necessary. His present activities in the political-cultural domain are the active expression of this long-standing preoccupation. The Maisons de Culture are designed to nurture future creative spectators.

The individual work of art is born out of a passion which is entirely personal. Malraux denies that "creating characters" is of any importance to the novelist. Rather, "he must create a coherent and particular world, like all artists. Not to rival the status quo, but to rival that reality which is imposed on him by 'life' . . . ."[13] Malraux frequently illustrates his conception of the novel as the expression of an author's obsessions by citing Georges Bernanos. Of Bernanos he wrote in 1928, "He lives in a particular world created by him. Sometimes he succeeds in making us believe in the existence of this world, in imposing it on us in an absolute way. . . . His essential gift . . . is intensity."[14] By combining intensity of vision with what Malraux calls "simplicity," Bernanos succeeded in imposing a particular reality reduced to its essential traits. Malraux's early appreciation of Bernanos reflects his consistent sensitivity to a type of fiction strongly resembling his own, one in which a sense of transcendency dominates the representation of quotidian reality. Several years later, in the mid-thirties, when his interests brought him into frequent friendly contact with the Communists, Malraux still held to a view of literature which departed radically from the

---

[12] "L'oeuvre d'art," *Commune*, No. 23 (July, 1935), 1,265. This speech was originally delivered before the "Congrès international des écrivains pour la defense de la culture" in Paris, June, 1935.
[13] *Malraux par lui-même*, 38.
[14] "*L'imposture*, par Georges Bernanos," *Nouvelle revue française*, XXX (March 1, 1928), 406.

growing theory of socialist realism which was to determine the direction of writers like Aragon for many years.

For Malraux literature is never the direct application of a social doctrine. Literature can be the affirmation or denial of a society, but it can never be determined by social forces. For a Communist public Malraux wrote in 1934, "It is only in the positive element of a civilization that the work of art finds its force." The artist does not paint the world, as Balzac tried to do; instead he tries to express "through images the development of a personal problem. *The Possessed* is not the portrait . . . of a revolutionary Russian milieu: it is the development of Dostoyevsky's ethical thought through a series of living characters. Like Nietzsche in *Zarathustra*, Dostoyevsky is a thinker who expresses himself in parables." [15] Malraux dates the emergence of the modern attitude of the artist toward his society, the indirect attitude, from the time of Rousseau. This attitude is not a break between the artist and his society; rather, it is a relationship in which the artist is compelled to create his genius *against* the values of his era. Malraux explained this phenomenon to an interviewer: "The revolt begins with Rousseau, when ethical predication becomes a function of literature. It is possible to see the Vicaire Savoyard as simply one heretic among others. . . . But the new fact exists that fiction (thus literary talent) then becomes the means for expressing the heresy. Trying to substitute ethics for a religion whose structure has become weakened, Rousseau also substitutes it for politics." [16] An artist's opposition to his society fosters his development. His opposition is a personal mode of reaction; it incites him to develop himself by opposition.

Malraux values the plot of a work of fiction far below the ethical or poetic urge which inspires it. In a preface to the French edition of Faulkner's *Sanctuary*, Malraux explained that he admired the American novelist's use of the "detective story" plot because it afforded ample opportunity for violence. Violence is a form of obsession; Faulkner's obsession marks him as a major novelist. Malraux then went on to state explicitly his conviction that the

---

[15] "L'attitude de l'artiste," *Commune*, No. 15 (Nov., 1934), 166–68.
[16] "Lignes de force," *Preuves*, No. 49 (March, 1955), 10. Reprinted from an interview with Albert Ollivier in *Combat* (November 15, 1946).

contemporary novel is fundamentally determined by an obsessive relationship between the novelist and his subject matter.

In literature, the supremacy of the novel is significant because, of all the arts . . . the novel is the least controlled, the one where the domain of the will finds itself most limited. How much *The Brothers Karamazoff, Les illusions perdues* dominate Dostoyevsky and Balzac can be seen by reading these books after the beautiful paralyzed novels of Flaubert. And the essential thing is not that the artist is dominated, but that for fifty years now he more and more chooses that which dominates him, that he organizes the means of his art as a function of it. Certain great novels were first of all for their authors the creation of the one thing which could overwhelm them. Just as Lawrence wraps himself up in sexuality, Faulkner flees into the irremediable.[17]

For Malraux, the novel is the form most suited to expressing that intensity which is the hallmark of the modern sensibility. Because it is a form with few strictures, the novel can be most easily molded to convey the author's intensity and the singular quality of his obsession.

In 1929 Malraux envisaged the transformation of the novel according to the emerging needs of literature as he understood them. In a review of Keyserling's travel journal he wrote, "The dramatic conception of philosophy, more powerful from year to year in all of the West . . . will perhaps lead to a profound transformation of fiction."[18] Gaetan Picon has situated Malraux within the major current of contemporary literature, that current which makes literature an instrument of metaphysical consciousness.[19] Malraux's reviews and prefaces reinforce this view. When confronted by a work which deals with problems and conflicts of a metaphysical nature, as in the cases of Bernanos, of Faulkner, and of Laclos, Malraux wrote critical essays which expressed his own "dramatic conception of philosophy" in the novel.

Malraux's own fiction has often been criticized for its failure to create characters independent of the author. He has replied that

---

[17] Preface to William Faulkner, *Sanctuaire*, in *Nouvelle revue française*, XLI (November 1, 1933), 745.
[18] "*Journal de voyage d'un philosophe*, par Hermann Keyserling," *Nouvelle revue française*, XXXII (June 1, 1929), 886.
[19] Gaetan Picon, *André Malraux* (Paris: Gallimard, 1945), 45.

fiction does not require autonomy of characters. Characterization and vocabulary are possible modes of fictional expression, but they are not necessities.[20] He suggests that what may appear to be psychological penetration in novelists like Dostoyevsky or Stendhal is in fact something quite different, because there is no such thing as *inner* knowledge of individuals. In *La tentation de l'Occident* (1926), his first major work, Malraux revealed his antipathy to the widespread interest in the unconscious which followed the growing influence of Freudian psychology. For him attention to and reverence for the unconscious was not merely too deterministic in nature to suit his own ante-existentialist emphasis on individual freedom; it was positively dangerous. "By accepting the notion of the subconscious, by according it an intense interest, Europe has deprived itself of its strongest arms."[21] Malraux preferred the search for "a coherent myth" to any oversubtle analysis of action as the result of subconscious drives. His critical writings reflect this same mistrust of psychology, this same preference for the mythological and abstract imagination.

"Do you think you know Mouchkine? And Stavrogin? Are you sure you understand Fabrice del Dongo, in the same way you understand Mr. Micawber? The word 'know' (*connaître*) applied to men has always made me wonder. I believe we know no one."[22] In novelists commonly called psychological novelists Malraux sees, instead of psychological analysis, a conception of the individual as a creature of will. One of Malraux's most revealing critical works is his essay on Laclos, published in 1939. Describing *Les liaisons dangereuses* as an intense intellectual novel, a "politics of persuasion," Malraux pointed out that Laclos' basic technical problem was to create characters determined by an "ideology." Laclos succeeded; he "made fictional characters act as a function of what they thought."[23] In the supreme confidence Laclos placed in the power of intellect and will, Malraux wistfully recognized a style of thought which diminished sharply during the nineteenth century.

[20] *Malraux par lui-même*, 38.
[21] *La tentation de l'Occident* (Paris: Grasset, 1926), 94.
[22] *Malraux par lui-même*, 48.
[23] "Laclos," *Tableau de la littérature française* (Paris: Gallimard, 1939), 420.

However, geniuses like Balzac, Stendhal, and Dostoyevsky introduced into the novel a new type of hero, one presaged by those of Laclos: the meaningful character. Malraux explains:

La Marquise, Valmont, Julien Sorel, Vautrin, Rastignac, Raskolnikov, Ivan Karamazov are special in this respect: they accomplish premeditated actions as a function of a general conception of life. Their fictional force comes from the fact that this conception lives in them exactly like a passion: it is their passion. . . . Such characters answer the deep desire man always has to act by controlling his action. With these characters, the hero ends and the meaningful character begins.[24]

Flaubert is Malraux's favorite illustration of the novelist of talent who artificially restricted his imagination by choosing characters of limited stature. What is actually "paralyzed" in "the beautiful paralyzed novels" of Flaubert is the will of the characters. To Malraux it seems inconceivable that a writer should *want* to depict creatures who are not motivated by strong will. The success or failure of their projects does not affect Malraux's preference. He admires willful characters for their "accusation of life." The passion is superior to the creation. Malraux is careful to distinguish between the mythology of will and the "will to prove." The latter implies a restriction on the author's part—he puts his creation in the service of a message, and thus destroys the ambiguity which should be the heart of a work of fiction. Malraux frequently criticizes novels of socialist realism because of their tendency to depict, to preach, rather than to discover.

In the preface to *Le temps du mépris* (1935), Malraux stated succinctly the aim of literature as he conceives it. He wrote, "One can prefer that the meaning of the word art be to try to make men conscious of the greatness in them of which they are unaware." He continued, "It is not passion which destroys the work of art, it is the will to prove. The value of a work is not a function of the passion or the detachment which animates it, but of the accord between what it expresses and the means employed. . . . This value,—and the *raison d'être* of the work, and its duration, even provisional,—lie in its *quality*." [25]

Malraux delimits certain techniques which he feels are proper to

[24] *Ibid.*
[25] Preface to *Le temps du mépris* (Paris: Gallimard, 1935), 9–10.

the modern novel. The major one is the use of *tone*, that quality which makes each of an author's work readily identifiable, which conveys the sound characteristically his. In a 1935 review of Gide's *Les nouvelles nourritures*, Malraux wrote,

In Gide what attracts me is almost always the tone of his voice—that flavor of intelligence . . . . This is the quality of the French moralists, and I understand why it is loved. It is precisely that which gives us the impression of intelligence in a living man. Experience scarcely teaches us to live and perhaps the most intense experience is evident in a man only by the sound of his voice, in a writer by the tone of his style— what fascinates us in Pascal or in Nietzsche even at the very moment when we reject their truths.[26]

In Balzac, his favorite novelist, Malraux notes the recurrent accent or tone as part of a symphony which is "less polyphonic than is generally believed." [27] For Balzac, for Gide, the world is "a more or less vast expression of a particular drama. The world of the modern artist is that of his affirmation." [28]

The modern novel uses dialogue in a manner different from that of earlier eras, Malraux insists. The dialogue conveys the author's tone, rather than the individual psychology of the characters. In the *Esquisse d'une psychologie du cinéma* (1946), Malraux offers a definition of the use of dialogue which reveals his predilection for dramatic scenes in the novel, for a mode of fiction closely related to the techniques developed by films. The dialogue is the third dimension of the novel, that which "makes of a man a great artist. Suggestive, dramatic, elliptical, suddenly isolated from the whole world as in Dostoyevsky, or linked to everything in the world as in Tolstoy. In each [the dialogue] is the great means of acting upon the reader. It is the way of making a scene *present* . . . ." [29]

Characters in modern fiction are not fully developed individuals; they are not monuments to the novelist's psychological penetration. Rather, for Malraux the characters are symbols of the author's

[26] "*Les nouvelles nourritures*, par André Gide," *Nouvelle revue française*, XLV (December 1, 1935), 935.
[27] *Malraux par lui-même*, 40.
[28] "*Les nouvelles nourritures*, par André Gide," 935.
[29] *Esquisse d'une psychologie du cinéma* (Paris: Gallimard, 1946), Pt. V, n.p.

personal obsession and vehicles for his questions. "I believe," he writes, "that for a great many novelists, and tragic authors, the character is produced by the drama and not the drama by the character. The heroes of Aeschylus like those of Shakespeare are 'possibilities' of their author, around which, like objects in some Surrealist paintings, moves a crowd in perspective." [30] To support this highly personal view of characterization, Malraux cites the example of Dostoyevsky. The Russian novelist's recently published notebooks support Malraux's interpretation. The notebooks reveal that Dostoyevsky kept shifting the agent of certain crucial actions and statements in the course of revising his novels. What was obviously primary was the personal obsession, the haunting meditation, rather than any attempt to construct a realistic situation or psychology. Malraux has never departed from his initial conception of fiction. In a recent interview he confessed, "I never wrote a novel in order to write a novel. I continued a sort of uninterrupted meditation which took successive forms, one of which was fiction. But the stories were all the same to me." [31] In Laclos, Bernanos, and Faulkner, Malraux finds a density of characterization which is the result of the author's meditation. He finds characters who have the intense ambiguity of typically modern creations. In other words, he finds a fiction which resembles his own.

Psychological realism is of little interest to Malraux, because what appears real in art is quite different from what would appear real in life. Fiction must provide "the mysterious dimension which is bestowed by the irreality of art. The more the hero of a novel is convincing, the more he is so by virtue of a life which is not at all that of men." [32] Malraux finds in the development of the modern novel a growing attention to dramatic psychology, "where secrets are suggested by actions, by half-confessions." [33] Dramatic psychology leaves large areas of character shadowy, ambiguous, and in this lack of clarity Malraux finds precisely that quality of fiction he most admires. "The part of mystery of every character who is

[30] *Malraux par lui-même*, 41.
[31] Interview in *Le Figaro Littéraire* (October 23–29, 1967), 13.
[32] *Malraux par lui-même*, 41.
[33] *Esquisse d'une psychologie du cinéma*, Pt. V.

shadowy . . . expressed by the mystery of the human face, gives a work that sound of a question . . . about life from which certain invincible reveries—for example Tolstoy's great stories—draw their grandeur." [34]

Malraux's preference for tragic art is well known.[35] His writings on art emphasize the perennial existence of tragic themes in all cultures. He finds in the fictional works he admires technical procedures which are the literary equivalents of a mixture of words, music, chorus, and masks proper to tragic theater. In Faulkner, for example, Malraux finds tragic drama. In Faulkner "there is no 'man,' no values, not even a psychology. . . . [There is only] Destiny standing behind all these so different and yet so similar characters, just as death stands behind a room full of incurables. An intense obsession destroys his characters as it strikes against them. . . . It stands behind them, always the same, and calls to them . . . ." [36] The modern fictional hero is a tragic figure like his author. The modern novel is "a privileged mode of expressing what is tragic in man; it is not an elucidation of the individual." [37]

Twentieth century fiction, Malraux believes, aims at something beyond realism. The failure of postrevolutionary Russian fiction is that it has not realized the possibilities open to the writer in our time, Malraux told a congress of Communist writers in the thirties.[38] "From the faces of the Saints to historical reconstructions, man's desire to represent has always been applied as much to what he has never seen as to what he knew," he wrote in the *Psychologie du cinéma*.[39] Recently Malraux reiterated this conviction when discussing the forthcoming definitive edition of *Les voix du silence*. In it he plans to push "to its limits" the theme of transcendency which underlies the *Antimémoires* and all he has written previously:

---

[34] *Ibid.*
[35] See for example: Frohock, *André Malraux and the Tragic Imagination*, Chaps. 3, 4, 5; Charles D. Blend, "The Rewards of Tragedy," *Yale French Studies*, 18 (Winter, 1957), 97–106.
[36] Preface to Faulkner, *Sanctuaire*, 754.
[37] *Malraux par lui-même*, 66.
[38] "L'attitude de l'artiste," *Commune*, No. 15 (November, 1934), 166–74.
[39] *Esquisse d'une psychologie du cinéma*, Pt. II.

I would say that one of the definitions of man is the fact that he is conscious of the human condition. And the fact of experiencing human servitude inevitably leads to a search for something which opposes servitude . . . the mysterious factor which transcendency gives rise to in man. . . . It was admitted for centuries that nature was the great point of reference and that it was a question of reproducing what one sees by imitating and idealizing it. But I believe that style is precisely the opposite of what one sees. Every work of art is at once something visible and something invisible.[40]

One of the most effective means available to the novelist for conveying the presence of a transcendency is symbolic confrontation. Malraux explains symbolic confrontation as a way of relating the physical universe to fictional characters, "uniting a moment important for the character to the atmosphere or the cosmos which surrounds him. Conrad uses this almost systematically and by this device Tolstoy has achieved one of the most beautiful fictional scenes of all time, the night when the wounded Prince André looks up at the clouds after Austerlitz." [41] Malraux uses the technique of symbolic confrontation heavily in his fiction, as we shall see. He presents nature for its ambiguous, suggestive possibilities; realism in the usual sense is relatively absent. The confrontation of man and nature is part of the general pattern of Malraux's theory of literature, a pattern which stresses tragic situation, concentration upon willful action, and significant dialogue. It deemphasizes psychological analysis, plot, and visual realism.

Malraux's long-standing interest in cinematic art is reflected in his criteria for modern fiction. In films he distinguishes that *selective use of reality* which reveals the creator's mastery of the means of his art. This same choice of significant detail is what distinguished Stendhal's fiction and made it a meaningful step into the future of the novel. Malraux calls the mass of facts available to the artist "chaos." Different arts choose different elements from this formless mass. For example, he writes in the *Psychologie du cinéma*, a film-maker might represent the fall of Robespierre quite differently from a historian. "Certainly, in any chaos there exist

[40] Interview in *Le Figaro Littéraire* (October 9–15, 1967), 14.
[41] *Esquisse d'une psychologie du cinéma*, Pt. V.

certain privileged moments, but they are determined by each of the arts which must express this chaos. At the instant when Robespierre can no longer make himself heard, the decisive accent is perhaps the distraction of one of the guards, engrossed at that very moment in kicking out one of the children or in looking for his lighter . . . ." [42] The phenomenon Malraux describes here is *dramatic indirection*, a technique admirably suited to the camera and sound recording. The silence of a voice against a roar of voices can be shown visibly and audibly.

Film and recording, two arts born in the twentieth century, are what Malraux terms arts of reproduction. That is, they assume their meaning and function only when reproduced. They must communicate immediately, and for this end poetic insight is essential. The simple reproduction of movement by a succession of images, combined with recorded stenographic sound, is not art. "I call art, here, the expression of unknown and sudden convincing relationships between beings, or between beings and things," Malraux writes. [43] These are poetic connections, intuitive insights into relationships and meanings. They are, to use the term Malraux applies to both cinema and the novel, an art of ellipsis.

Applied practically in the novel, ellipsis can take the form of *reportage*. This narrational technique has been present in the French novel from the time of Balzac and Zola, Malraux points out. In the twentieth century reportage has assumed a larger role in fiction, replacing the omniscient author of the nineteenth century. Malraux describes the technique as "the intrusion of a character into a world which he reveals to us while discovering it himself." [44] In some ways reportage resembles the strict first or third person narrative. However, it is distinguished from either by its *indirection*. What is discovered is not stated, judged, or interpreted directly. Instead, the technique juxtaposes *facts*; it is a kind of journalism of the novel. What distinguishes this technique from journalism proper is the quality of vision, the poetic insight of the novelist. The modern novelist as Malraux conceives him is ideally a

[42] *Ibid.*   [43] *Ibid.*, Pt. VI.
[44] Preface to Andrée Viollis, *Indochine S.O.S.* (Paris: Gallimard, 1935), vii.

kind of dramatic poet, a philosopher-journalist who questions the events of his time by that which transcends those events. He reveals the presence of an enigma.

It is not surprising that Malraux values highly direct experience of action and of historical events. His biography and his fiction testify to his fascination with the more adventurous aspects of twentieth century history. "There is not a single good war novel written during the war by a peace-time novelist," he writes. "To write during peacetime is to wring from peace its hidden tragic element. In war, one must wrest from the tragic its unknown or strange aspects." War is a dramatic setting, a heightened illumination of man's eternal condition. The novel about war is therefore "a series of tableaus coordinated by a fatality." [45]

Malraux has always been concerned with the artist's role in the life of man. The artist should be a shaper of culture, a pioneer of sensibility, a voice for the inarticulate mass of men. "Joy or misfortune, it is the destiny of the artist which makes him cry out, but it is the destiny of the world which determines the language of these cries." [46] The *matière première* with which the artist works is the available cultural heritage. The originality of the artist's work, Malraux explains, echoing Goethe, lies in evolving a style which moves from imitation to conquest, which assimilates and transforms the past into a "significant difference."

One finds a curious note of fatalism in Malraux's conception of the artist's relation to his work. The word *destin*, destiny, appears like a leitmotif in Malraux's critical and fictional writings. Death is significant because it transforms life into destiny. Destiny stands behind man and gives his actions tragic significance. We notice here an important aspect of Malraux's thinking: the fact that he uses abstractions frequently, elliptically, often inconsistently. *Destin* is one of Malraux's poetic words; it takes on meaning in a context. When Gaetan Picon noted that Malraux's own future was curiously prefigured in his early novels, Malraux replied, "This relationship between the work of certain writers and their life is

[45] "*Les traqués*, par Michel Matveev," *Nouvelle revue française*, XLII (June 1, 1934), 1,014–15.
[46] "Sur l'héritage culturel," *Commune*, No. 37 (September, 1936), 2.

striking. . . . It is not so much that life supplies the previously invented event, but that it provides the novelist with an equivalent. Life rediscovers not the fact but its example." [47]

The artists Malraux admires were men of action such as Sophocles, Dante, Bacon, Cervantes. "Henry James and Flaubert," Malraux remarked dryly, "do not represent the eternal prototype of the artist." [48] Action and art seek the same end, to translate the widest possible experience into consciousness. The whole of art and of cultural history demonstrates the same fundamental human urge, "to transform destiny into consciousness." [49] The tragic poet "expresses what fascinates him, not in order to be delivered from it . . . but in order to change its nature. For by expressing it along with other elements, he brings it into the relative universe of things conceived and dominated." [50]

The human experience which most strongly symbolizes man's condition is imprisonment. In those artists who personally knew imprisonment—Dostoyevsky, Cervantes, Defoe—Malraux finds the paradigm of the artist's role with respect to other men: "All three wrote the book of solitude, the book of a man who rediscovers men alive and absurd, men who can live forgetting that somewhere exist prison and the pillory. And all three wrote the revenge of solitude, the reconquest of the world by the man who returns from hell, . . . [by] transforming into a conquest for the artist, into the illusion of a conquest for the spectator, the experience which was suffered." [51] In his own lifetime Malraux has been imprisoned at least three times. The experience of reemerging into the world of free men is one he highlights in his novels. Whereas Albert Camus concluded from a meditation on the artist in prison that the experience reveals the solidarity of men, Malraux concludes instead that the privileged experience of incarceration and humiliation is in fact a special crucible for the further purification of the superior individual, the sage or *Shaman*.[52]

[47] *Malraux par lui-même*, 26.
[48] André Malraux and Spencer Byard, *The Case for De Gaulle, A Dialogue between André Malraux and James Burnham* (New York: Random House, 1948), 70.   [49] "Sur l'héritage culturel," 9.
[50] Preface to Faulkner, *Sanctuaire*, 746.   [51] "Sur l'héritage culturel," 3.
[52] Frohock discusses the shamanistic aspects of Malraux's thought in *André Malraux and the Tragic Imagination*, 137–49.

Malraux's conception of the artist's role is linked to his preoccupation with Spengler. Malraux belongs to a generation which accepted as an axiom Nietzsche's declaration that God is dead and which felt deeply Spengler's assertion that the West was moribund. The disunity of European thought after the First World War plagued Malraux and his contemporaries. The essential question which underlay *La tentation de l'Occident* was whether or not Spengler was right. In an essay of the same period as *La tentation*, "D'une jeunesse européenne," Malraux wrote, "What will be the destiny of this violent youth, marvelously armed against itself, and freed of the base vanity of giving the name grandeur to a life to which it cannot attach itself?" [53] In the language of 1926 and 1927 Malraux was talking about engagement, many years before Sartre's novels and Camus' essays. For the young Malraux the fundamental problem was first one of choosing oneself, rather than of making practical political choices. Faced with the Spenglerian negation, he had to decide actively that he was free and then to demonstrate that the culture of which he was a product was not doomed to extinction. The obsession with the past which has been characteristic of all of Malraux's writings has its roots in this anti-Spenglerian stance adopted in his youth. The enthronement of will, the obsession with salvation in art, the search for transcendent aspects of man in action are all offshoots of this fundamental desperate affirmation that Spengler was wrong, that he had to be wrong.

Interpreted in the light of *The Decline of the West,* Europe in the 1920's offered a spectacle of death and discontinuity. Malraux's earliest reply, *The Temptation of the West,* indicated by its very title that the downward movement led to a fatal fascination with death and destruction. For Malraux the hero of the Occidental world was the artist. Creator of a new reality, he alone could reconcile the separation between thought and feelings, between actions and passions which undermined the unity and strength of Western man. "The mind gives the idea of a nation," Malraux wrote, "but it is its community of dreams which creates its sentimental force. Our brothers are those whose childhood unfolded following the rhythm of the epics and legends which dominated

[53] "D'une jeunesse européenne," in André Chamson and others, *Écrits,* "Les Cahiers Verts," No. 70 (Paris: Grasset, 1927), 153.

ours. We have all felt the freshness and the morning fog of Austerlitz . . . ." [54] The legends of history and of literature reveal the
historical consciousness common to European culture. The creative artist who understands these legends, these heroic myths, can
reinforce the failing nerve of Western civilization; he can provide
new myths and dream-stuff for the imagination. As an artist assimilates and transforms the work of the past, he also expresses his own
epoch.

From his experience with the Surrealist and other artistic movements lively in Paris in the early twenties, Malraux quite early
became convinced that the subject matter of art was becoming as
elusive as the historical justification for Western civilization. He
felt it necessary to affirm a unity which was on the verge of
disintegrating. In "D'une jeunesse européenne" he wrote, "We
must today find once more the harmony between man and his
thought, without making man conform to thought posed a priori.
Doubtless the price these recent years have put on the possible
arises out of this need. The possible, ancient domain of the fantastic and of madness, with its people of dreams, suddenly rises to a
bizarre royalty. It reigns alone over the plastic arts of Western
Europe and almost uniquely over all of Western poetry." [55] The
artist more than any other man is capable of making out of the
chaos of existence forms which can affirm man's continuity and his
will. "Each of us must recreate in his own domain the heritage of
phantoms which surrounds us . . . and create . . . human consciousness with the millenary anguish of men." [56]

Malraux has continued to stress that the *imagery* of civilizations
differs greatly, while man remains constant. This is one of the most
interesting and successful aspects of the *Antimémoires*, where he
unites series of personal memories of different countries and times
with images out of his mental museum of world art in order to
illustrate the recurrent patterns of human experience. In 1946
Malraux suggested this technique: "Beneath the particular forms
of civilization . . . there are in men eternal feelings; those born of
the night, the seasons, death, blood (the whole great cosmic and
biological domain). These have permanence . . . [but] this cosmic

[54] *La tentation de l'Occident*, 95–96.
[55] "D'une jeunesse européenne," 150.   [56] "L'oeuvre d'art," 1,266.

domain only assumes its full force by being incarnated in the particular metaphors of each civilization." [57] The artist not only transforms into consciousness as vast a *personal* experience as possible; he also simultaneously creates the consciousness of other, less gifted men. In this way, Malraux suggests, the continuity and permanence of man can be affirmed against the Spenglerian negation.

Heroes and myths are the creative forces which express and shape morality and dreams. The artist can be a maker of myths in his writings. He can also embody a myth in his life. Malraux often calls the writers he admires mythmakers or moralists. The terms seem to be interchangeable. If the artist is as Malraux would have him be, a moralist, he is also a "rectifier of dreams." This emphasis on the moralist and his myths is Malraux's answer to the vogue of the psychologist and his complexes. In the notes to *Malraux par lui-même* he comments, "In 1910, everyone was digging into the subconscious to find demons there; in 1953 people are beginning to find angels (or heroes) there. This could take us a long way." [58] Preferring to emphasize those elements in man which demonstrate his nobility and self-transcendence, Malraux has always been fascinated by heroes. The artist can create heroes in his work. The artist can also become a living embodiment of an essential truth, "a myth" in his own person. Politics, revolutions, war are the ideal climate for the birth of living mythological heroes. Symbolic types "are born from the clash, at certain moments in history, of attitudes which up to that time seemed irreconcilable. . . . Every great form of politics which surpasses the politics of the politicans creates its particular human type." [59]

Malraux's description of the artist as a mythical hero seems an apt description of his own life. In "Le démon de l'absolu" he writes,

The mythical person [is] born from all the writings he has signed. . . . The image we have of such personalities is that they were able to answer by what they wrote the questions put to them by life and by men. They have an answer for everything, because for everything they have only one answer. They have reached a summit of mind which com-

<hr/>

[57] "Lignes de force," 12. [58] *Malraux par lui-même*, 84.
[59] *The Case for De Gaulle*, 62–63.

mands all avenues . . . this "summit" has but one name: a truth. A great
personality, in this slightly blurred realm where art and thought are
fused, is a man through whom an essential truth is expressed.[60]

T. E. Lawrence, Saint-Just, De Gaulle, the characters of Laclos, are
some of Malraux's preferred mythical-literary heroes. These men
are for a moment "masters of their own destiny"; they belong to
the same mythology of will which underlies Malraux's artistic
preferences and informs his critical theory.

Malraux believes that the masses, that is, those who do not
create, those who only consume art, are most likely to be touched
by what is symbolic and intuitive in art. Therefore it is the artist's
duty to supply them with myths which will awaken the grandeur
lying sleeping within them. The ideal popular art form would be
something combining "the grave accents of primitive poems," the
terror of Greek tragedy, and the *brio* of a contemporary detective
story. The modern novel as Malraux defines it in his critical writings would seem to fill the bill. However, as Malraux has recently
admitted, the novel as he conceives it seems at this moment to
have lost its power in the face of the direct diffusion of actual
events by the press. "This crushing quotidian reality has no preced-
ent. . . . The fiction of the nineteenth century is much more
exciting than the reality the readers knew; but what is twentieth
century fiction in the face of daily events, atom bombs, wars,
revolutions." [61] Instead of writing novels, Malraux prefers now to
foster what he feels will be a cultural climate for enduring
values.

Malraux's present program for cultural diffusion in France is the
natural outgrowth of his concern with a new humanism as expressed in his speech before UNESCO in 1946. In this speech,
"L'homme et la culture artistique," he outlined explicitly his notion of cultural pluralism. He asked again the question which
underlay his last novel, *Les noyers de l'Altenburg:* Is any notion of
Man possible? The speech was Malraux's most impassioned effort
to refute Spengler and was no doubt very moving in the troubled
years immediately following the Second World War. His twenty-

[60] "Le démon de l'absolu," *Panorama de la nouvelle littérature française,*
ed. Gaetan Picon (Paris: Gallimard, 1949), 299–300.
[61] *Le Figaro Littéraire* (October 23–29, 1967), 14.

year-long personal meditation seemed directly occasioned by recent events. He began by asserting that cultures of the past are not to be regarded simply as hypotheses, for while it is true that we may understand nothing of the inner psychological reality of an ancient Egyptian, we nevertheless appreciate and retain certain transmissible values from the past. What we *can* understand from cultures of the past is "the quality of humanism which each culture bore." If we conceive of cultures as "modes of permitting man to achieve a harmony with himself," then our interest in the past and in the present is the same—to intensify man's "destiny." [62]

Man's destiny is always defined by opposition to something, to gods, to the devil. When, Malraux noted, the "idea of man" began to appear in history, it took the form of an accusation, an attempt "to escape the human condition by drawing from man himself the deep strengths he had formerly sought outside of himself." Thus, culture and the art which shapes it enable man "to organize himself as a function of what he recognizes is divine in himself." [63] Man's divine part is his creativity. The museum is the handbook of man's own divinity, the place where "the quality of humanism" in all cultures is evident. Malraux ended his speech by calling for an "effort to create man." This was his elliptical way of stating that European culture needed to be rebuilt out of the ruins of war. He found the challenge crucial and perilous. "We can found a humanistic attitude only on the tragic because man does not know where he is going; and on humanism because he knows his starting point and his desire." [64] Tragic humanism, the attitude Malraux described in 1946, has been his own since the mid-twenties, since the days when he began to write his first novel, *Les conquérants*. His fiction has richly illustrated his effort to accomplish what he asked of all art: "to explode (*faire éclater*) the human condition by human means." [65]

Malraux has written six novels. *Les conquérants* (1928) is based on the Canton insurrection of 1925, and deals primarily with the adventurer Garine and his role within a revolutionary historical

---

[62] "L'homme et la culture artistique," *Les conférences de l'UNESCO* (Paris: Editions de la Revue Fontaine, 1947), 77–78. The original lecture was delivered at the Sorbonne on November 4, 1946.
[63] *Ibid.*, 78.   [64] *Ibid.*, 87.   [65] *Ibid.*, 88.

situation. Malraux's second novel, *La voie royale* (1930), centers around another adventurer, Perken, who joins the young aesthete Claude in a search for lost sculptures along the ancient Cambodian "Royal Way." *La condition humaine* (1933) evokes a much larger cast of characters caught in the Shanghai insurrection of 1927. It chronicles the defeat of the Communists just as Chang Kai Shek was taking power. *Le temps du mépris* (1935) is primarily the account of the imprisonment and eventual release by the Germans of Kassner, a Czechoslovakian Communist. *L'espoir* (1937) is a vast panoramic novel of the early days of the Spanish Civil War. It has a great many characters, alternating scenes of action and dialogue, and the most strongly developed analysis of the problem of action of any of Malraux's novels. *La condition humaine* remains Malraux's most popular novel. *L'espoir*, vaster, more episodic, is certainly more characteristic of his art and may well be his most aesthetically satisfying novel. Malraux's last novel, *Les noyers de l'Altenburg* (1943), is a work which lies halfway between his fictions of action and the later meditations on art. An account of several generations of the Berger family, the novel examines by means of a series of scenes and colloquies the conflict between art and action present in the earlier novels.

Malraux's "uninterrupted meditation" on man's fate makes it possible to discuss his novels, with the exception of *Les noyers*, as a group. "The stories were all the same to me," he said. More than any other novelist in this study, André Malraux seems, once his major themes and ideas took shape in the twenties, to have modified his thinking not at all. He exhibits a consistency of preoccupations and of technique which is almost frightening. Whether the obsessive unity of his fiction is the sign of a unique and lasting genius we cannot know at this moment. Certainly Dostoyevsky, whom Malraux has always admired, exhibited some of the same terrible consistency. One might also judge Malraux's consistency as a lack of development. His fiction is perhaps too limited in its scope. One of the greatest obstacles to any objective judgment of the novels *qua* novels is their *apparent* force as historical documents. As more information about Malraux's own life comes to light, however, we begin to find out that he was not an eyewitness to most of the events he described so vividly, that the documents were more imaginative than historical. And we marvel at his prophetic power and his ability to create fiction out of the brutal realities of the wars and revolutions which convulsed the world in the years between 1925 and 1943.

Malraux's novels share that "dramatic conception of philosophy" he recognized as a hallmark of modern fiction. Elements of high adventure, philosophical discussion, poetic glimpses of cities and stars, torture, agony, death, illuminated by reminiscences of paintings, music, and sculpture constitute the flesh of these novels. Their style is alternately abrupt, spare, journalistic, and rhapsodic, strangely poetic. Their unity lies in the unity of Malraux's private world, in the power of his personal obsession. Armand Hoog has called Malraux "the only *photographic* genius of the French novel." [66] This is perhaps true with respect to some of the individual details of violence and action which stud the novels. However, there are serious gaps in Malraux's accounts of events, moments when he supplies unexplained affirmations in place of logical connections.

Malraux's art is an elliptical one. He confronts human actions with their metaphysical significance, omitting the analysis of motivations common to psychological, social, or historical novels. The overall effect of such gaps is an immediacy which plunges the reader into the heroes' anguish with extraordinary force, as R. M. Albérès has noted.[67] Malraux's elliptical approach to the representation of reality is a reflection of his fundamentally ambiguous conception of existence. Ellipsis is a mode of thought as well as a mode of art. The poetry of cataclysms which forms the substance of *Les conquérants, La condition humaine, L'espoir* reveals the ambiguities of action and the mystery of man. These war novels are series of "tableaus coordinated by a fatality."

The telegraphic structure of the opening pages of *Les conquérants*, for example, makes remarkable use of the technique of report-

[66] Armand Hoog, "Malraux, Möllberg and Frobenius," *Yale French Studies,* 18 (Winter, 1957), 87.
[67] R. M. Albérès, "André Malraux and the 'Abridged Abyss,'" *Yale French Studies,* 18 (Winter, 1957), 47–48.

age as Malraux conceived it. Radio communiqués, segments of action, snatches of scenery follow one another in rapid succession. *La condition humaine* is organized by oddly spaced date indications. *L'espoir* is divided into numerous scenes without explicit narrative connectives. These narratives appear to discover directly a turbulent world whose meaning is nowhere stated or explained. The narrator of *Les conquérants* sees Saigon in a series of disconnected observations, as one might quickly note details in unfamiliar surroundings, without passion or judgment: "Desolate deserted provincial city, with long avenues and straight boulevards where the grass grows under vast tropical trees. . . . In front of me in the middle of a wide street covered with grass a small railroad wanders. 37, 35, 33 . . . stop! We stop in front of a house like all the others in this quartier: a 'compartment.' Some kind of vague agency. Around the door are affixed signs of obscure Cantonese commercial firms." [68]

Another important device of reportage is relating a face to a landscape. For example, the speaker looks at his interlocutor, then allows his gaze to move further into the distance. Suddenly, the other speaks, while the presence of an ominous landscape or background grouping of objects remains, endowing the spoken words with a special effect of intensification. Albérès has noted that this technique is highly cinematic, with shifting angles of vision and "cutting." It is curious to note that in 1928, when Malraux published *Les conquérants*, films had not yet discovered this device. The total effect of Malraux's cutting and montage is an intense impression of being inside of the protagonist's mind. Never is the reader supplied with a minute description of a landscape as a full stage setting for the action to follow. He sees only what the character sees, participates with him in the action. Nothing is explained, nothing is analyzed. Time *is* experience and has the shocks and discontinuity of experience at times of great stress. The movement of Malraux's novels is their meaning; the characters are our only guides. Unlike Hemingway's antipoetic characters, Malraux's lead us to intense intuitions, to poetic insights.

[68] *Les conquérants,* in André Malraux, *Romans* (Paris: Bibliothèque de la Pléiade, 1952), 11.

The most notable fault in Malraux's novels is absence of psychological explanation. His characters seem totally formed when the narratives open. They do not develop; they do not assume greater depth as their experience accumulates. This fact is due of course to Malraux's fundamental skepticism with respect to psychology. As we have noted earlier, he feels that psychological realism is neither desirable nor attainable. His "dramatic psychology" instead *suggests* through actions and half-avowals. André Rousseaux has noted that the impression left by Malraux's characters is that of "silhouettes in dialogue, without human substance, all cut from the same model: a bomb or a revolver in their hands, and a metaphysical brain for meditating on man's destiny while other men running all around are falling under the machine gun fire." [69] Rousseaux's observation is striking. However, it takes into account neither the diversity of Malraux's race of would-be supermen nor the fact that they do indeed have different faces and different voices. The tone of metaphysical questioning which underlies Malraux's fiction has many pitches and variations. As we shall see later, it tends to ask basically the same question; but the replies differ widely.

Physical descriptions of characters fall into two major types. The major personages are depicted as portraits in action. They are always seen through the eyes of someone else, as, for example, Garine through the eyes of his companion as the two walk along a Canton boulevard in the Oriental midday heat. The mask of action which is Garine's is faintly disintegrated by his obvious fatigue, then recomposed by his will as he begins to speak. Claude in *La voie royale* notes a similar transformation in Perken: "The expression of his look: heavy, enveloping, but of a singular firmness when an affirmation for an instant tightens the tired muscles of his face." [70] This physiological modeling is visible evidence of the dramatic psychology Malraux substitutes for psychological analysis.

The other principal group of characters is composed of crowds,

[69] André Rousseaux, "André Malraux," *Revue de Paris*, No. 10 (October, 1946), 123.
[70] *La voie royale* (Paris: Grasset, 1930), p. 21.

of the nameless and generally faceless men who inhabit the half-shadow world of the novels' background. Occasionally they emerge for a moment; then they serve the visual and psychological function of providing contrast for the heroes. The crowds are man in general, undifferentiated, only vaguely conscious of the human condition, almost subhuman. At a political rally in Les conquérants the crowd seems to bark like one huge animal. In the streets, on the battlefields, crowds in motion seem to symbolize the density and indistinctness of human life for the majority of men. Only when a crowd seems to recall a pictorial procession out of the sculpture of the Middle Ages or the paintings of Breughel, as in some scenes of Les conquérants, L'espoir, and Les noyers, is it described with some humanization; then it is transformed into a canvas against which the destiny of the willful hero assumes eternal proportions.

Malraux's use of dialogue is extremely limited. His heroes speak only of fundamental issues; they ask ultimate metaphysical questions. They all have the tone of their author, the tone of anxious moralists. The dialogue is made to serve an unusual narrative function: it stands in place of temporal continuity and psychological explanation. It would perhaps be more accurate to call Malraux's dialogues multiple monologues, since very few characters seem to be listening to what their companions have to say. They each speak their "truth" with a peremptory dogmatism which allows for no mediation. Albert Camus once aptly called these dialogues "passionate geometries." Each voice seems to be arguing with itself, confronting understanding of what is with desire for what ought to be. The total structure of L'espoir, as Victor Brombert has pointed out, is a dialogue, a dialogue between thought and passion, between war scenes and intellectual discussions.[71]

The actions and dialogues of Malraux's novels are set off by careful use of light and shadow. Soldiers running in the street are seen as silhouettes against the triangle of light cast by auto headlights, silhouettes striped with the black shadows of guns. The theatrical lighting of the opening scene in La condition humaine,

[71] Victor Brombert, "Malraux, Passion and Intellect," Yale French Studies, 18 (Winter, 1957), 72–73.

the scene in which Tchen commits his first murder, is achieved by artificial light from an electrical sign out in the street. A roomful of revolutionaries is eerily lit and metamorphosed by a swinging lamp, so that faces appear and disappear with changing expressions. All of Malraux's climactic scenes are composed with nocturnal lighting which intensifies the features of his heroes, deepens the lines in their faces, gives their gestures a relief similar to that of the plastic arts. The scenes are tableaus, isolated in time by the lack of explicit narrative connectives, isolated in space by the use of lighting. The heroes are endowed with a symbolic presence, an immensity which formal realistic description could never achieve. As Guernico of *L'espoir* wanders in the temporary headquarters of the secret police, he is silhouetted against the staircase and, by a superimposition of images, transformed into an incarnation of the Christian knight. The crowds, subhuman in the full light of day or under electricity, become by night symbols of the will of a city as they build barricades in the Madrid fog, transformed into "a silent phantasmagoria." Other crowds move over abandoned fortifications in a tragic nocturnal ballet.[72]

The most memorable scenes of Malraux's novels are those which symbolically incarnate the abstract words threading his prose—destiny, fate, fraternity, eternity. These vague terms are essential to Malraux's vision and by his fictional techniques he imbues them with the quality of mystery he believes fundamental to the most meaningful aspects of human experience: death, will, and art. These scenes are "accusations of life" in which man confronts that which surpasses him and rises to cosmic grandeur. This victory has of course nothing to do with any real victory. Malraux's tales chronicle a vast spectrum of defeats. The dramas are tragic. But, by what Frohock has called a logic of the opposite,[73] Malraux affirms the contrary of what reason reveals to be true. As defeat falls like a transfiguration on his heroes, he fashions triumph out of doom. The wounded aviators descend the mountain in *L'espoir*'s most moving scene: "And this procession of dark peasants, of women with their hair hidden under ageless kerchiefs, seemed less to be

[72] *L'espoir*, in *Romans*, 694.
[73] Frohock, *André Malraux and the Tragic Imagination*, x.

following the wounded than to be descending in an austere triumph. . . . It was not death, at that moment, which was equal to the mountains: it was the will of men." [74]

The precise meaning of such scenes is not accountable in words. It is impossible to say why the defeated aviators are victors; why the agonizing death of Perken is a victory over death; why Tchen's ludicrous suicide has the accent of a heroic gesture. In part, the transformation of defeat into victory, of death into eternal significance is achieved by an act of the novelist's will. Things are so because he wants them to be so. Another facet of Malraux's logic of opposites lies in the particular character of his visual imagination. Behind each of his symbolic scenes stands the world of painting, sculpture, and music which has obsessed him since his youth. By juxtaposing the wounds of defeat with ancient immobilized images of stigmata, the mournful procession down the mountain with the processionals of medieval art, he makes these painful moments from this century timeless and painless, objective as works of art.[75] His symbolic scenes use nature as a backdrop which at once underlines man's finitude and suggests that hidden grandeur of which he is unaware. A starry sky, some mountains, passing clouds reveal the cosmic import of the fictional drama.

In the preface to Le temps du mépris and in his speech on "L'homme et la culture artistique," Malraux emphasized that it is the artist's function to awaken men to their innate greatness. This greatness sleeps in them unnoticed until certain privileged moments of intense action, of courage, anguish, fraternity, will. As a novelist, Malraux attempted to fulfill this function by wresting from the wars and political turmoils of the twentieth century an image which was to be its transfigurative epic.

As an imaginative re-creation of some of the major political and social upheavals of our age, Malraux's novels present a disquieting assessment of the efficacy of action. They record varying modes of

[74] L'espoir, 836.
[75] For a more complete discussion of the synaesthetic aspects of Malraux's fiction, see: Rima Drell Reck, "Malraux's Novels and the Arts," Studies in Comparative Literature, ed. Waldo F. McNeir (Baton Rouge, Louisiana State University Press, 1962), 219–38.

endeavors, that of the terrorist, the adventurer, the political activist, the professional revolutionary, the aesthete. Of these, only the hero whose primary form of action is the creation of objects which endure beyond a single life span appears likely to transcend the defeat which accompanies action like a shadow.

"What is to be done with a human soul if there is neither God nor Christ?" asks Tchen of *La condition humaine*.[76] Each of Malraux's heroes undertakes to answer this question by his mode of existence. Goaded by an intense consciousness of man's limitations, each reacts in an individualist fashion. Whether in the realm of action or of art, Malraux's heroes are, in his own word, *mythomanes*. They are, like the characters of Laclos, significant heroes, that is, they carry out premeditated acts as a function of their general conception of life. Their fictional force springs from the fact that "in them this conception lives like a passion; it is their passion. . . . Such characters answer man's constant and profound desire to be master of his own actions." [77] They are myth-makers because they model themselves according to their self-images: they act in two domains at once, in their mythical image and in their living image. Malraux calls such characters demigods and adds that a literary work composed of them is a kind of mythology. In his own novels, Malraux weighs political and social action against individualistic action through heroes who propound their points of view like prophecies for all men. The clash of contradictory myths transforms Malraux's scenes of dialogue into a dialectic on the meaning of human existence.

The terrorist, a recurrent hero in Malraux's novels, while finding a measure of self-expression within the context of a revolution, is in fact fundamentally isolated from those among whom he fights. In war he seeks a Nietzschean liberty, not victory. For Hong of *Les conquérants*, bred on misery and hating the rich because they respect themselves, hatred becomes a mode of existence, a duty. This hatred which can express itself only through action finds the revolution too slow a vehicle. "Politics," says Hong, "doesn't interest me." [78] He is single-minded: he must not waste the one life he

[76] *La condition humaine*, in *Romans*, 226.   [77] "Laclos," 420.
[78] *Les conquérants*, 106.

has. The terrifying and intoxicating sense of having something unique obsesses him. "A single life, a single life . . . this had not given him a fear of death . . . but the profound and constant fear of spoiling this life which was his and of which he could never erase anything." [79] Hong gives form to his one life through terrorism, and his death has the savage and sterile glow of his life.

Tchen, religiously educated, later turns from religion under the tutelage of the aesthete and opium-eater Gisors. For a while Tchen finds in revolutionary political action "the satisfaction of his hatreds, his thought, his character. It gave a meaning to his solitude." [80] However, once he has committed murder he finds a form of action more closely suited to his personal thirst—terrorism. While experiencing no satisfaction in communal action and remaining indifferent to questions of methods and aims in the revolution, Tchen discovers a curious reconciliation with himself in destruction. The sense of solitary action gives to this man immured in an anguished personal quest "the sense of life . . . the complete possession of himself." [81]

The anarchist Le Négus of L'espoir reacts in much the same way as Hong and Tchen to questions of strategy and doctrine. "We do not want to make a state or a church or an army. We want to make men." [82] While the anarchist is more willing to act within a group than is the terrorist, his essential concern is no less personal. For Le Négus revolution is a state of being in which one can live without concern for victory or the future. Garcia, a practiced Communist organizer, is quick to note the element in the anarchists which will eventually destroy what it helped to found: "When one wants the revolution to be a way of living in itself, it almost always becomes a way of dying. In that case, one is as content with martyrdom as with victory." [83]

The terrorists seek to found a religion of which they are themselves the martyrs and prophets. With a wild look Hong asks that after his condemnation to death the young people be told to imitate him. Going to his death with a bomb under his arm, Tchen thinks of the oppressed Chinese, whose state he wishes not so

[79] *Ibid.*, 26.   [80] *La condition humaine*, 227.   [81] *Ibid.*, 316.
[82] *L'espoir*, 604.   [83] *Ibid.*, 603.

much to alleviate as to endow with a meaning in itself: "To give an immediate meaning to the hopeless man and to increase assassinations, not by an organization but by an idea: to have martyrs rise again . . . ." [84] Malraux's terrorists want immortality in a single transfigurative gesture, exaltation, or vengeance, living at their highest intensity for a moment before extinction. Tchen is motivated by the myth of man as absolute proof of God's nonexistence, much like Kirilov in Dostoyevsky's *The Possessed*. And the death which Tchen conceives as an absolute appears as ludicrous and absurd as that of his Russian counterpart.

The adventurer is one of Malraux's most striking heroic types. Malraux defined the type thus:

The adventurer is . . . outside of the law. . . . He is opposed to society to the extent that it is the *form* of life; he is less opposed to its rational conventions than to its nature. . . . In the same manner as the poet who substitutes for the relationship of words to one another a new relationship, the adventurer tries to substitute for the relationship of things to one another—for "the laws of life"—a particular relationship. The adventure begins with exile, at the end of which the adventurer will be a madman, a king, or totally isolated. [85]

The adventurer protests against the *form* of life by creating in action an image of himself which his society is incapable of nurturing. For Garine it is the revolution as an Apocalypse, for Perken the destiny of primitive tribes to be shaped. Each seeks to make out of the ordinary substance of life a destiny sufficient in itself and owing nothing to anything other than the self.

Garine finds a form of power within a revolution in its earliest stages, when it is still "a state of things." Fundamentally opposed to clear social forms, Garine is associated with the revolution in Canton only incidentally, almost by accident, their momentary aims being the same. "My action," he says, "makes me apathetic to everything which is not my action, beginning with its results. If I associated myself so easily with the Revolution, it's because its results are distant and always changing. At bottom, I'm a gambler. Like all gamblers, I think only of my game, with stubbornness and

[84] *La condition humaine*, 353.   [85] *Malraux par lui-même*, 78–80.

with force." [86] Although Garine's work within the revolution may be efficacious, his attitude arouses justified suspicion and mistrust in Borodine, a doctrinaire Communist. Garine does not want to better society; he wants to show that it is absurd. He cares not at all for the men in whose behalf he fights. Adventure is the satisfaction of "a perfectly despairing passion" which must spend itself in the attempt to prove that nothing is worth conquering, that the passion is at all times superior to the form of action it inspires.

Perken boasts that he has gambled his life on a game greater than himself. He carves a personal empire among primitive tribes in order to leave "a scar on this map." Perken is more interested than Garine in the actual results of his action. His ultimate purpose, however, is the same: to express through violent action the self, the will. We meet both characters at the beginning of their downward curve in life, when *la vie* begins to become *destin*, when what has happened can no longer be changed and begins to take on the shape of what was fated. As advancing age makes Perken aware that he is becoming a prisoner of his own life, he sees "the limited, irrefutable destiny which falls on you like a sentence on a prisoner: the certainty that you will be this and not something else, that you *will have been* this and not something else, that what you haven't had, you will never have. And behind you, all your hopes, those hopes which are under your skin as no living being ever is . . . ." [87] Ill and aware he is dying, Perken becomes more concerned with "shaping his death" than with shaping his life.

Perken voices the basic concern of the adventurer. The actions in which he and Garine engage are designed to prove the absurdity of death by giving the appearance of roles played for eternity. Both are obsessed with the futility of the world and the utter unacceptability of death. Thus they take it upon themselves to prove death absurd by acting *as if* it had no meaning. Garine affirms that one defends oneself only by creating; his life is his creation. Perken affirms his own existence above the fact of death: "There is no death. . . . There is only . . . I . . . I . . . who am going to die." [88] Living by the myth of man's will and its ability to override for a

---

[86] *Les conquérants*, 143.   [87] *La voie royale*, 85.   [88] *Ibid.*, 268.

moment the absurdity of the world, the adventurer chooses a desperate game. The creativity of his action is negated precisely by that fact which makes it admirable—its mortality.

The political activist is an important heroic type in Malraux's novels. This hero chooses to act politically in communion with his fellows. He practices a politics geared to precise aims in the future. He believes in the fraternity of man. This type of character was of course most attractive to the Communist milieus Malraux frequented in the thirties. Borodine of *Les conquérants* is an instance of the type, later more fully developed in Kyo of *La condition humaine* and Garcia and Manuel of *L'espoir*. Léon Trotsky's criticisms of Garine were not to the point. Garine was not intended to be the model for a revolutionary hero.[89] Borodine, Kyo, Kassner, Garcia, Manuel are Malraux's true political activists. It is important to note that Malraux judges the value of the adventurer's action neither higher nor lower than that of the true revolutionary. In his often quoted and frequently misread preface to *Le temps du mépris*, Malraux made his position clear. "The individual is opposed to collectivity, but he is nourished by it. . . . It is difficult to be a man. But not more difficult to become one by deepening one's communion with other men than by cultivating one's difference— and the former mode at least as forcefully as the latter nourishes that by which a man is a man, that by which he surpasses himself, creates, invents or conceives himself."[90]

To orient one's action toward social aims is *one* of the ways of "being a man" and not the only one. In Malraux's mythology, socially oriented action is a form of shaping one's destiny. Political action is a valid means of self-expression, but no more valid than the individualist ways of the adventurer. By his treatment of their situations, Malraux implies that the action of his Communist heroes is perhaps fundamentally equally personal, that communal action is simply another form of self-expression. Kyo is therefore not to be admired any more than Tchen. During the thirties

[89] Trotsky's criticism of *Les conquérants*, "La révolution étranglée," appeared in *Nouvelle revue française*, XXXVI (April 1, 1931), 488–501. Malraux's reply appeared in the same issue, 501–507.
[90] *Le temps du mépris*, 11–13.

Malraux was regarded for a time as a Communist novelist. No doubt those who thought of him in this way neither read his novels very carefully nor listened attentively to his speeches before Communist audiences. For him the essential values were then, as they have always been, apolitical and aesthetic. If Malraux so often used political settings for his novels, it was because such settings provided the modern décor for man's eternal situation. "Tragedy, in this age, is politics," Malraux said, quoting Napoleon.[91]

"The individual is opposed to collectivity." Those who direct the stage work of the modern tragedy do not always fully realize this fact. Borodine attempts to stir the Chinese by appealing to their class consciousness. Sensing that this sort of propaganda will not move them, Garine tries a different approach. He achieves an almost frightening success "by giving them the possibility of believing in their own dignity, in their importance. . . . This revolution is in the process of giving each man his life." [92] Garine compares the appeal of the revolution with that of Christianity: each allows men to become aware of their particular, distinct lives. Borodine is able to act successfully because the nascent individualism of the Chinese makes them revolutionaries, not because his program appeals directly to them. In *Les conquérants* Borodine is always portrayed in disadvantageous contrast with Garine. Borodine wants to produce revolutionaries "assembly-line fashion." His logic goes so far as to conclude, "There is no place in Communism for the man who wants above all . . . to be himself . . . to exist separate from others . . . ." [93] Borodine is too limited and single-minded a character to be sympathetic.

In *La condition humaine* Malraux creates his first fully rounded political activist, Kyo. Kyo's early education instilled in him the conviction that ideas should be *lived*, not thought. Therefore he had chosen action "gravely and with premeditation. . . . The sense of heroism had been given him as a discipline. He was not anxious. His life had a meaning and he knew it: to give each of these men dying of hunger like a slow plague, the possession of his own dignity. . . . Individual questions posed themselves for Kyo only in

[91] "Laclos," 419.   [92] *Les conquérants*, 15–16.   [93] *Ibid.*, 150.

his private life." [94] Unlike Tchen's heroism, Kyo's is not a justification of life. His almost complete serenity, unbroken except by his wife's infidelity and his reaction to the solitude of prison, is at times rather wooden beside the anguish of Tchen, the metaphysical questions of Gisors, the hard-won and difficult heroism of his fellow Communist Katow. Kyo sees things primarily in terms of the future. For him the revolution has meaning because he believes it will ultimately succeed. His action is informed by the myth of man's fraternity and man's future in society.

Kyo is unwilling to recognize certain aspects of man which disturb his certainties. He momentarily loses his composure when he sees his fellow prisoners as something less than human. "These obscure creatures who were swarming behind the bars, disquieting as the crustaceans and enormous insects of his childhood dreams, were no longer men. He found total solitude and humiliation." [95] But he puts this solitude out of his mind and plans his suicide (he will take cyanide) as an exalted act resembling the life he had chosen, to be set in the place of horrors which is also filled with "virile love." Kyo's ritual suicide is beautifully described. It falls into a slightly ironic perspective, however, when contrasted with the death of Katow, who relinquishes his chance for a peaceful suicide and marches to be burned alive, watched by the very men Kyo thought of as he quietly took his poison. Kyo's death for "the virile fraternity" somehow seems a dodge compared to Katow's bravery in total isolation and anguish among, Malraux writes, "all these brothers in the mendicant order of the Revolution." [96]

L'espoir portrays the man of political action most sympathetically of all Malraux's novels. Manuel is aware of the needs of the men with whom he fights; he learns the burdens of discipline, the isolation which comes with leadership. He is a character with many inner conflicts and doubts. He carries out his share of "things to be done on earth" with dignity and without self-deception. Manuel leads men who want, like the old Spanish peasant Barca, not to be despised. The novel's central theme, the grandeur of man in hope and in defeat, is expressed from many points of view.

[94] *La condition humaine*, 227.   [95] *Ibid.*, 389.   [96] *Ibid.*, 403.

Garcia is the spokesman for the technicians of this revolution which has so many disciples. He recognizes how diverse are the aims which make men fight; he is also aware of the gap between their actions and the eventual aims *he* conceives. Garcia says to Hernandez, "The Communists want to *do* something. You and the anarchists, for different reasons, you want to *be* something . . . . That is the drama of every revolution such as this one. The myths by which we live are contradictory: pacificism and necessity for defense, organization and Christian myths, efficacity and justice. . . . We must put these myths in order, transform our Apocalypse into an army, or perish." [97] Garcia can see no hope for Hernandez and others like him who seek solutions to personal problems in political action: their gestures are aimed at something unseen and unseeable. Garcia insists, "Political thought exists only in weighing one concrete thing against another concrete thing . . . an organization or another organization—not an organization against a desire, a dream or an 'Apocalypse.' " [98]

The *means* of political action will always displease the idealist, the dreamer, the intellectual, the man in search of an absolute, because, Garcia points out, all action is Manichean. What Garcia fails to note is that every action *with a concrete aim* is Manichean. The actions of Hernandez, of Tchen, of Garine have no possible future expression in concrete fact. Their actions exist only in the present and only for the agent; they do not need to be double. "Every true revolutionary is a born Manichean," says Garcia. "And every man of politics." [99] His statement merely underlines the fact that few of Malraux's adventurous and political heroes are true revolutionaries or men of political action. When *L'espoir* ends, the pragmatics of Garcia have little relevance—the war is almost lost, the social hope is almost totally defeated. The novel vindicates the nobility of the act by which a man dies "for that which does not exist."

The hero who engages in aesthetic and cultural speculation, whose form of action is primarily reflective, is a recurrent figure in the novels of Malraux. Like the activist the aesthete also ultimately meets a dead end. However, his essential preoccupation is most

[97] *L'espoir*, 613.   [98] *Ibid.*, 614.   [99] *Ibid.*, 761.

characteristic of Malraux's own. The aesthetic obsession underlies all of Malraux's fiction, leads to his writings on art, and presently shapes the pseudopolitical career in which he is engaged. Malraux and his aesthetic heroes seek in art the single, final answer to the human situation.

The somewhat ill-defined and awkwardly presented character Claude of *La voie royale* is the first of Malraux's aesthetic heroes. He is actually a figure of compromise between the life of action and the life of artistic contemplation. He is an adventurer whose efforts seek something enduring in the stone forms lying unseen in the Cambodian jungle. To Claude the statuary represents a kind of *substantial* salvation. Claude's struggle to transport the huge bas-reliefs reveals a commitment which goes far beyond the simple desire for an artistic "find." "It was his life which was threatened. . . . His life. All the stubbornness, the tense will, all the mastered fury which had guided him across this jungle, led to discovering this barrier, this immobile stone standing between Siam and him." [100] Claude eventually abandons his sculpture to go with the dying Perken, fraternity in this instance triumphing over the artistic obsession.

Gisors of *La condition humaine* is one of Malraux's most fascinating fictional embodiments of the aesthetic hero. He has all the essential qualities of the type, crowned by the "saving vice" of opium. Malraux treats Gisors with an ambiguous affection bordering on irony. "For twenty years he had been applying his intelligence to making himself loved by men by justifying them, and they were thankful to him for a goodness which they never suspected took its roots in opium." [101] Gisors' fine sensibility for Chinese art and landscape, his ability to understand the motivations of men, are wearing thin as his obsession with death grows. Opium is his last refuge, as terrorism is that of Tchen. Gisors is significant not for his vice, but for the reasons which drive him to it. Understanding that death is the basis for men's anguish, Gisors is sympathetic to the frenzies of action and madness which surround him. He is Tchen's mentor because he alone fully understands the implications of terrorism. His hold over his son Kyo is less strong because

[100] *La voie royale*, 120.   [101] *La condition humaine*, 209.

Kyo avoids Gisors' disturbing ability to dissipate the firmness necessary to resolute action. Kyo has to believe that his political action
has a practical purpose, that suffering and death are not in vain. He
acts aided by an illusion of purpose and futurity. His death is veiled
by the same illusions. It is Gisors who must ultimately face the
naked, unjustifiable fact of Kyo's death in one of the novel's most
moving scenes. Malraux describes Gisors' anguish: "The world had
no meaning, no longer existed: the irreparable immobility of . . .
[Kyo's] body which had bound him to the universe was like the
suicide of God. . . . The child was the submission to time, to the
flow of things; doubtless, at bottom Gisors was as much hope as he
was anguish, hope of nothing, waiting, and his love had had to be
crushed for him to discover this fact." [102] With the death of Kyo,
Gisors' life turns full circle and he returns to his original interest—
the history of art. He explains to Kyo's widow that he was momentarily attached to Marxism because it seemed a fatality to which his
anguish over death suited him temporarily. From his present
perspective Gisors no longer fears death and has no further use for
politics. He flees into the Olympian perspective of opium
dreams.

L'espoir, Malraux's most experimental novel in technique and
most poetic in narrative tone, projects fully the theme of art's
essential function. While the Spanish Civil War rages under the
windows of his Madrid apartment, Alvéar tells Scali why he is
indifferent to politics and to the possibility of his own death. He
does not feel that political action has anything to do with his
essential concern with "the quality of man." He feels that the
fundamental in man is not involved in revolution. "Man engages
only a limited portion of himself in action; and the more total the
action aspires to be, the smaller the engaged portion. You know
well that it is difficult to be a man . . . more difficult than the
politicans believe." [103] Gisors' reasoning is the same: "What is most
deep-seated in a man is rarely that by which one can make him act
immediately." [104] With the perspective of age Gisors and Alvéar are
able to judge the limitations of action, the gulf between a man's

[102] Ibid., pp. 413–14.   [103] L'espoir, 704.
[104] La condition humaine, 209.

commitment in the world and his inner needs. Alvéar points out that for many men revolution in this era plays the role that hope of eternal life played in the past; it is an *anti-destin*.

The "hope" which fills the pages of *L'espoir* is not hope of any specific political gain, since for the most part the novel is a record of defeats; it is not hope of eternal life, since death is the largest figure in the novel. Rather, the hope is inspired by a vision of man independent of the vicissitudes of action. For Alvéar art alone can touch the fundamental in man; art alone can express it. His belief is Malraux's own most consistent one: art is the tool which can awaken man's "unself-conscious grandeur." In art is to be found man's divine part. "It is not the gods who created music . . . but music which created the gods." [105] Alvéar's attitude is not exemplary in terms of the political and physical reality in which he lives. He dodges some essential questions. He admits the inadequacy of most of his books in face of the terror in the streets outside. But in his ideas on art Alvéar represents the strongest strain in Malraux's thinking. From *La tentation de l'Occident* to *Les voix du silence* Malraux has shown himself to be in essential accord with Alvéar that in art above all other forms of action can be found the essential in man.

The political settings of Malraux's major novels are secondary to the myth of man eternal which they contain. The novels chronicle a passionate search for liberty and many histories of defeat. The actions of Malraux's heroes find appropriate dead ends. Tchen fights with a revolutionary movement whose eventual aims will little suit him. Seeking fraternity in war, Magnin of *L'espoir* discovers instead the absolute isolation war generates. Fascinated with the release death appears to offer, Hernandez witnesses a grotesque comedy of execution of which he is a part and finds death utterly meaningless. What makes action *heroic* also tends to nullify it *as action*, that is, as an effective means to a given end. Action becomes the art for art's sake of existence. All of Malraux's heroes seek an issue from death, in political action, meditation, opium, art. There is none. Death continues to live *in them*, beyond the reach of their impassioned refutations in action. The personal,

[105] *L'espoir*, 706–707.

hallucinatory quality Malraux demands of fiction is expressed in his own work in the intensity of revolutions, wars, deaths which fill its pages. "Every man dreams of being God," Gisors says. Each of Malraux's *mythomanes* defies this absurd universe and tries to deny it in favor of a new world of which he is the creator.

After the momentary brilliance of man's affirmation in action, death triumphs. Action as a metaphysical quest leads always to a checkmate. But representation of this checkmate is itself a form of conquest. The true face of a man becomes apparent only after he has been dead an hour, an old Spanish saying maintains. In the welter of dead bodies on the streets of Spanish towns Malraux appears to find a peace and poetry largely absent from his earlier novels. A dead woman seems to sleep with her curly hair nestled in her arms. "Anarchists, Communists, Socialists, Republicans . . . [sleep] in the fraternal depths of death." [106] The art of the novel transforms the reality of death into the myth of man. "What interests me," says Claude in *La voie royale*, "is the transformation of works of art, their most fundamental life, made of the death of men. Every work of art . . . tends to become myth." [107]

Malraux's last novel, *Les noyers de l'Altenburg*, is in many ways different from those which precede it. The events described, while based as in the earlier novels on twentieth century history, are seen in retrospect; they are events most of which Malraux did not witness personally. The immediacy of *Les conquérants* is absent and in its place we find a meditative mood set by the introductory section. There Vincent Berger's son, prisoner at Chartres in the Second World War, sets out to write about the experiences of his father in 1917. Surrounded by men writing letters they know will never reach their destination, the young Berger seeks in the act of writing the meaning of his experience. The novel's structure is circular, so that the full import of the opening pages can only be grasped when one has read the last part and reread the beginning in its light. The symbolic scenes are not presented with that aura of immediacy and personal discovery which characterizes *La condition humaine*. Instead, each symbolic vision is set off in a section

---

[106] *Ibid.*, 723.   [107] *La voie royale*, 61.

by itself, prepared, carefully proportioned, as if the oracular significance of the scene were not merely suggested, as in the past, but
now stated in a form which is permanent, like the images of art.

The intellectual character of the novel is focused in the colloquium at Altenburg, where the issues underlying Malraux's work
are debated: Does man have a self-identity throughout history? If
so, in what forms can it be discerned? The earlier novels propose
that man affirms himself by choosing between gesture and image,
between action and art. *Les noyers* states explicitly in its dialogues
that the most efficacious victory over the human condition lies in
art. "The greatest mystery is not that we are thrown by chance
between the profusion of matter and that of the stars; it is that in
this prison we draw from ourselves images powerful enough to
negate our nothingness." [108] Those gathered at Altenburg agree that
one can know man by one of two means: by his culture, which is by
definition the product of a few for Malraux; or by *la charité du
coeur*, which takes the form of a symbolic intuition in *Les noyers*.[109]
The struggle between the man of action and the man of reflection
groups itself along these lines during the course of the argument.

Les noyers does not present simple either/or choices. The very
topic of the colloquium is undermined by ambiguity. The original
theme was to have been "the eternal elements of art," but, riddled
by more fundamental doubts, the participants have changed their
topic to "the permanence of man." We learn that the original
theme would have clearly demonstrated the second by showing
that what is most permanent in man is his desire to be more than a
man, to transform his life in art. The secular patience of Berger's
fellow prisoners, writing their letters which will be scattered to the
winds, is an aspect of this desire. Another dichotomy, between the
life of action and the life of art, is similarly shown to be illusory.
Art can combine action with a product which is lasting, can supply
a gesture which defines itself in an image. And finally, the argument over whether man is the individual, the *moi*, as Walter

[108] *Les noyers de l'Altenburg* (Paris: Gallimard, 1948), 98–99.
[109] Frohock calls the scene of this intuition "the poem of the walnuts." See
W. M. Frohock, *Style and Temper* (Cambridge: Harvard University Press,
1967), 62–77.

Berger believes, or the *other*, as Vincent Berger maintains, is never settled. Both are right. Man is the individual whose creations affirm his meaning. He is also the mass whose symbolic and biological continuity is the overall structure of the human adventure whose mystery pervades the novel. The imagery of *Les noyers* offers the answer to the question, Is there an eternal man?, in the walnut trees and in peasant faces.

The mystery of life is unexplainable and the mystery of man within it can only be revealed. *Les noyers* is a series of such revelations. Vincent returns to the world from a forest rotted by poison gas. The narrator, young Berger, rediscovers the world after a night in his overturned tank. Imagining that the old peasant woman he meets is smiling ironically at death, Berger thinks, "With a dark smile the mystery of man reappears, and the resurrection of the earth is no more than a trembling décor." [110] There is more description of nature in *Les noyers* than in any other of Malraux's novels with the possible exception of *La voie royale*. There nature is a jungle choking with luxuriance, teeming with insects, a constant spectacle of horror and menace. The color and shape of leaves, the smell of ferns, new branches against the sky— *Les noyers* abounds with the presence of growing things, with a perception of them which is direct and extremely vivid. And in each image nature is finally subordinated to man. It becomes a "trembling décor" for the human adventure.

In prison at Chartres in the novel's final section Vincent's son thinks "of the mystery which unites the unformed part of the prisoners to those songs which stand up before the eternity of the night sky, of the nobility which men ignore in themselves. . . ." [111] The young Berger has a knowledge of art which informs his vision of fundamental man in the Gothic faces which surround him. He has been restored to an intuition of the mystery of creation by his encounter with near-death. In action and in art he finds the mystery of man.

Malraux's earlier novels present action as a form of defiance man can assume against the human condition. These novels also suggest

[110] *Les noyers de l'Altenburg*, 291–92.   [111] *Ibid.*, 250.

that action has great limitations, that another form is possible and perhaps more satisfactory. *Les noyers de l'Altenburg* weighs this evidence, and concludes that action is perhaps not the most effective form of defiance. It is, after all, the intellectual Berger who is able to discern "the unformed part" of his fellow prisoners. Underscoring a subtle theme in the earlier novels, that in art and the contemplation of art man achieves self-affirmation and finds proof of his self-identity throughout history, *Les noyers* states that man's victory over his human condition lies in art.

Malraux is consistent. His fiction has been a continual meditation on several fundamental questions. His career has been and still is simply another mode of the same metaphysical inquiry. His varying adventures in politics belong to the same obsession which has inspired his writings on art. Despite the strikingly active, historical quality of his novels and of his life, Malraux remains committed only to a lifelong meditation on action and art as suprahistorical phenomena. In a letter to a critic, he made his position clear. "You are right in insisting on what you call my permanence . . . I think that *Altenburg* rewritten would only pose more clearly the problem that underlies everything I write: how to make man aware that he can build his greatness, without religion, on the nothingness which crushes him. Says Walter, 'In that prison we draw images from ourselves that are powerful enough to negate our nothingness.' " [112]

[112] Hoog, "Malraux, Möllberg and Frobenius," 95.

Index

PQ
671
.R4

Reck, Rima D
    Literature and
responsibility

3340

The Library
Lynchburg College
Lynchburg, Virginia 24504

PRINTED
IN
U. S. A.